Making a Difference the Right Way

Hazelvern Publishing—Baltimore, Maryland
ISBN: 978-0-578-78672-8
Library of Congress Control Number: 2022904064
Title: *Making a Difference the Right Way*
Author: Stewart W. Russell
Digital distribution | 2022
Paperback | 2022

This book is a memoir, and covers real-world events and circumstances. Some names, incidents, and places have been omitted for privacy purposes.

Making a Difference the Right Way

Stewart W. Russell

Dedication to My Family

As we have come to see in this world family can be an early foundation structuring our lives. For me the love I received was very special, as were the people on both sides of my families. Along with that love came expectations of learning responsibility, concern and compassion for others, always doing the best you could, and above all, honesty. Many of my family related experiences are as vivid to me now, as they were when they happened. That love and care was for all of the kids growing up in the various cities and towns regardless of where we lived. Summers, holidays, growing up in the church, and personal tragedies all rolled into one, helped determine what was to become of us years later. As the seasons go by, and we get older, sadly we start to lose those who loved and took care of us. If we are lucky, we get to take care of them. But as we go along, we keep our memories of them in our hearts, and remember them for the difference they made in our lives. Here's to the Russells, Smiths, Johnsons and Browns on my dad's side of the family, and on my mom's side the Hills, Butlers, Johnsons; and Chaneys, Davises, Joneses, and Francises. To my own immediate family my thanks and love go to them for all they endured all through the years on and off the job. My wife Karen, our son Jordan our soon to be daughter in law Emma, and last but not least our Yorkie Mr. Kyu (pronounced "Q").

Table of Contents

Forward

My friendship with Lieutenant Colonel (Ret) Stewart Russell has been over many years, beginning with our time in the Maryland State Police. As a young man, Stewart had a desire to become one of "Maryland's Finest" and his persistence certainly guided him through one of the toughest state police academies in America. I watched his progress with much interest as he was always willing to take on any task as a state trooper. He always made the most of any opportunity to enhance the reputation of the MSP, as the very best and professional police agency in the state of Maryland.

As an investigator, he combined knowledge and instincts to get the job done. His transition from trooper to supervisor, help form his outlook to make positive changes within his area of responsibilities. As a supervisor and commander, he was a constant mentor, encouraging the troopers under his command to do their jobs professionally, but always safely. During his executive command tenure, he weathered rough political seas that high ranking state police officials must face during the course of their duties. When confronted by challenges, he used sound judgment in his decision making to gain the best outcomes.

His integrity and professionalism were recognized by many in the law enforcement community. Rising through the ranks, he never forgot where he came from. He was admired by sworn and civilian employees alike, who respected his concerns for them and love for the MSP. As one of his first supervisors, I was present at the start of his 35 years with the MSP. It gives me pleasure to endorse the publication of this state trooper's memoir.

Walter W. Wassmer
Maryland State Police (Ret)
Chief of Police (Ret)
Prison Warden (Ret)

Chapter 1
I Couldn't Have Done It Without Them

This book is based on actual cases and events that I was directly involved with, or had knowledge of. There are times where I voice my outrage in recalling the dishonorable behavior by some of those I've encountered throughout my career. I decided not to mention the names of those who were negative factors in my career; or of those who were described in embarrassing situations; or those who in my opinion failed to honor the badge they wore. Instead, I would rather mention the names of those who proved my desire to choose law enforcement as a career was the right decision.

No public safety story can be complete without recognizing the invaluable contributions of our civilian employees. Their dedicated service and skills, helped make what we do possible. My part in this story is about the pride I felt being a Maryland State Trooper. These are the recollections of my experiences and views, where sometimes I found myself inexplicably dealing with more than just crime.

The Maryland State Police (MSP) is a way of life. Those who live it faithfully never regret doing so. The strength of my career was based on the principles I learned from family early on in life, and from those I worked with, who understood the true meaning of leadership and integrity.

This is my affirmation to those who used their wisdom and positions to do the right things for the right reasons; not to the pretenders who were merely content to say, "I got mine." It is a tribute to my colleagues who were protectors and mentors; and to those who let their promotions and positions be more than just a title, only benefiting themselves.

My story is one full of controversy and repeated irony. It's about respecting the importance of integrity, and taking a stand against those who had none. This is an acknowledgement to those who served the law enforcement community with distinction. This isn't just my story. It is a story about all of the dedicated men and women I served with; especially for those we have lost along the way.

On behalf of all of the sworn and civilian members of the MSP, and to those in the allied agencies I spent a combined 37 years serving alongside of, I hope their names and actions will resonate with the respect they have earned. Their devoted service to public safety and the citizens we served, is truly a story worth telling. I couldn't have done it without them.

Chapter 2
Never Compromise Your Integrity

From the day you begin the academy, there are certain things impressed upon you by your instructors that go beyond the performance of your basic functions. These matters were referred to as: "The things that could get you fired." A great emphasis was placed upon telling us about several situations you would undoubtedly face at some point in your career; and that you should avoid if you valued your job.

For example, some of the more prevalent ones are as follows: Intentional mishandling of property, stealing, sexual relationships while on duty, driving impaired while on or off duty, inappropriate use of force with or without your weapon, just to name a few. One's own prior experience may have determined your sense of urgency in accepting this advice.

Those warnings resonated with me during my initial law enforcement career while attending the Baltimore City Police Academy. They became exceedingly clear in the state police academy. I had no intentions of losing my opportunity with the state police, having spent nearly two years trying to get there. I knew it was best to go about my own sense of priority. However, as you will discover, even my best efforts wouldn't go unchallenged throughout my 35 years with the MSP.

It didn't take long to realize not everyone met my idea or definition of a sound trooper, supervisor, or executive officer. Regardless, I discovered you can learn much about yourself, even from those who exhibited a lack of propriety. So when faced with hypocrisy, racism, envy, unscrupulous behavior, and the ever-present political expediency, I found you had to grow up in the reality of the world you chose.

Whether it was taking a stand to do the right things for the right reasons, or speaking out against egregious conduct, I would have to address such matters even up to the last few months before I retired.

I was blessed to achieve the ranks of trooper first class to lieutenant colonel before retiring in 2012. In all, I worked in 19 different assignments, supervising or commanding in 10 of them. I served under 11 superintendents, and seven governors. Four of the governors served two four-year terms.

MSP majors and lieutenant colonels, are appointed under a "serve at the pleasure of" clause, by an appointing superintendent, and can be reduced to their last rank without cause. Not surprisingly, I was removed from my position as a lieutenant colonel/bureau chief, after I was unwilling to accept the dubious conduct of my last superintendent, whose self-expedient decisions, clearly threatened the safety of our troopers, in my opinion.

As I was never the purported weight rack spotter for a future governor, I had to rely on my integrity, and ability to keep me warm at night. The way I saw it, who wouldn't want a senior executive on their staff that tried keeping them, or the department from the appearance of impropriety or worse? Obviously, only someone who counted on people being complicit, indifferent, or a "yes man." I recall one time in 2004, when I wanted to bring a troubling matter to the attention of the superintendent, Colonel Thomas E. (Tim) Hutchins.

Although I was on the colonel's staff, I approached him prefacing that it may not have been my place telling him what I thought he needed to know. Without hesitation, Colonel Hutchins said, "Captain, I expect you to tell me what I need to know, not just what you think I want to hear."

After informing him of the predicament, I then offered a solution to the problem. The colonel acknowledged my idea as a worthy solution. But then he gave me the facts on why he had to take a different direction. Colonel Hutchins respected my position, and treated me as though I was capable of processing the view from his level. Need I say anything more about his leadership qualities?

Make no mistake about it, I greatly valued my "serve at the pleasure of" major and lieutenant colonel positions. At that level, you can generally get things done and help those in need. Although I didn't go around looking for trouble, I wasn't going to ignore it when it dropped in my lap either. So as a commissioned officer, when I encountered civilian employees being placed in compromising situations, troopers being retaliated against, or when data regarding our unsafe issued sidearm was being ignored by a superintendent, I met the moment, and acted accordingly.

Generally speaking, some may have thought I was being insubordinate, or even defiant. To the contrary, I had the utmost respect for rank, even holding myself to higher standards as a commissioned officer. However, I developed the stance that someone's higher rank didn't make them right if they were wrong. Having the last word didn't mean they were right, either. I remember being warned once about a subordinate I was to inherit. This individual had a habit of keeping notes on his supervisors. I told the person warning me, it didn't bother me as long as the notes were accurate. If I required a person to do something inappropriate, why shouldn't they protect themselves? I certainly would if necessary.

My story is no homily, nor is it about being a whistleblower after the fact. Some of my colleagues and detractors, felt I was my own worst enemy when it came to somethings I said or did. Referring to my candor, one day my academy classmate Rick Norman said, "You're brutally honest; and when you're honest, you're brutal." (What a joy to be comprehended.) There were times when I found it necessary to be incongruent with some people, especially, when they summarily spoke to me as if I were stupid, beneath them, or couldn't see what my eyes were telling me.

Having to deal with all sorts in my career, I wasn't totally tactless. I just wouldn't play games with self-important people. But my concerned colleagues and friends apparently knew better than I did, that being right in the end, wouldn't save me from those who had the last word.

Chapter 3
TFC Namon Brown and My Fate Riding the Number Eight

Growing up as a native of Baltimore, Maryland, I benefited from having a normal and loving environment all through my early life. At a young age, I was fascinated by television shows with law and order themes whether fantasy, westerns, or detective dramas. I can still recite the opening narration to the 1950s "Highway Patrol" television series. I was captivated with crime fighting units, like those portrayed in the 1950s "Untouchables" television series.

Being a traditionalist even at a young age, meant that culture and professionalism would certainly dictate my choices in life. I went to high school at Baltimore City College, from 1971 to 1974, where I was by no means an academic wizard. After graduation, I got a summer job in the landscape crew with the Baltimore City Housing Authority, thanks to Mr. Robert Johnson, the crew's supervisor. Mr. Johnson was the father of one of the neighborhood's families.

During the late 1960s and early 1970s, I spent summers with my grandparents Charlotte and Joe Butler, in Turners Station, Baltimore County. I remember seeing two different troopers who were Black, drive by their house on Sollers Point Road. Years later, I learned the first was Trooper Nat Alston. The second was Trooper Manuel Lewis.

Although Trooper Alston had resigned, and continued his career with another police department by the time I joined the MSP, I would actually get to work with "Manny" Lewis who was assigned to the Special Service Division's (SSD) Intelligence Unit in 1983. Manny achieved the rank of lieutenant before he retired.

The transit bus I rode to high school, traveled along a street named the Alameda, in Northeast Baltimore City. One day I saw a yellow marked state police vehicle parked in front of a section of row houses not far from the school. Initially, I thought the trooper was there on business. When I saw the vehicle there several days later, I assumed the trooper lived there. I remember whenever I saw that state police vehicle, I moved to the rear of the bus, and knelt on the long back seat just to get a good look at it. After becoming a trooper, I learned that was Trooper First Class (TFC) Floyd Jones who lived there. Floyd later became a detective sergeant, who I worked with in the SSD before he retired.

In order to get home from my job with the housing authority, I had to catch the number eight bus that traveled along York Road, to the Govans area of the city were we lived. One day, I was standing at the rear exit as the bus neared my stop at York Road and Woodbourne Avenue. Transit buses displayed various mid-sized advertisement placards horizontally just above their windows. As we neared my stop, I noticed a placard that immediately captured my attention. It was a recruiting advertisement for the Maryland State Police.

The color placard featured a Black trooper in his dress uniform, standing behind the driver's side front door of his patrol vehicle. The top of the placard highlighted the slogan, "Be One Of The Best." The trooper was sharp, proud and confident looking.

Seeing a Black person representing the state police on that placard gave me quite a thrill. I memorized the telephone number on the placard, and immediately ran home to tell my mother Miss Hazel, I knew what I wanted to do for a living.

Albeit an honorable consideration, going into something dangerous like law enforcement didn't exactly thrill my mother. Very soon, she realized I was serious about it. As I moved closer to being accepted, my mother reluctantly, but lovingly continued supporting her oldest child. Being a career Licensed Practical Nurse (LPN), she understood doing something you loved for a career was important.

State police superintendent, Colonel Thomas Smith, selected TFC Namon Brown to appear on that recruiting advertisement. TFC Brown's image was seen on billboards all around Baltimore, and catapulted the department's minority recruiting efforts significantly. I know several troopers of my generation who were also inspired by the sight of that recruitment poster. To me and many others, Namon is an MSP legend. He was a Marine and Vietnam veteran, whose MSP stories still make me smile with admiration today.

By the time I arrived in the academy, he was a corporal. As well as being a recruiter, Corporal Brown was also one of our associate instructors in the academy. Like me, he began his law enforcement career with the Baltimore City Police. Namon retired as a Lieutenant in 2005.

After a lengthy illness, the legend passed on to his eternal greatness on February 12, 2021. It was my extreme pleasure to have Namon as my friend, who I loved and admired. I was honored when Namon's family asked me to speak at his funeral. In my remarks, I quoted what former superintendent, Colonel "Tim" Hutchins wrote when he learned of Namon's passing. The colonel said the following: "Namon was there during my entire career. He was a benchmark for what it is to be a trooper. He made a difference for me."

As it is with somethings you want in life, they don't always come when you want them to. Fortuitous circumstances, perseverance, and the department's desire to recruit minorities, made my entry into their ranks a reality within two years after I initially applied.

My family's expectations as well as my own, led to an appreciation of what it took to get where I wanted to go in life. Through my family, I learned the importance of character, compassion, respect for others and yourself; and what to avoid if I valued my future. These and other factors, provided the opportunity for me to seek a way of life that was more than just a job.

Chapter 4
The Career That Almost Never Happened

Immediate employment with the state police was not readily available by the time I reached 21 years of age. I was told I'd be placed on a waiting list. I thought there may be a long wait before a position became available. My start in law enforcement actually began thanks to two of my best City College High School friends, the late Tyrone Francis (who sadly passed in 2018), and Warren Cooper, who were Baltimore City police cadets. City police cadets are uniformed civilian employees 18 to 20 years of age, who perform administrative tasks at the city's police headquarters. Once a cadet reached the age of 21, they became eligible to continue their employment by entering the police academy.

In 1975, Tyrone and Warren persuaded me to join the cadet program. Like most of the cadets, I was assigned to central records working at the "Hot Desk," running record checks for officers on the street. My intent was to become a city officer, and make myself a better candidate for the state police to choose from. That decision turned out to be a pivotal one, and would affect my status during the MSP's hiring process.

On July 20, 1976, the final phase of the selection process was held at the state police headquarters gymnasium in Pikesville, Baltimore County. Candidates had to take the "California Psychological Inventory," pass a timed agility demonstration, and pass a physical examination. This organized stress began that morning at 7:00 a.m. Once all of your data and test results were collected, your information was placed in a folder. We were then called alphabetically to a series of joined tables where uniformed members of the training academy's personnel were seated.

My final reviewer was Lieutenant John Sawa. Lieutenant Sawa took pause with something in my folder. My records indicated that the index finger on my right hand had to be amputated, after it was injured accidentally. This happened when I was three years old. Lieutenant Sawa asked to look at my hand.

Lieutenant Sawa (who was a firearms master in his own rights) formed the qualified opinion that it was unlikely I would be able to safely discharge a weapon. Therefore he could not recommend my acceptance. When I informed the lieutenant I was an armed Baltimore City police officer, he quickly looked up at me. After I showed him the holstered weapon underneath my suit jacket, Lieutenant Sawa looked at me again. Lieutenant Sawa immediately apologized, and said, "Good luck son."

In the ensuing months of the academy, I came to appreciate Lieutenant Sawa. Undoubtedly, he was the highly respected elder statesman of the academy staff. He was straight forward, trim, and immaculate in his uniform; and always a gentleman. In retirement, Lieutenant Sawa passed in 1999.

While I was in Baltimore City's academy, the same issue over my amputated finger gave their instructors doubts as well. My initial firearms training scores, caused concern over my ability to properly use a handgun. One of the academy's firearms instructors Officer Ray Butler, watched me closely during a training session. Officer Butler deduced my amputation wasn't the main problem.

He noticed that when I pulled the trigger, I flinched in anticipation of the recoil, rather than concentrate on my sight alignment and the target. Officer Butler said this was common for those who weren't use to proper shooting techniques. However because of my amputation, I would have to learn to shoot differently from others, he said.

Officer Butler recommended I begin strengthening the middle finger on my right hand that now served as the trigger finger in place of my missing index finger. Officer Butler cut a pencil in half, and had me place it between my thumb and middle finger. Officer Butler said by squeezing the pencil between my thumb and finger, I would build up the strength in my middle finger. The man knew his stuff. It worked like a charm. As I was no longer a novice at handling a handgun, that exercise helped steady my trigger pull, and my scores reached the passing range.

When Officer Butler retired, he began working for the state lottery system. Years later, our paths crossed one afternoon. I reintroduced myself to him, and asked if he remembered helping me back in 1976.

Officer Butler didn't exactly remember, but that's ok. I'll never forget it. At the time I was writing this book, I learned that Officer Butler passed in 2019. I can't thank him enough. He certainly made a difference in my career.

After graduating from the city's academy in 1976, I was assigned to the Northeast District. Eight months later, I entered the Maryland State Police Academy on January 17, 1977. I wasn't unaware that I had been accepted, until one afternoon when my background investigator the late TFC John Hubbard, saw me standing on my 416 foot post on Erdman at Bel Air Avenues.

TFC Hubbard wanted to know if I received my letter of acceptance. I told him that I hadn't. He knew I had been accepted, but told me to call the recruiting office and check with Corporal Brown, to make sure. After shaking his arm out of its socket, I hurried to the nearest pay phone.

Corporal Brown assured me that I had been accepted. He said they were late getting the acceptance letters out in the mail. He advised me to immediately put in my notice of resignation. I used my portable radio to call the central dispatcher, and requested to have a unit transport me to the district. The dispatcher asked if I was ok. I advised, I needed to address a personnel matter. The dispatcher acknowledged my request, and sent Officer Paul Kelly to pick me up. Officer Kelly was my personal mentor all through my time there. He was the only one who knew I wanted to be a trooper. When he heard my good news, he said, "Now go show them how to be a good cop!"

Paul has been my friend throughout these many years. He taught me how to subtly anticipate potentially dangerous situations, and other valuable ways to survive on the streets. I owe him as much as I owe anyone. He was there for me when it all started. Once I got cut loose from my state police field training, I invited Paul to ride along with me during a night patrol shift. For the few hours Paul rode with me, he really enjoyed sneaking up on the unsuspecting motorists we caught speeding.

When word got out around the district I was headed to the state police, some officers wanted to know why I wanted to be a "glorified ticket writer," or "AAA with a badge." Even the administrative lieutenant cautioned me during my exit interview. He warned they might not take me back if I didn't make it in the state police, and decided I wanted to return to the city police. I told the lieutenant politely, I didn't plan on not making it. When I arrived home that evening, there it was, one of the most important letters I would ever receive. January 17, 1977, couldn't come fast enough.

Chapter 5
"The Gospel According to the MSP"

The MSP Academy is like being in a military boot camp. I can say this with without reservation. There were several former military veterans from the Army, Marines, and the Navy in our class who also said so. One of the recruits who was an Army veteran, eventually dropped out. He said he didn't want to go through that type of training again. Our class was unusually diverse given the times. Although previous classes had its first females, and some had its first Black recruits, our class had a substantial cross section of diversity within its 70 candidates.

We had six state police cadets, who as 18-to-20-year-old uniformed civilians, assisted troopers in the field at truck-weighing stations throughout the state. When a cadet reached 21 years of age, they were eligible to go right into the academy (as it was with the Baltimore City Police Cadet Program). The class also had two former civilian MSP Police Communication Officers (PCO). PCOs are the department's version of dispatchers in other police departments.

Including myself, and another former Baltimore City officer, 10 of the recruits were former police officers. Two were from New York, one was from Washington, D.C. one from Frederick, Maryland and four were Baltimore Washington International (BWI) Airport Police officers. There were some recruits with college degrees, and like myself, some without. Many of us were in our early 20s, and some a few years older. Obviously, many of us were from Maryland. There were some recruits from New York, Pennsylvania, Washington D.C., and maybe one or two other states as well.

As the majority of our class had no prior military, or police background, I'm sure it had to be both exciting, and a bit scary for many of them. The academy was six months long; a combined 22 weeks. Compared to Baltimore City's academy which was five months (or 19 weeks), the state police system of constant pressure and physical requirements, made the two academies different from one another.

Another difference, is that the MSP's academy is a "residential academy." You are there 24 hours a day. It was the only police academy in Maryland that had such a requirement. We were off on Saturdays and Sundays. You only got to go home when you didn't accumulated 10 or more demerits during the week. Demerits were given for any breech of policy, or failure to satisfactorily carry out any order, or duty assignment during the course of the day.

These duties included but were not limited to cleaning details, policing your quarters, being prepared for class, or for any noted misconduct, such as uniform untidiness. I can personally attest to the demerit system thanks in part to Recruit Heber Watts. Heber was less than a minute late entering the classroom on our very first day. He was immediately cited by the academy first sergeant, Pat Bucher. First Sergeant Bucher who was a no-nonsense individual, awarded Heber with 10 demerits, insuring Heber wouldn't be going home that weekend.

Heber, sat in the open seat next to me. Having a kind nature, I voiced my concern for his misfortune. This didn't escape the notice of the first sergeant, who was addressing the class. First Sergeant Butcher felt since Heber and I had become such good friends, he gave me 10 demerits too. That way I could keep Heber's company. Discipline was the key element stressed. Maintaining it, would factor in your survival while in the academy, and later after you graduated.

Each recruit was assigned a roommate for the first three months, and then another for the last three months. My two roommates were different as night and day. My first roommate Scott Flowers, was a Marine veteran helicopter pilot. He was very private, and very anal about the cleanliness of our room. My second roommate was the recruit who got me my first weekend, Heber Watts. Heber was more outgoing than Scott, and a Maryland resident who like me, grew up in Baltimore City. Apparently Heber and I loved the thought of being in the academy so much, I believe we combined to accumulate more demerits than the entire class. That distinction allowed us the privilege to stay several weekends, and attend to various cleaning details.

Our class was the 76th academy class in the history of the department. In perspective, as of this writing the MSP just graduated its 152nd class in our history. The department was established under the Commissioner of Motor Vehicles (CMV in 1921. In 1935, the MSP separated from the CMV becoming its own agency, as we know it today.

What I later grew to appreciate about our academy, was the idea of being required to work, and live within a diverse little community setting with 70 hopeful candidates for six months. By design, you learned to interact with different personalities, races and genders. You had to work within a team concept, but when necessary, function independently. You had to get along with those who were different, and some who may have not cared for you…at least not at the start.

The fact you couldn't leave, provided the onus to snap to, and get with the program if you expected to survive those six months. Having the instructors in your face at any given moment, always kept you focused. In the end, it was up to the individual to understand the importance of discipline and integrity. You were expected to do things the right way, without being watched, or told to. Years later, I coined the phrase referring to those principles, and others we learned in the academy as: "The gospel according to the MSP."

One of the things I loved most about being a trooper, was our military bearing. Besides the art of saluting and close-order drill, another military courtesy we had to perform, occurred when an instructor entered the classroom. Whoever saw the instructor first yelled out, "Class, a ten-hut!" Everyone stood up in unison to attention. Reaching the front of the classroom, the instructor would take a few seconds to look over the class before saying, "Seats." Again in unison the class would be seated.

Of all the instructors, the academy's assistant commander, Lieutenant Edward Clark's deep and slowly voiced command of "Seeeats," was the most memorable. TFC Dave Franklin's, sternly enunciated, "Seats people… seats," was the runner up. TFC Franklin retired at the rank of captain in 2000. Dave went on to continue his career as a lieutenant colonel with the Maryland Transportation Authority police, before fully retiring from law enforcement, and becoming a full-time pastor at his church in Reisterstown, Baltimore County.

Our curriculum included criminal and motor vehicle law, the geography of Maryland, departmental rules and regulations, officer safety, report writing, and learning the ten codes. Ten codes are used over the radio to succinctly transmit requests for information, or when describing an incident, or your actions. We learned how to conduct criminal and accident investigations, and how to operate a police vehicle in pursuit, or defensive driving modes.

During firearms training, we were taught the proper use and care of our six inch .38 caliber revolvers, and pump-action shotguns. After we qualified, depending on your overall qualification scores, you earned a pistol badge to be worn on your uniform after graduation. The designations were "Pistol Master," "Pistol Expert," or "Pistol Sharpshooter." I was able to maintain a pistol expert level throughout my career.

There were practical exercises on basic first aid, crime scene preservation, arrest and fingerprinting techniques, and tactical responses to civil disobedience training. Back then, troopers fingerprinted, and processed their own prisoners before taking them to the district court commissioners, for an initial bail hearing. Then there was close-order formation and marching drills. Sometimes in the beginning, unannounced sessions were held in the parking lot at 2:00 am.

I vividly recall one of the important lesson we learned during our first week. While we were performing close-order drill exercises in the gymnasium, one of our female recruits just happened to be standing on the painted MSP shield in the middle of the floor. From out of nowhere, First Sergeant Bucher yelled at her from the top of his voice: "What are you doing standing on that shield? Don't you know men have died for that shield?"

With that, he ordered the entire class to drop to the floor, and start doing pushups until he said stop. I think everyone found out three things at that moment: First, never let the first sergeant see you stand on that MSP shield as a recruit. Second, traditions of honoring our fallen heroes were to be taken seriously. And last but not least, you didn't mess around with First Sergeant Bucher.

Several of the academy's curriculums awarded you Associates of Arts college credits. Those classes were taught by Dr. H. Freimuth,

Loyola College, and Dr. B. Mayo-Wells, University of Maryland. Then there was the long time academy legend, Dr. Alvin J.T. Zumbrun, Catonsville Community College. "Dr. Z," as he was affectionately known, taught criminal justice.

He sported seersucker suits, and had a teaching style that added to his unique, and delightful manner. Dr. Zumbrum retired in 1994, and was made an honorary trooper in 1995. After years of providing educational service to law enforcement, and the public safety communities, Dr. Zumbrum passed in 2014. He will be fondly remembered by the generations of troopers he taught in the academy.

All together we had a total of 49 MSP associate instructors. There were 41 from the ranks of captain to trooper, and eight civilians from different sections in the department. Our compliment of local guest instructors were from the Anne Arundel County Police, Baltimore City Police, Montgomery County Police, Prince George's County Police, Baltimore County District Courts, the Maryland House of Corrections, the Maryland Medical Examiner's Office, Maryland's Fire Marshal's Office, and the University of Maryland Hospital System.

The academy also invited guest instructors from the federal government such as Alcohol Tobacco and Firearms, the Federal Bureau of Investigation, U.S. Customs, the U.S. Secret Service, and the National Auto Theft Bureau. From the private sector, there were representatives from the C&P Telephone Company to help complete our training.

Several weeks later, we were visited by tailors from the Howard Uniform Company; a Baltimore uniform supplier under contract with the state. We were fitted for our dress blouses paired with the Sam Browne cross strap that attached to your gun belt. Additional uniformed clothing included patrol outerwear coats, trousers, felt and straw Stetson hats, and long and short sleeved shirts. The company even inserted a tailor's tag inside the jacket pockets, and on the trousers' pocket linings with your name typed on them. Now that was class.

Troopers were noted for our distinctive uniforms. Our uniforms consists of brown jackets, beige shirts, black ties and olive-drab green trousers with a medium black stripe down the leg. The crowning jewel of the uniform was the beige Stetson hat. Getting to wear that sharp uniform, was another reason I wanted to be a trooper. The old saying after you graduated was: "You get to wear the big hat, long gun, and sunglasses."

The academy's regular weekdays began by rising at six in the morning, policing your room, and making your rack (bed) just as they do in the military. Next we quickly moved to our assigned details within the various locations in, and outside of the academy. After that, there were calisthenics, and inspection of our rooms, uniforms, and detailed assignments for proper cleanliness. Next in an orderly formation, we headed to breakfast. We were seated in a designated area of the department's cafeteria reserved for recruits.

The rest of the day consisted of classroom time, or class related field trips, physical training, showers, lunch, more classroom, taking tests, dinner, and study hall. Our class obligations were generally over around seven in the evening. Finally, there was downtime.

Downtime gave you the opportunity to use one of two pay telephones to call family and friends, time to study for an upcoming test with classmates, work out over at the gym, social time, or just time to unwind by yourself. Recruits secured in their rooms at 10:00 p.m., also known as "Lights Out."

Within the following days, one of our details became what was referred to as "Night Watch." "Night Watch" required securing the compound by ensuring all the doors to the buildings around the headquarters grounds, as well as the academy building were locked. If there were any noted issues, you alerted the academy instructor spending the night in the instructors' bedroom. When all was secured, you notified the uniformed headquarters duty officer in the "Executive Building" across the parking lot.

The detail also included keeping a headcount on the inmates from the state's correctional pre-release facilities. These minimum risk inmates, were used to maintain janitorial functions, and augment landscaping around the grounds with our facilities management employees. The inmates were supervised by a correctional officer until the end of regular business hours. Once the correctional officer secured for the day, the inmates were taken to the lower level of the academy building, where their designated quarters were maintained for meals and sleeping. The inmates were on an honor system, and were paid for their work hours by the state. They were there only during the week, and returned on Mondays.

Academy classes were divided into several groups just as it was at the barracks. By groups, we were assigned to two-hour shifts during "Night Watch," beginning after "Lights Out." When it was my group's turn, it was just my luck to always get the last two hours right before the start of a new day. A few years after we graduated, the inmate program was discontinued.

Throughout the day, we quickly moved through the hallways, and outside on the compound, going to and from our scheduled destinations. Anytime along the way you encountered any sworn or civilian personnel or visitors, you had to perform the ritual called "Stand By." Upon someone approaching a recruit in the building, you were expected to briskly stand with your back against the wall at attention, and loudly shout, "STAND BY!"

Any recruit in the area also had to comply. You had to stand clear until told to "carry on," by the approaching person. If you were outside at the time, you shouted "STAND BY" and stopped in your tracks. You stood at attention until told to carry on. Humorously, this embarrassed some of our civilians who'd say, "Please, please go on." Some of the poor visitors not familiar with this ritual were startled, and didn't know what to make of it. A passing sworn, or civilian employee, would tell us to carry on, and off we'd go at the double to our destination.

The physical training which was a badge of honor to complete, consisted of circuit training. Circuits featured sets of weight lifting, pull ups, pushups, sit ups, dips on the parallel bar, and rope climbing. As the weeks advanced, so did the number of sets you had to complete in order to receive a passing grade. There was also boxing, judo, swimming, and long distance running. This was all designed for officer safety, and to get you in the best shape possible, while preparing you for the grueling five-mile run. The five-mile run which was at the very end of the academy, was a requirement that had to be completed within 45 minutes or less, in order to receive a passing grade.

As the weeks went by, we would see a few class members leave for various reasons. After our second week, we even experienced the unannounced late night disappearance of one of the female recruits. When it was discovered she was missing the next morning, the staff naturally had a concern for her wellbeing. We had to search the entire facility looking for her. Thankfully, it was just a case that she no longer wanted to be in the academy. She was a member of the 75th class, which our class had overlapped. She was allowed to enter our class, after leaving the 75th class for personal reasons.

Speaking of the 75th class, they were in the final days of their six months. As several recruits returned from their recent field training assignments, a few of them felt it necessary to exert their seniority on us. I guess they couldn't wait till after graduation, and had to practice using their newfound authority on someone.

Chapter 6
Is This the End of Another Soul Brother?

Within the early weeks of our class, the Black male recruit who was also a former Baltimore City police officer, was terminated for allegedly using marijuana during a weekend stay. After the recruit was terminated, one of our White male recruits found it necessary to celebrate by saying, "They got rid of a soul brother." The marijuana incident was actually observed by other recruits, and rightly reported to the academy staff.

No one in the class felt this recruit shouldn't have been terminated, or tried to suggest it was racially motivated. Those who even cared, asked how this guy could be so stupid. I believe both of those recruits exhibited the nature of their respective characters. Neither was anything to be proud of.

As we neared our final weeks, I fell awkwardly, and slightly strained my right foot during a judo session. It happened the day before we were to perform the five-mile run. Not wanting to miss it, I received permission to skip the next morning's calisthenics from the physical training instructor, TFC Dennis Supik. I didn't want to put any unnecessary strain my foot before our scheduled run. The five-mile run, was the last major physical hurdle to get by before we graduated.

If any recruit had a confirmed illness or injury, they were excused from physical activities while incapacitated. Your name would be placed on what was referred to as the "Sick, Lame and Lazy List." Insensitive as it seems now, that's what it was called back then. Those recruits would stand on the sideline, while the rest of the class engaged in calisthenics during morning physical training (PT), or any other physical activities during the day. I was lucky enough not to have been injured, or miss any of the classes' activities up to that point.

The next morning's duty officer was a corporal, who was assigned to the Public Information Office's television studio. His duties included videotaping MSP activities, as well as being one of our instructors. When the corporal saw me standing on the sidelined with the other three or four injured recruits, he walked over to where I was standing.

The corporal asked me why I wasn't participating in calisthenics since my name wasn't on the limited duty list. I explained that I was excused by TFC Supik just for that morning only, after straining my foot in judo. I said I was resting my foot, so I could participate in the five-mile run later that evening. Looking at me suspiciously, the corporal muttered, "We'll see about that."

Knowing I was telling the truth, I gave no more thought to the matter. Later that evening, we began the test at the Randallstown High School in Baltimore County. In order to complete the required five miles with a passing score, we had to run 20 laps around the quarter-mile track, within 45 minutes or less. That was one brutal test, but I made it with 10 minutes to spare.

By that time, most of the class enjoyed a closer camaraderie. Several of us stayed on the track running beside the remaining fellow recruits who were struggling, encouraging them not to give up. In the end, we all made it. Many of us felt a big weight had been lifted off our shoulders.

The next afternoon, we were in class watching a film on the Bell and Howell two-reel film projector, during a traffic accident investigation class. I can still recall the film: "Mechanized Death," produced by the Ohio Highway Patrol. The "Charge of Quarters" (CQ) tapped me on the shoulder, and directed me to follow him out into the hallway. The CQ is another duty each recruit had to perform while in the academy. The CQ was the liaison between the recruits and the instructors, and helped coordinate recruit activities for the day.

The corporal was standing in the hallway, and ordered me to follow him to the part of the building that housed the academy staff's offices. Inside the office of Lieutenant Clark, were the academy's commander Captain Lemuel Porter, and two other uniformed instructors. They didn't look too friendly, but as they never did, that didn't initially concern me. That all changed when I found I was being accused of feigning an injury, and making a false report of an authorization to skip calisthenics. Such infractions especially while on probation warranted termination, and without the legal recourse of LEBOR (Law Enforcement Officer Bill of Rights).

In Maryland at that time, police officers were covered under the Law Enforcement Officers Bill of Rights, or LEOBR. LEOBR was intended to protect Maryland's law enforcement personnel from investigation and prosecution, related to an officer's conduct, during official performances of their duties. LEOBR provided officers with privileges based on the rights of due process under the law, in addition to those normally provided to American citizens. Officers in a probationary status were not covered by LEOBR, except in the cases of an alleged act of brutality. Maryland was the first state to pass a LEOBR in 1974. As of 2021, Maryland was the first state to repeal it.

Although I was somewhat alarmed initially, I figured a simple explanation would resolve any misunderstandings. However, when I heard the corporal say he had spoken with TFC Supik, and TFC Supik said he never gave me permission to stand down from PT, my alarm turned to total fear. The corporal made his accusations, and his version was apparently all they needed to hear. I respectfully asked to be heard, and was granted liberty to speak. I immediately pointed out that the one person who could bear out my innocence was absent. I had to request to have TFC Supik report to Lieutenant Clark's office.

Back then, Pikesville's phone system featured an intercom that when activated, could be heard throughout the entire compound inside and out. Lieutenant Clark directed TFC Supik to report to his office. It seemed like an eternity, but TFC Supik finally reported to the lieutenant's office. Before the corporal could put his spin on anything, I asked TFC Supik, if he recalled granting me permission to skip PT the next morning, after I injured my foot. I reminded him that I wanted rest my foot, because I didn't want to miss the five-mile run.

TFC Supik deliberated a second looking upward trying to channel his recollections. Finally, he recalled giving me permission. I stood there numb until dismissed. I was so relieved I was able to keep my composure, and calmly stand my ground. By the time I was back in my seat, I felt a combination of relief and queasiness.

A few minutes later, the CQ taped me on the shoulder again. He told me the corporal wanted to see me. Foolishly, I allowed myself to think the corporal was going to apologize. The corporal said despite what TFC Supik admitted, he still thought I was lying. The corporal then mockingly told me he was giving me 20 demerits. This meant I wouldn't be going home for the following two weekends.

With a smirk on his face, he asked me, "What are you going to do about it?" When recruits received demerits, instructors noted them inside a pocket-sized card bi-fold. You were being put on report. As you received demerits, they accumulated until you reached 10. When applicable, a new card would be initiated for any subsequent infractions.

Once you've reached the magic number of 10 demerits, you received an all-expense-paid weekend, performing different cleaning details at the academy. I asked the corporal for a pen. While signing both cards, I reminded the corporal we had just finished the five-mile run. Unemotionally, and without looking at him, I told the corporal that meant we were almost finished, and he nor anyone else was getting me kicked out.

After signing both cards, I asked him was there anything else I could do for him. He snapped back, "Get back in the class." For the remaining time I was in the academy, I never shared that experience with anyone in the class, nor tried reporting the corporal's actions to academy command staff. I decided not to make an issue out of it. Instead, I reminded myself I asked to join them, they didn't ask for me. Admittedly, I was not happy. After all the talk about integrity, and treating people fairly, this corporal harassed me because he couldn't admit he was wrong.

I assumed the corporal thought I would lose my temper, and act insubordinate, giving him another opportunity to have me terminated. He was wrong for a second time that day. Having survived that, I convinced myself that if this is the game I have to play, then so be it; I was not going anywhere.

Life in the academy wasn't always filled with such personal drama. I credit that time with generally making the right impression on me, and understanding that being an MSP trooper, was a privilege not to be taken lightly. I also developed an attitude that any negativity perpetrated against me by individuals, would never reflect poorly on the department. I would view the state police as all the great things, and people I knew had to be out there. Something I wanted so badly, certainly had to be worthy my loyalty.

Occasionally, there were some tense moments amongst the recruits. By design, the academy was a pressure filled environment, intended to create a sense of urgency within the class. At times the instructors instigated spirited, but good natured competition amongst the recruits. But in the end, you knew this was not about fun and games. It was about discipline. It was about your survival both academically and physically. You had to perform at an accepted level, or it was all for nothing.

Although you learned to work as a group, there were times when you had to rely on your own abilities, and act independently. All in all, by the end of our six months, our class had become a functioning unit, thanks to the academy's time honored system of entrance-level training.

As in any community, or society there were cliques. Some willing separation by race, gender, or by where you were from. So unless you developed a particular relationship with someone, generally there was little chance of getting very close to your other classmates. Sometimes, that closeness came only if you had an opportunity to work with them personally after graduation. This was certainly the case in my own experiences with just a handful of my classmates.

One of the final practical requirements of the academy's curriculum, was for recruits to undergo a brief period of field training. We were paired with selected troopers from barracks, and other uniformed assignments across the state. Depending on who you were assigned to, your field training could have been at a barrack, or as it was in my case, patrolling the Baltimore Beltway near the academy.

Those recruits whose troopers were from barracks further out across the state, got to stay in the barrack's dorms during the duration of their field training. Because we were from the Baltimore area, Recruit Watts and I got to go out with TFC Edward E. Johnson. He was assigned to the Automotive Safety Enforcement Division. TFC Johnson had Heber and I patrol the Baltimore Beltway I-695, and parts of I-70, from Baltimore County to the Howard County line. TFC Johnson would drive, and sometimes he would let me and Heber take turns driving.

TFC Johnson took notes on our driving habits, our ability to observe, and our acquired knowledge of the state's motor vehicle and criminal laws. Standing close by, TFC Johnson also watched us approach stopped vehicles. He checked our issued written warnings to violators, and noted how we reported disabled vehicles over the radio. At the end of our training for the day, TFC Johnson would critique our performances, while he filled out our individual field-training observation reports.

Although only 43 years old, TFC Johnson's hair was mixed gray. He said after he finished with Heber and me (mainly me), his hair really turned gray. One early evening we were on a traffic stop on the beltway. My straw Stetson blew off my head, and into traffic. Just like a little kid running after a ball, I ran after my prized Stetson. Fortunately, there was only light traffic, and a woman operating her vehicle swerved just missing my Stetson. TFC Johnson was beside himself, and asked me was I trying to give him a heart attack.

A day later, Heber was driving westbound on I-70. TFC Johnson was seated in the front passenger seat, and I was in the rear. An old pickup truck was just ahead of us, and TFC Johnson told Heber to get closer behind the truck. Unbeknownst to us, TFC Johnson had spotted a violation. TFC Johnson told Heber, to activate the emergency lights and siren. After we pulled the truck over, TFC Johnson approached the driver's side.

When he returned with the operator's information, TFC Johnson told us to go locate the violation he had observed. Heber and I looked all over, and couldn't find what TFC Johnson saw. He told us to look at the rear registration plate. TFC Johnson pointed to the validation sticker in the upper right-hand corner of the plate. The sticker was expired in violation of "Transportation Article 13-411D."

After I graduated, I could spot an expired sticker in my sleep. Other than speeding citations, I think I wrote more expired tag related violations than any other kind. TFC Johnson ingrained an awareness of that violation in my head from that day on.

TFC Johnson would retire at the rank of sergeant in 1996. "Double E" as he was famously known, passed in 2018. I got to spend a Sunday watching the end of an NFL game with him, at his care center. I reminded him about the days when he trained me and Heber, and took us by his house that he referred to as "Johnson Terrace." In his deep raspy voice, he would jokingly warn us to stay away from his house, and his daughters. Unfortunately, "Double E" passed early the next morning, the day after our visit.

Finally, the day that made this all worthwhile arrived: June 17, 1977. Out of the 70 recruits that entered, 66 graduated. The uniform of the day was our Class "D" summer uniforms consisting of straw Stetsons, short sleeved shirts, and summer weight trousers. Our families, friends and invited guest were greeted by the superintendent, Colonel Smith. Colonel Smith, was the first trooper to be appointed superintendent back in 1970. Prior to Colonel Smith, the previous superintendents had been majors or colonels in Maryland's National Guard; and in one case, the state's Secretary of Public Safety and Correctional Services.

During the program in our gymnasium that doubled as an auditorium, the audience got to see slides of our individual photos shown on a big projector screen, as our names were announced by the academy's commander, Captain Porter. Reception of our class as the newest members of the Field Operations Bureau (FOB), was accepted by the bureau chief, Lieutenant Colonel Thomas Veditz. In unison, we took the "Trooper's Oath of Office," administered by the deputy superintendent, Lieutenant Colonel Carroll Cook.

At the conclusion of the ceremony, there were smiles, and people taking pictures. We congratulated one another, and introduced each other amongst our families and friends. Warmly, and in some cases customarily, we wished each other the best of luck. The harsh realities of a career in law enforcement was far from our thoughts that day.

Little did we know at the time, that some of our classmates wouldn't make it to the age of normal retirement time. Some tragically by an on-duty death, some through debilitating on-duty injuries, a few leaving for other police agencies, and professions; And yes… some were terminated for violating the law; One of those things that could get you fired, that we were warned about.

I am proud to recognize our two classmates who gave their lives in the performance of their duties. Corporal Greg May, who while piloting one of our medic-vac helicopters, perished in a crash along with the medic/observer TFC Carey Poetzman. Always quiet, Greg never had to stay a weekend. Amazingly, he accumulated a total of only nine demerits through the entire six months.

TFC Eric Monk, was struck, and fatally wounded by an oncoming vehicle while conducting a traffic stop. Eric was one of the two recruits I had to take on, during two separate boxing tests. He hit me so hard, I thought there were two of him in the ring at one time. Although I never got to know either one of them very well, or saw them much after graduation, I know they were two of "Maryland's Finest."

There were four of our classmates who suffered on-duty career ending injuries precipitated by traffic accidents: Connie Harris, Leonard Glenn, Jr., Vonzel Ward and Denise Bays. Vonzell would go on to be elected sheriff of Calvert County, after he retired from the MSP.

Looking back, I know we were being prepared exactly for the nature our required duties. To me the state police academy embodies a great tradition, and culture second to none. From day one, it was instilled in us to recognize how fortunate we were, to be a part of an organization steeped in a history of excellence, and achievement. Matters about integrity and dedication to duty, was an integral message woven through lectures time and again. The question of if you can't be trusted in a controlled environment, what will you do when you get cut loose, was always a central theme.

One of my earliest reminders of how important your presence in our uniform can be, came unexpectedly one day after work. Before going home one evening after my early patrol, I stopped by a shopping center near my home. After leaving, and heading to the parking lot, I noticed an elderly Black gentleman walking towards me on the sidewalk.

The man was walking with a cane and looking down. As we neared I said, "Good afternoon sir." The man stopped, and looked up at me for a second. Then he looked me up and down, as if he were inspecting my uniform. Putting his hand on my arm, he looked at me and said, "Boy I don't even know you, but I'm so proud of you, [because] when I was your age, there was no such thing."

I cupped his hand with both of mine, and sincerely thanked him. As he slowly walked away, I just stood there watching him. I thought about what he said with both humility, and pride. That is still such an emotional moment for me to recall. That made it very clear to me, what being a trooper in this state could mean to so many people.

I know all of my family was very proud of me, especially my late grandfather Joe Butler. He always held state troopers in the highest regards. When I graduated, I think he was prouder than I was.

On July 12, 2018, my retired classmate, brother trooper, and friend, Captain Heber Watts, passed unexpectedly. At his funeral, I said he was a man with many talents. After I remarked about how intelligent Heber was, with tongue-in-cheek, I said, "So much so, that sometimes only God, and Heber knew what in the world [Heber] was talking about." Much like all the greats who have passed on, Heber will be remembered for his dedication to public safety, and his love for the MSP.

Chapter 7

"Once a Highway Man, Always
a Highway Man"

My first assignment was at the John F. Kennedy Memorial Highway Barrack "M" (referred to as JFK or the Highway). The barrack was responsible for traffic and criminal enforcement, as well as other related public safety activities on Interstate 95's 43 miles of highway, from mile marker 000 in Baltimore County, through Harford and Cecil Counties, to mile marker 043 at the Delaware State line.

Barrack troopers also patrolled and answered calls for service at the two traveler and truck stop plazas: the Maryland House in Harford County, and the Northeast Plaza in Cecil County. The JFK Highway Barrack's activities were funded by the Maryland Department of Transportation (MDOT). Because toll fees had to be collected at the main tollbooths, and the unmanned coin baskets situated on the off and on-ramps, some of our duties involved safeguarding the MDOT employees who collected that revenue.

There were two barrack distinctions depending on its mission within Maryland's 23 counties patrolled by the department. Barracks responsible for patrolling interstate highways, and some state routes nearby, were referred to in the field as "traffic" barracks. This was mainly because, their responsibilities relegated them to interstate highway enforcement and motorist safety duties. Troopers assigned to "traffic" barracks still had full statewide law enforcement powers, and could affect arrest throughout the state.

Our criminal and traffic apprehensions at JFK, usually resulted from detecting those engaged in the illegal possession, or transportation of drugs and weapons, or other illegal contraband, or vehicle and other property thefts. We also arrested individuals wanted on outstanding warrants (in or out of state), motorists operating under the influence of an alcoholic beverage or other substances; and motorists operating on a suspended or revoked driver's license, as well as incidents occurring at the two travel plazas to name a few.

The other barracks were known as "full-service" barracks. Like other police agencies, troopers at those barracks patrolled neighborhoods, and handled all calls for service within those neighborhoods, and business communities served by the barrack.

My four years at JFK, were spent learning the intricacies of the department, while trying to survive and get along with all sorts; while somewhere in between, learning how to become a trooper. The department has a two-year probationary period for recruits/troopers beginning when you enter the academy. The first period of your probation begins with your first six months in the academy. Upon graduation, you have an additional 18 months to successfully complete your probation, and become a permanent employee.

New troopers are required to undergo a field training period. When I graduated, the department had no formal field training trooper (FTT) designation as it would in later years. Therefore you rode with all the members in your group, who were senior to you. Your performance in the areas of driving, radio etiquette, knowledge of the area, courtroom preparation and demeanor, officer safety, contact with the pubic, report writing, investigating traffic accidents, issuing citations, arrest procedures, and your powers of observation, were all being reported on for inclusion in your probationary personnel file.

A trooper's field training period generally lasted eight weeks depending on the individual trooper's progress. That gave you roughly another 70 weeks of probationary status. However, after you completed your field training, you were allowed to patrol on your own while still on probation.

Each group included at least five troopers, a corporal, and a sergeant. The sergeant was referred to as the duty officer (DO), or shift commander. The sergeant oversaw the barrack's patrol activities, along with the Police Communications Officer (PCO) during your shift. The corporal had a duel role. Normally, they acted as the patrol group's first-line supervisor. In the sergeant's absence from the desk, the corporal would assume the role of duty officer. Within the group's structure, there's the senior troopers at the rank of trooper first class (TFC), followed by troopers, and finally in my case, trooper probationers. So with the exception of a fellow classmate, everyone was senior to me.

One of the great things about being a trooper in Maryland, is you are assigned a vehicle that you can take home, and use within reason off duty. Troopers could also enforce the law in an off-duty capacity, while operating their assigned vehicles. Back then, troopers were the only ones outside of high-ranking officials in other departments, who had take-home vehicles. That added to the prestige of being a state trooper. Today, several county and sheriff's departments in Maryland also allow their officers that privilege.

Unlike today, only the supervisors, and senior troopers got first consideration for vehicle assignment, especially for newer vehicles. However, at some point after completing your field training, you got to use someone else's vehicle. Generally, a new trooper wouldn't be considered for a permanent vehicle assignment, until they successfully completed their field training, and began patrolling on their own.

One morning, while off duty, I was sitting at a traffic light in another trooper's vehicle. I noticed a White male operating the vehicle to my right, kept looking over at me. When he suddenly tapped his horn at me, I thought he needed assistance. I rolled down my window. The man actually asked if I was a trooper. I said yes I was, and asked could I help him.

The man just took off after the light turned green. Minutes later, I was stopped by a local police officer asking to see my identification. Shortly afterwards, the barrack began calling me over the radio, asking if I was ok. It seemed that the concerned citizen at the traffic light notified the police, that a young Black male had stolen a state police vehicle. I guess I just didn't look old enough to be a trooper to that concerned citizen.

On your official first day reporting for duty, you had to drive your own vehicle. I had never driven through that part of the state before. But as the barrack was on I-95, heading north towards Delaware, I figured I couldn't miss it. The first mistake of my day as a new trooper, came when I mistook a building with a huge radio tower next to it, and two or three of our marked patrol vehicles on the parking lot, for the barrack. The building was on the southbound side of I-95, just south of the Maryland House Travel Plaza.

I drove through the crossover, and parked on the lot. When I entered the building, I was taken aback on how small the open floor plan was. There were two desk about, and a man sitting at one of them, dressed in a short sleeved shirt and tie. Although I didn't think he necessarily looked like a trooper, I assumed he was an investigator.

The man asked if he could help me. Saluting and standing at attention, I said, "Trooper Russell reporting for duty sir." Laughing politely, he told me the barrack was further north of the Tyding's Memorial Bridge, in Cecil County. The man was the maintenance shop supervisor.

The barrack's vehicles were serviced by two MDOT garages that also serviced their own vehicles, and performed other highway maintenance, and related safety matters. They were referred to as Maintenance-one in Harford County, and Maintenance-two in Cecil County. Fortunately I left home early enough, and still made it to the barrack to report on time.

Chapter 8
There Was More Than One Kind of
Minority in the MSP

During my time at the barrack, I experienced some challenges to my nature and perseverance. It would be my first official post-graduation test dealing with blatant, and sometimes subtle racism. Even then, I felt these incidents had to be the exception, and not the rule. In 1977, there were still some individuals who found it hard to accept the movement towards racially diversifying the MSP. There were six to seven troopers who were Black assigned to the barrack, including one of my academy classmates.

Within my own group, there was one trooper who occasionally tested my patients with his alleged inquisitive conversations inquiring about Black people, and their stereotypical behavior. If that wasn't bad enough, I had another trooper in my group allegedly say he didn't want any "niggers" driving his assigned vehicle. One evening, I was being driven home by a TFC from another group. The 1978 Ford LTDs in use at that time, suffered from vapor lock in the summer, causing them to occasionally hesitate.

I was sitting in the front passenger seat, resting with my Stetson over my face, but I wasn't asleep. Along the way, the vehicle's engine began sputtering. The TFC banged on the dashboard saying, "This car acts just like a nigger." My initial reaction was to respond in kind, instead I decided to pretend not to hear him, taking the sting out of his vile conduct.

Before heading to work early one afternoon, I was directed to stop by Pikesville, and pick up the barrack's mail, and the mail for Bel Air Barrack "D" and North East Barrack "F," on my way to work. As Bel Air was on the way before I reached JFK, I decided to drop off their mail personally. Entering the barrack, I was buzzed into the radio room by the corporal. After we saluted, the corporal asked me to put the mailbag at the foot of the wooden coat tree near the radio console. As I got near the coat tree, I saw an 8x10 sheet of paper hanging from one of the brass hooks.

The paper had some type of drawing on it. I could immediately tell it was some crude attempt at racism, and payed no direct attention to it. As I was about to leave, the corporal asked me if I had seen the drawing. I told him I hadn't noticed it. He then redirected my attention to the coat tree, suggesting I go back and look at the drawing. In front of the PCO, I went back, and took a closer look.

The drawing depicted a cartoon-like figure of a White male uniformed trooper, with an alligator on a leash, as though it were a K-9. The alligator had its two front legs on a lamp post, trying to climb it. At the top of the lamp post attempting to escape the alligator, was a caricature of a Black male drawn with a monkey's tail, looking back anxiously at the alligator. As I walked back towards the corporal, he asked me what I thought about the drawing. Smiling at the corporal, I just said, "How about that sir." I continued walking out of the radio room as if nothing happened, and left the barrack. I don't think that was the desired effect the corporal was hoping for.

These things were all perpetrated to get under your skin, and perhaps discourage your desire to stay. Quitting wasn't an option. So when occasionally confronted with that type of ignorant behavior, I learned not to respond; especially while I was new. While you were on probation, you were best suited to learn your job, stay safe at all times, and try not to kick up too much dust along the way.

Those who harbored a distain over racial diversity, would soon learn they were just wasting their time on me and others. Outnumbered, and out ranked, I developed the stance that as long as they knew better than to put their hands on me, and backed me up when I needed help, they'd just have to deal with it. No pun intended here, but as I would soon discover, those types of individuals were the real minorities in the department.

Chapter 9
Getting on the Right Track

As a new trooper back then, you didn't graduate from the academy with a certification allowing you to use the department's speed detecting devices. As a probationer, your traffic enforcement efforts mainly relied upon your own observations, or working personally with someone in your group who was certified to run radar or VASCAR (Visual Average Speed Computer and Recorder). You could also participate on "stopping teams," run by the senior troopers in your group.

After coming off probation, you could request to attend related classes, and become certified, once you passed the test administered at the end of the class. Nearing the end of my probation period, I hadn't distinguished myself to the complete satisfaction of supervision, or command when it came to my traffic enforcement measures. Although my other measures of performance were satisfactory, my traffic enforcement output was lacking in their expectations.

A senior TFC named Raymond Grissett, was transferred from Randallstown Barrack in Baltimore County, to the JFK Highway Barrack. TFC Grissett was assigned to my group. One morning he pulled alongside of me in a crossover. After assessing my status, he said, "All right young man, let's get you on the right track."

To say TFC Grissett was a high writer of citations even by today's standards is an understatement. The tractor-trailer operators use to refer to him as the "Hatchet Man," on the CB (Citizen Band) radio. The department installed CB radios in our vehicles to monitor conversations about traffic conditions, and other safety related concerns, being reported by the tractor-trailer operators, and others motorists with CB radios.

For Ray, 20 citations a shift was an average day for him. Remarkably, he would call out 10 to 13 stops for me to issue the violators citations or warnings, and still get his stops. This clearly made a difference in my traffic enforcement output. After my probation, I was able to obtain my own certification for use of the radar equipment.

While assigned to patrol a major interstate highway for eight hours, there were expectations that expressed the necessity to earnestly enforce the traffic laws, in order to maintain the safety of motorists who traversed it. Even though there were a few sarcastic remarks from violators about end of the month quotas, these same people wouldn't want to trade places with motorist who lost their lives, due to their own, or someone else's negligent driving habits.

Thanks to TFC Grissett's leadership, and concern, I was released from probation at the scheduled timeframe, along with most of the troopers in my academy class. We became what was referred to as a "slick sleeve." That's a trooper with no stripes on their sleeves, who is now off of probation. My graduating class was eligible for automatic promotion to trooper first class (your first stripe), in January 1980.

In the years to come, Ray went on to achieve the rank of lieutenant before he retired. He commanded the Glen Burnie Barrack, and the Golden Ring Barrack respectively. In 2003, I was able to return his earlier kindness, when I requested Ray's transfer to one of my units, making him my assistant commander, prior to his retirement.

Untimely in 2016, Ray passed. He would be laid to rest joining his late wife Evelyn, and their two sons, Kirk and Rodney. Ray certainly left his mark on the MSP, and my career. You can't think of a consummate lead-by-example individual, without thinking of the original "Hatchet Man" himself…. Ray Grissett.

Chapter 10
M-21 Highway, 10-41

The 10 code used to report for duty is 10-41. When I was finally assigned my first permanent vehicle, it was M-21; a yellow 1978 Ford LTD II. It belonged to my sergeant who got a newer vehicle with a different number. It took almost a year before I got my own assigned vehicle. Even when you were assigned a vehicle, sometimes troopers had to leave their vehicles for use by a trooper on the next shift; especially if there was a shortage of vehicles, due to maintenance needs, or accident damage, causing a shortage to the barrack's fleet.

If you were required to leave your assigned vehicle at the end of your group's work week, your corporal or senior TFC took you home, and picked you up when your leave was over. Sometimes if the senior trooper didn't feel like taking you home, they would drive to their residence, give you their spare keys, and let you take their assigned vehicle home. With the keys, you received the warning: "Don't let anything happen to my vehicle or else." Even if you received the vehicle soiled, you were expected to have it cleaned before you returned it. You did have the option to leave your personal vehicle at the barrack, and drive it home when your group went on leave.

By the time I got M-21, the lower half of the doors began to rust from exposure to the road salts used during the winter months. That didn't bother me much. I could be seen in front of my house, gladly waxing that rust. There was a humorous oddity about that particular shade of yellow. Sometimes as I drove through different parts of Baltimore City, people on street corners would start aggressively waving at me. When I pulled over asking what was wrong, they would do a double take and say, "Oh, I thought this was a cab."

After I got cut loose from field training, my first tense moment came when I stopped a vehicle with Delaware registration for speeding, on northbound I-95, in Baltimore County. I was en route to begin my night patrol (12 midnight to 8 a.m.) shift. After calling out my location and the vehicle's registration number, I approached the vehicle. Including the operator, I could see there were at least three other occupants inside.

When I received the operator's driver's license and registration card, I returned to my vehicle to run his information over the radio. I wanted to ensure there were no open warrants, or suspensions on him. This is the normal sequence of events during a traffic stop. Depending on the name on the registration card, a stolen check may also be requested.

As I sat inside my vehicle, the operator and his three passengers, got out of their vehicle, and began walking towards my vehicle. I stepped out and ordered them to stop, and get back inside their vehicle. They stopped, and started shouting at me menacingly. Sergeant Larry Musial, who was also assigned to the barrack, was in the area. When he heard me call out the stop over the radio, he responded to my location. After Sergeant Musial pulled in behind me, he instinctively sensed what was going on.

With his long steel flashlight in hand, Sergeant Musial quickly jumped in. He told them to get back in their vehicle. Sergeant Musial said, "If you think this trooper was by himself you just made a big mistake!" All four of them quickly got back inside the vehicle, and never said another word. Sergeant Musial told me he would stand by while I finished writing my citation.

Afterwards, he told me to not take any unnecessary risks, and call for back up in the future. This was a great example of the leadership, and concern for one another I came to appreciate, and eagerly emulate. Sergeant Musial would go onto make captain before retiring. We got to work together again in the Bureau of Drug and Criminal Enforcement, and again when he became a major with the Cecil County Sheriff's Department, after he retired from the MSP.

During another night patrol, I was dispatched to the scene of a 10-50 (accident), southbound on I-95, in Cecil County. By the time I arrived, the operator was outside of the vehicle. The vehicle had run off the road, and into a guardrail on the right shoulder. The operator was sitting on the guardrail.

My partner from the adjoining patrol also arrived. The operator was somewhat incoherent, but jovial, and appeared to be under the influence of something. Looking around with his flashlight, the senior TFC observed a large, clear plastic baggie containing a green vegetable-like substance in the grass near the vehicle. It had been raining earlier, and the bag was only wet on the side lying against the grass. We believed it was enough probable cause to connect the bag to the operator.

It was later determined that the substance in the bag was parsley flakes laced with phencyclidine (PCP), a drug used for its mind altering effects. The operator was arrested, and charged with possession with intent to distribute. The bag of PCP weighed just over two pounds, and at that time, had a street value of $2,000. The operator was identified, and found to be a known active member of the Pagans Motorcycle gang. He was also known to our Intelligence Unit.

Corporal Walter Wassmer, the barrack's ID section supervisor, and only full-time investigator, was called out to assist me with processing, and storage of the PCP. This was my first major arrest. In order to perform field tests on a suspected controlled dangerous substance (CDS), the department used reagent drug testing kits, to aid in the preliminary identification of a suspected CDS.

The type of suspected CDS, determined what kit was used. The kits were made up of small, squared, thick clear plastic packs. The packs contained small glass ampules filled with liquid reagents. A minimum sample of the substance is placed inside the pack. After you closed the flap, with the pressure of your thumb and forefinger finger, you pressed and cracked the ampules in the directed sequence. A chemical interaction identified the presence of a CDS, by changing to a specific identifying color. The kit's instructions indicated the correct colors that should appear after the chemical reaction took place.

Next, the suspected PCP was put inside a plastic evidence bag, heat sealed, and finally placed in a locked storage container. The evidence was then forwarded with the attached analysis request/chain of custody (MSP Form 67A) to the crime lab, by a crime scene technician. The substance is then analyzed by one of our chemists, whose findings are officially documented, and presented as evidence in court during the subsequent trial if necessary.

While you are still early in your career, even after you are cut loose from field training, you must pay attention to everything that happens around you. The senior TFC who was at the scene with me, decided to open the bag for a closer inspection. Needless to say the contents emitted a strong odor, and that was good enough for me.

The TFC took a deep whiff of the contents, and for the next few days he was out on sick leave, suffering from diarrhea caused by inhaling the contents of the bag. That early lesson impressed upon me you have to use great care when examining the things you find; especially chemical substances.

On another night patrol, I was traveling southbound on I-95, in Cecil County, when I stopped a speeding vehicle, on the right shoulder. Before I could exit my vehicle, the operator quickly sped off continuing south, reaching speeds over 80 miles per hour. Thankfully, there was not much traffic on the road due to the early morning hours. Operating in the dark at those speeds, could have been hazardous in heavy traffic.

I called out the various numbered mile markers along the route of the pursuit. The barrack was advised to have the southbound tollbooth collectors on alert should we reach that point. In his reckless attempt to avoid being stopped, I was concerned that the operator may crash into one of the occupied tollbooths.

Before reaching the toll plaza, the operator sharply took the off-ramp to the last exit before reaching the tolls, Route 222, to Port Deposit/Perryville. Due to the operator's speed, he was unable to negotiate the ramp's curvature, and collided with the unmanned toll-basket console on the left shoulder of the ramp. The operator got out and attempted to flee on foot. I was able to catch, and apprehend him in the grassy acreage behind the console.

The arrestee was identified as a 17-year-old runaway from Massachusetts. The vehicle belonged to his grandmother, and was taken without her permission. The arrestee admitted he burglarized two residences, stealing property and money, on his way south. In order to gain entry into the residences, the arrestee said he used whatever was available to break and enter through sliding glass doors in the rear of the residences.

In one case, he said he threw a cinderblock through the sliding glass door, and hid out for a few minutes. When he was sure no one was home, he entered the residence. He then stole money, and other things he wanted. His plan was to drive to Florida, and meet a friend. He said that he passed all kinds of police without a problem.

The arrestee told TFC Bob Stein (the acting criminal investigator), and me, the only reason he was speeding, was because he was tired, and trying to find somewhere to rest. Unfortunately for him, just a few miles south from where the pursuit began, we passed the Northeast Travel Plaza. There he would've been able to rest in one of the many parking spaces on the lot, most likely undetected.

Because of his juvenile status, the arrestee was turned over to the county's juvenile services. After contacting the authorities in Massachusetts, it was decided to put the arrestee on a plane with someone from our juvenile services, and return him to the custody of their local authorities, who would be waiting at the airport.

All seemed to be going well for me, until one afternoon when I was directed to respond to a vehicle fire south on I-95, in Harford County. I observed the operator of a Volkswagen Beetle on the right shoulder, with his rear engine compartment's hatch up. By the time I arrived, the flames had fairly subsided. I used my vehicle's fire extinguisher to douse the remaining flames.

After interviewing the operator, I learned that he was traveling south, when he began smelling smoke. He immediately pulled over onto the right shoulder. After responding to the rear and opening the hatch, he said the engine suddenly caught fire. Had the vehicle caught fire while it was being driven, it would've been considered a vehicle accident, requiring a written Accident Report (AR/MSP Form 1).

Under the circumstances, I reported the call as a 10-46 (disabled vehicle). A 10-46 call required no report. The PCO would open a Complaint Control Card (CC-Card) for service, and note the disposition on the card as towed, self-repaired, or abandoned until further notice. The card would then be closed, except in the case of an abandoned vehicle.

While I was calling in the 10-46, another trooper pulled in front of the Volkswagen. This particular trooper was actually in my academy class, but due to personal issues, he dropped out. He later reapplied, and was "recycled" through the next class.

I observed him speaking to the operator. I thought nothing of this, until he came back to my vehicle. Apparently while speaking with the operator, the trooper developed the opinion that this was an accident call, not one for a disabled vehicle.

Standing by my driver's window, he said, "Russ this was a 10-50. The driver said the vehicle caught on fire while he was driving it." Although I didn't have to provide an explanation to him, I explained to the trooper, that I went over the matter twice with the gentleman, explaining the differences. I told the trooper the matter was as I reported it. I continued calling in my request for a tow truck to remove the vehicle off the shoulder.

Apparently that exchange didn't satisfy the trooper. Unbeknownst to me, he went to nearby Maintenance-one, and telephoned the PCO while I was still at the scene. He told her I improperly coded the incident. Standing on the shoulder speaking with the gentleman, I heard the barrack call, "Highway M-21," on my outside speaker. Excusing myself, I went to answer the radio. The PCO requested I give her a 10-21 (telephone call) at the barrack.

By then the tow truck had arrived, and I left the scene. Using the telephone at the maintenance shop, I called the barrack. To my surprise the PCO began questioning me about the incident, inquiring whether I had properly coded the call for service. I knew this had to be instigated by that trooper. I repeated the same information to the PCO, ensuring her that the disposition was as I initially reported it.

Assuming I was not going to hear the end of this, I decided to write an Incident Report (IR), even though one was not required in this instance. An IR is used to report miscellaneous, or noncriminal matters. I informed the PCO that I would report the matter on an IR, and asked her for the complaint control number (CC#) to write on the report. I told her that should satisfy the matter, because it was not an accident.

The irony of all this was that it would have been easier to do a single-vehicle accident report, rather than an IR. But I was not going to be coerced, and change my initial coding. I drove back to the scene in time to catch the tow truck, and obtained the owner's information for my IR. I had no idea of the escalation this matter would take on a few days later.

During barrack staff meetings, it was customary to select a trooper to attend, and make the command and supervisory staff aware of any issues from the rank-and-file. After the trooper made his allegations against me, he was invited to repeat his claim before the gathered administrative staff. Probation or not, such infractions can be punishable by termination.

After my corporal become aware of the allegation, he radioed for me to 10-25 (report) to the barrack. My corporal who I always got along with and respected, approached me in a heated fashion. Although I found it necessary to accept less than professional conduct from others while I was on probation, it was most undesirable now. I was troubled by the manner in which I was spoken to by my corporal.

Without giving me the opportunity to provide my side, he lashed out at me in a fit of anger. Actually, I was more hurt than angry. Our voices could be heard in the hallway from the trooper's room, even with the door closed.

The barrack commander stuck his head in the door, and looked in a few seconds before closing it again. I didn't say anything insubordinate; I just wanted to know why my corporal was willing to take the word of another, without hearing my side before accosting me angrily. With no answer in sight, I was dismissed by the corporal. As it was the end of my shift anyway, I headed for home.

The next morning, I found myself in the barrack commander's office. I got a stern lecture from the lieutenant because of my behavior towards my corporal. I was unaware the barrack commander assigned a sergeant from another group, to conduct an inquiry into the allegations that I made a false report. I didn't realize it, until I passed Sergeant Paul Hamm in the hallway later that afternoon. It was then I learned I had been under investigation.

Using the information provided on my incident report, Sergeant Hamm contacted the owner/operator of the Volkswagen by telephone at his home in New Jersey. The gentleman confirmed my version, instead of what was reported by the trooper and PCO. Very casually, the sergeant said he was glad they could trust me. I never received an answer as to what they were going to do to the trooper who falsely reported my actions. Looking for those answers got me nowhere, so it was time to move on.

These people were incredible. It was hard to believe they all thought I would risk termination, by being too lazy to submit a simple accident report. A report where under the circumstances, all I had to do was fill in the blanks, write a short narrative, and draw a small diagram of a vehicle on fire.

Before I knew it, my corporal retired, and my sergeant was promoted to first sergeant, and transferred to another barrack. A newly transferred corporal and sergeant, became my supervisors. It was apparent from the start, neither were enamored with me. I took the hint that it was time to move on. I felt confident enough to seek a transfer to a "full-service" barrack. Thankfully, in 1981, I was transferred to the Westminster Barrack in Carroll County.

When word got out I requested to leave, a senior TFC told me I was crazy to leave, and go to Westminster. I asked why he thought so. He responded by asking me why I wanted to go a barrack, where I'd be doing more work than I would at JFK, for the same pay. I simply told him I had plans, and JFK was no longer in them.

I don't want to paint my tenure at JFK as undesirable. There were some excellent opportunities to learn as a new trooper, and some exceptional people that would be a positive influence throughout my career. Mainly, the barrack's ID section supervisor; corporal, later to become a detective sergeant: Walter Wassmer.

As I mention in the next chapter about my time at the Westminster Barrack, I had a brief assignment to the barrack's ID section. I called the JFK Barrack to tell Corporal Wassmer the news, and he was elated for me. A few days later, I received a package in the barrack mail. Corporal Wassmer had put together a booklet with examples from some of his cases, and other related documents, as a guide to help me with my transition into the criminal section.

Attached to the booklet was a typed 3X5 card. It was a personal note from Corporal Wassmer congratulating, and encouraging me to take it slow at first, and always ask questions of the senior investigators. The note went on to say my acceptance in the ID section made him proud. Corporal Wassmer said that I was one of his men who enjoyed doing good criminal work. I still have that booklet today.

In 2008, when I was appointed to lieutenant colonel, I met Walt for lunch in Harford County one afternoon. I asked Walt if he remembered the booklet he made for me. He said he had forgotten about it until I reminded him. When I showed Walt the booklet, he couldn't believe I kept it all these years. I told him it was one of the most treasured mementos I had in my career.

Walt is a veteran of the U.S. Air Force, and a former Wilmington Delaware Police officer. There is no finer example of a trooper, leader, or dedicated professional in the MSP. As it is with several others I mention, Detective Sergeant Wassmer represents everything

I love about the state police. After his retirement from the department, Walt went on to become the warden at the Cecil County Detention Center. After that, he became chief of the Quarryville, Pennsylvania Police, before finally retiring. Walt and his wife Jane also had their own private investigation business as well. I am extremely blessed to have Walt and Jane as dear friends all these years later.

There was also a corporal named Johnny Hughes assigned to the barrack. Although I didn't work in his group while I was there, I found him to be an excellent supervisor, and a sincere down-to-earth individual. Corporal Hughes would retire as a major, and later became the 33rd U.S. Marshal in the history of our District here in Maryland. U.S. Marshal Hughes was appointed in 2002, and has served under six presidents. At the time of this book, he is still serving in that same capacity, and he is still the same gentleman today, as he was back when we met.

My group's corporal and I, shared a good working relationship prior to that false report allegation. After that, the relationship of trust and respect was no longer there I guess. We were never the same after that.

The group's second-line supervisor was Sergeant Don Hash. Back in those days, you had very little interaction with your sergeant. You pretty much dealt with the senior TFC first, and the corporal second. But for the interaction we had, I had a respect for the sergeant, and his calm demeanor. It was always good to hear him go 10-7 (out of service the barrack. Sergeant Hash would retire at the rank of lieutenant.

Two of the senior TFCs in my group, TFC Guy Williamson and the late TFC George Glenzer were very helpful to me as well. I got to work with a new trooper named Roswell (Eddie) Jones. Eddie was a second-generation trooper following in his father's footsteps. I mean this in a good way: Eddie had one of those colorful, eventful, and adventurous careers that not many people could have survived. Eddie was a good trooper who enjoyed his job, and those who worked with him enjoyed him too.

Chapter 11
"If You Can Work at Westminster,
You Can Work Anywhere in the State"

In 1981, I began my tenure at the Westminster Barrack "G," in Carroll County. Back then, Carroll County was rural and wide open, not like today, where the county is populated by major shopping centers and business, restaurants, auto dealers, schools, churches and all types of luxury housing. I would have to learn an all new geographic locality. There were towns named Union Bridge, New Windsor, Taneytown, Manchester, Hampstead, Mt. Airy, Eldersburg and Sykesville to name a few. The barrack shared jurisdiction with the sheriff's office, and the various town police departments, except those that had an exclusive municipal jurisdiction.

Unlike the Baltimore areas where I grew up, many of the county's rural areas had no street signs, or street lights illuminating certain roads at night. The patrol areas were so expansive, a Carroll County "ADC Street Map" guidebook, became an essential part of my equipment. Public pay phones were our unofficial callboxes. If there was a message too lengthy, or sensitive to put out over the air, you were told to 10-21 the barrack. After finding a nearby pay phone, you'd radio the telephone number to the barrack. The barrack telephoned, and gave you your message.

It didn't take long to see how the barrack got its reputation as being one of the busiest, if not the busiest in the state. You hardly had time to finish one call for service before receiving another. There were times where I would be taking a report, and before I could finish, the PCO telephoned the residence giving me one or two other calls for service.

After your shift was over, it was common to see troopers gathered in the troopers' room on the second floor. Due to the volume of calls for service, reports were hard to finish during your shift, especially on day shift. The troopers' room is where we gathered to complete our reports, or pick up your mail. On one side of the room up against the wall, was a large wooden compartment mail organizer. Each trooper had their own designated slot. This is where troopers received their mail, court summonses, returned disapproved paperwork, and other assigned duty related directives, or notifications.

We'd all be sitting at the long battered wooden table, trying to finish reports before we secured for the day. Some on typewriters, and others handwriting reports. This was a far cry from the JFK Barrack. But I knew this was the best way to gain experience.

In those days, most of the supervisors and senior TFCs, were seasoned veterans. Unlike today, there was a measurable age difference between them, and most of the graduating troopers. My first immediate supervisor was Corporal Bob Crawford. The first thing I will always remember about him, came after our initial meeting. Sitting in the office shared by the barrack's corporals, Corporal Crawford confided something to me which immediately sealed my loyalty to him.

It appeared that one of my admirers from JFK, contacted Corporal Crawford prior to my arrival. Someone tried warning him I was the worst trooper of all times. Being a standup person, Corporal Crawford told the caller he was capable of making up his own mind about me. Corporal Crawford assured me he was giving no credence to the call.

I told him I was grateful, and assured him they were the problem not me. Corporal Crawford told me how he didn't like that type of ambushing another person, and figured it was personal. The corporal said, "Now Russ I don't know you at all, but you will have every opportunity to be successful, as long as you do your job."

It's these types of moments that speak volumes about someone's character and leadership, you don't soon forget. I knew he was giving me the benefit of the doubt by telling me about that call. It didn't take long for me to realize Corporal Crawford was the type of supervisor you would give your all for. I saw firsthand how much he cared about his troopers… and we cared about him too.

Functioning effectively at Westminster was something to be proud of. The barrack investigated everything from misdemeanors to felonies. Calls for service ranged from malicious destruction of property, disturbances, fights, forgeries, burglaries of homes and business, citizen and business armed robberies; sexual assault offenses, child abuses, and homicides. Patrol troopers also investigated motor vehicle accidents from fender-benders to fatalities. Troopers are also the initial responder to accidents involving aircraft. Those investigations are subsequently turned over to the National Transportation Safety Board (NTSB). The county also had its share of suicides, attempted suicides, and those who suffered from a loss of mental stability.

The barrack had a top-notch criminal investigation section that was second to none. The investigators assumed control of the more serious cases for follow-up, or initiated their own investigations. In certain investigations, you conducted your own follow-up with their help, if needed.

One of the more unusual duties I encountered, was in November 1981. During a period of organized inmate unrest at the Hagerstown Correctional facility in Washington County, troopers were directed to respond to the facility located in the western part of the state. We were directed by our superintendent, to supplement correctional officers dealing with the unrest. My group was just about to end night patrol, when an order came out over the radio stating no one could secure at the end of the shift. From the barrack, we drove in a caravan to the prison later that morning.

We were soon joined by other troopers, who had also been on night patrol from other barracks in the region. We stood in the various corridors watching the prisoners move along the corridors. One of the correctional officers pointed out Arthur Bremer to us. Bremer was convicted for his attempted murder of former Alabama Governor George Wallace, in 1972. Secreted in the crowd, Bremer shot presidential candidate Wallace at a campaign rally in Laurel, Maryland.

I was on late patrol (4:00 p.m. to midnight) during a particularly deadly Christmas Eve. Unfortunately, the barrack investigated an accident involving several fatalities, and a suicide. In all, seven people died in the county that day. I responded to an attempted suicide handled by another trooper, as his backup. Later that evening, I investigated the reported suicide call.

A family north of Manchester, was having a Christmas Eve visit from the father's parents. During the visit, the grandfather excused himself to the bathroom. When it was noticed he had been in there for a while, his wife (the grandmother) called out to him. Receiving no response, the bathroom was checked.

They found that the grandfather had hung himself from the shower curtain rod. A check of his person revealed a "pink slip" in his pocket. The grandfather had been laid off from his job. After such an experience, it's not hard to imagine how Christmas Eve would never be the same again for that family; especially the children.

One night patrol, the barrack received a call reporting that a stabbing occurred outside the Melrose Tavern, north of Manchester on Route 30. I was assigned the call. When I arrived, I observed there was no one around, except for a White male sitting on the front steps. He was leaning forward with his arms and head on the top of his knees.

Walking past him, I checked the front door, and found the tavern was closed. Turning my attention back to the subject on the steps, I asked him if he was ok. He kept his head down, so I leaned to his level again asking if he was ok. He was mumbling to himself, and I could smell the odor of an alcoholic beverage coming from his breath.

A few minutes later, Corporal Crawford quickly pulled onto the parking lot. He hurriedly called me over to his vehicle. Corporal Crawford told me that the subject on the steps was the suspect in the stabbing. The color drained from my face, I'm sure. I asked the corporal how he know that.

The duty officer had Corporal Crawford call the barrack from a pay phone, and gave him the details before sending him to back me up. The victim suffered multiple wounds, but was still alive. The victim had been taken to Hanover Hospital in Hanover, Pennsylvania. Maryland Route 30, ends at the Pennsylvania line, and Hanover is a short distance from there.

Corporal Crawford and I approached the suspect. After a probable cause search of his person, we found the suspected weapon used on the victim. The knife wasn't something that jumped out at you as a serious weapon, but it apparently did the job. The suspect was placed under arrest. Corporal Crawford transported the suspect to the barrack, while I responded to the hospital to get information for my initial report. The case was subsequently turned over to the ID section. I was less than happy with the duty officer (sergeant).

Unknowingly, I placed myself in a compromising position with a suspect still in possession of a weapon he had just used in a crime.

If the sergeant had information that the suspect was still on the scene, why would he send me on the call without the benefit of knowing that? If it was perilous enough to have my backup phone in for those details, I should have been given some indication as well. The sergeant could have easily emphasized using 10-0 (caution) until my corporal arrived, if he didn't want to put that information over the air. That would have at least provided me with some measure of suspicion, that something else may be amiss at the scene.

I decided not to air my opinion about my concern over the sergeant or his lack of judgement. Instead I thanked my blessings that nothing bad happened. That was a clear message not to take anything for granted again. I promised myself if I ever became a supervisor, I would never intentionally be so careless with the safety of my troopers.

Of course the way things were currently with the promotional system, I knew it would be a good while before I was ready, or eligible for promotion. Besides, I had enough to worry about, just trying to keep up the hectic pace, working at Westminster.

A case of declining mental health would be the bases of a call for service I responded to in Hampstead, during a subsequent late patrol. The complainant telephoned the barrack when his visiting father began acting unusual, and wouldn't release his physical hold on one of the children. When I arrived at the residence, I heard Corporal Crawford on the radio advising the barrack he was en route to back me up.

The complainant advised me that his father started hugging his small daughter, and suddenly began squeezing her too tightly. This began to frighten her. The son attempted to release his daughter from his father's grip to no avail. When the grandfather began a continuous, indiscernible chant while hugging his granddaughter, this heightened the family's concern.

When I approached the grandfather who was seated on the living room sofa, I leaned over (but not too close), and asked if he would let me take his granddaughter. I told him she needed to go to the bathroom. He just pulled the child even closer.

By this time the little girl began crying. Again, I asked him if I could please take her because she was afraid. I told him I knew he wouldn't want that. Suddenly, the grandfather inexplicably began an incoherent chant saying: "This Black man is causing spots before my eyes… you can't fool me." Fortunately by this time, Corporal Crawford arrived.

Along with the son, we decided it was necessary to have his father committed to the psychiatric ward at Carroll County Hospital, on an Emergency Petition Order. Using the telephone in the living room, Corporal Crawford updated the duty officer, and requested the local volunteer emergency medical services (EMS) respond to transport the grandfather to the hospital. Anticipating we were in for a struggle, Corporal Crawford also requested an additional trooper as well.

Turning our attention back to the grandfather, we learned he was a retired steelworker. Although elderly, and shorter than average height, he was burley, and had extremely thick forearms. The first thing we had to do was forcibly pull the grandfather's arms apart so the son could safely secure his daughter.

Once the child was safe, next we had to get the grandfather situated to be transported. Corporal Crawford attempted to communicate with him. But again, the grandfather just chanted about spots, and this Black man not fooling him. As it was apparent he was not going voluntarily, we knew he had to be secured with handcuffs.

I said to the corporal, "I don't think he wants to go."

Corporal Crawford replied, "That's too bad Russ, he's got to go."

After a quick glance at each other that signified we were ready, the corporal and I lunged at the grandfather, attempting to grab his arms. The struggle was on. We wrestled the grandfather to the floor, and he threw us backwards. We jumped back on him, and now he was half way off the sofa. Still struggling, we maneuvered him back onto the floor. He was in a push up stance with us on his back.

After what seemed like an eternity, we were able to get him handcuffed. Finally TFC Tim Selby arrived, as did the EMS personnel. Thank goodness the grandfather was just resisting, and not fighting us. It took six of us to strap him onto to a wooden board used to carry him to the ambulance. I rode in the back of the ambulance, while Corporal Crawford followed us to the hospital. While en route to the hospital, the man continued his delusional utterances. I hadn't seen anything like that before.

Dealing with the mentally incapacitated, is something of a great challenge for police officers. In this case, although the grandfather was not trying to fight us, he could have posed a deadly threat to himself, and the police as well. In order to avoid an unnecessary catastrophe, the correct amount of physical force had to be used under the circumstances. Thankfully, I had an experienced supervisor like Corporal Crawford there as a backup. We were very fortunate it ended as it did.

Chapter 12
A Case of Mistaken Identity

The most direct route to the barrack coming from my part of Baltimore City in the 1980s, was MD Route 140, which ran west from Baltimore City, through Baltimore County, and into Carroll County. In those days, troopers passed each other along Route 140 in the two counties, like ships at sea. As I said earlier, I have always loved our military bearing. When troopers drive by one another, we salute. Other police departments didn't seem to stress such courtesy; So it was more noticeable, especially to the public, who identified it as part of our professionalism and culture.

One morning, after reporting 10-41 for early patrol (8:00 a.m. to 4:00 p.m.), I was told to 10-25, and contact the first sergeant. First sergeants (or the "First Shirt"), and detective sergeants (or "D/Sarge"), are the highest ranking noncommissioned officers in the department's rank structure. First sergeants run the daily administrative functions, and other noncriminal activities at the barracks; while detective sergeants command criminal investigative units and sections, and oversee their related administrative functions. Both fall just below the rank of lieutenant.

After reporting to First Sergeant Charlie Fowler's office, I was informed there had been a complaint lodged against me. It had been alleged, I was late for duty on a previous early patrol shift. The complaint was initiated by a former TFC assigned to the barrack, who had recently been promoted to corporal. While en route to his new assignment that particular day, the corporal thought he saw me enter Carroll County from Baltimore County, on Route 140.

Based on the time of day, the corporal assumed that I was late for patrol. There certainly could have been a legitimate, or approved reason for me arriving on patrol past 8:00 a.m. However, the new corporal felt obliged to report his observations. As I hadn't been late for patrol since being at Westminster, I had no idea what day the corporal was referring to. After being confronted by First Sergeant Fowler, I requested to know the date in question.

The corporal who was also present, decided to give me a lecture about the importance of being on time. Most of the patrol troopers kept track of their scheduled shifts in a pocket-sized calendar booklet. After checking my own dates with that of the first sergeant's master schedule, it appeared I was off that day. I wasn't even in the county for a scheduled off-duty court appearance. It was obvious that the new corporal saw a Black male, and decided it was me.

At that time there may have been four or five Black males at the barrack, including my academy roommate TFC Heber Watts. None of them even remotely looked like me. This was just another example that I would see time and again: Supervisors who either forgot, or didn't know the basic elements of checking their facts first. The kind who felt their ranks made them right, not facts.

I watched the corporal foolishly trying to excuse his error, saying it was an easy enough mistake to make. I'm sure it was for him. If he had simply checked the first sergeant's master schedule book first, all of this would have been avoided. I just looked at him and thought, "The poor thing…he just had to display the awesome power of his new rank."

Chapter 13
You Can Always Judge This Second Lieutenant
By His Cover

Although it was my day off, one snowy morning, I had to go to court and testify against a defendant I had arrested earlier for DUI. While en route to the barrack one night patrol, I observed the defendant's failure to operate his vehicle within a single lane, westbound on Route 140, in Baltimore County. After the defendant failed a series of sobriety test, he was arrested for DUI.

One of the great things about being a state trooper, is that you have statewide arrest authority. It is undoubtedly a benefit to the public's safety. The operator was processed at the Security Barrack. Security Barrack had replaced the defunct Randallstown Barrack in 1980. Route 140, was on their side of Baltimore County.

While on my way to Security Barrack to get my case file for court, I had to stop and assist a few motorists whose vehicles were disabled on the shoulders of the beltway, due to the snowy conditions. By the time I reached the barrack, some additional snow had resurfaced on the rear of my patrol vehicle. While I was in the barrack some additional accumulation of snow had also covered my rear window.

After I got the file, and exited the rear door, I saw the assistant barrack commander, looking at my vehicle. As I approached the second lieutenant, I saluted him. Returning the salute, he then asked me was that my vehicle with the rear window, and lights covered with snow. I said, "Yes sir it is." Obviously I was going to take my snow brush, and clean off the vehicle before leaving the parking lot.

The second lieutenant began reminding me that I shouldn't be operating my vehicle in that snow-covered condition. He said it was my responsibility to keep my vehicle in proper order at all times. Even though the snow had mainly resurfaced while I was in the barrack, I didn't argue the point, and told the second lieutenant he was right. Evidently, the second lieutenant arrived after me. He said he heard me go 10-7 the barrack, just before arriving at barrack himself. Noticing my "G-4" tag number, the second lieutenant assumed I had been operating my vehicle without properly cleaning off the snow.

In what I thought was a nice gesture, he said, "Now trooper, I'm not trying to give you a hard time, but you can hardly charge someone if you do the same thing." Again, rather than contradict the point, I thanked the second lieutenant and asked him to excuse me, as I was running a little late. I finished cleaning off the snow, and headed to court in Owings Mills.

As I drove off, I remember thinking about some of the negative things I overheard others say about that second lieutenant. He seemed ok to me; and I was usually a good judge of character…at least 97% of the time anyway.

Westminster Barrack had what was referred to as a "Resident-Trooper" program. Through a mutual contract with the state, salaries and equipment for the program, were subsidized by a participating town, to augment the state police presence in their community. The troopers were designated as "Resident Troopers," and exclusively patrolled in those communities.

When I returned from leave, I was told to report to First Sergeant Jack Bowman's office before going on patrol that morning. First Sergeant Bowman was one of the two resident program's first sergeants. First Sergeant Bowman is physically very tall, and equally tall as a gentleman.

First Sergeant Bowman said he was aware that I had been at Security Barrack recently, and asked if I experienced any issues with the second lieutenant. I said I had been there to pick up court documents, but I had no issues with the second lieutenant. I told First Sergeant Bowman about the snow on my vehicle, and what the second lieutenant said to me about it.

I advised First Sergeant Bowman that even though the snow resurfaced while I was in the barrack, I chose not to contradict the second lieutenant, and immediately cleaned off my vehicle. It wasn't worth discussing, so I just listened respectfully, and said nothing disagreeable. I even mentioned how I thought the second lieutenant was a pretty nice guy.

Inexplicably, the second lieutenant telephoned the barrack, telling First Sergeant Bowman I had given him a hard time. I wondered what in the world was wrong with that second lieutenant. I now understood why I heard nothing good about him from others. Fortunately, First Sergeant Bowman had enough dealings with me, and thought the second lieutenant's version of events sounded extreme.

First Sergeant Bowman also knew that second lieutenant very well, and told me to forget about the complaint, as it would go no further. First Sergeant Bowman kindly reminded me to be sure and keep my vehicle appropriately maintained at all times. I thanked the "First Shirt" for his confidence in me. I walked out of the barrack thinking that second lieutenant was out of his mind. That little bit of insanity on the part of that second lieutenant, certainly lowered my percentages in the category of correctly judging someone's character.

First Sergeant Bowman was promoted to second lieutenant shortly after I left Westminster in 1983. When the second lieutenant's rank was abolished, Jack was one of three left. In 1995, when the department promoted the three remaining second lieutenants to the rank of lieutenant, I was on the lieutenant's promotion list as well. I had the honor of sharing the stage with him at the promotional ceremony.

After Jack retired, he returned to the MSP as a civilian, and we are better for his continued presence, leadership and experience. I'm happy our friendship continues today. He is still tall, and still very much a gentleman.

In another bit of unexpected irony, very soon, I would have another experience indirectly with that same second lieutenant who falsely reported my conduct. One I'm sure he never saw coming.

Chapter 14
Guess Who's Not Coming to Dinner?

One late patrol, I responded to a complaint involving an assault on a police officer, at the state's mental health hospital facility in the lower part of the county. The officer was part of the hospital's security. When I arrived, the officer identified one of the nurses as his alleged assailant. The officer who was not hurt, reported that he responded to a complaint by staff members, when the nurse began acting disorderly. When he tried to intervene, she struck him several times. The nurse was in police custody, inside their office.

When I went to speak with the nurse, she was crying, and visibly upset. I asked the officer to remove his handcuffs. I told the nurse it wasn't very nice going around assaulting police officers. Jokingly, I said to her, "What am I going to do with you?" I asked the nurse to calm down, and bought her something to drink from a vending machine, hoping to ease her tension.

The nurse asked if I was going to arrest her. I told her as the assault was minor, and wasn't committed in my presence, the officer would get a summons for her to appear in court. I advised the nurse that I would have to take a report on the alleged assault. I also informed her, that she would have to leave the premises as requested by the management, when we were through. Prior to filling out my report, she asked me if I knew her husband.

I said, "No ma'am I don't think so."

She said, "He's a lieutenant in the state police."

I asked, "Really, what's his name?"

Surprisingly enough, her husband was that same second lieutenant from the last chapter. After telling her I knew him very well, I called the barrack, and asked the duty officer to contact the second lieutenant, so he could come and get his wife. She was in no condition to drive. Subsequently, the officer at the hospital secured a criminal summons charging the second lieutenant's wife with assault. As I was the responding trooper in that case, the summons was assigned to me for service.

I wanted to give the second lieutenant, and his wife the courtesy of letting them know I needed to serve the summons, before dropping by their home unannounced. I requested that the barrack telephone their residence, and ask if I could stop by and do so. When I arrived, I was greeted by the defendant at the door. She remembered me, and warmly hugged me before inviting me inside.

She called for the second lieutenant to come in, and meet the trooper who was so nice to her. Although the second lieutenant barely made eye contact with me when he entered the room, I was sure he recognized me. Here was the trooper he lied about to First Sergeant Bowman standing in his living room. What an awkward turn of events this had to be for him.

After issuing the summons, I was graciously asked by the second lieutenant's wife if I had my dinner yet. I said, "No ma'am." She said I must stay and have dinner with them, as they were about to eat. I had to hold back my laughter, when the second lieutenant abruptly put an end to his wife's invitation. He said, "I'm sure the trooper is too busy to stay dear." I started to say I wasn't, but I didn't want to make her the center of this ironically funny situation.

I thank her for the kind offer, and said I had to go on another call. She hugged me once more, and thanked me again for being so kind. She invited me to stop by anytime I was in the neighborhood. Smiling at the second lieutenant, I saluted and left. I didn't want to ruin his appetite. That was the best dinner I never ate.

Chapter 15
The New Barrack "G" CID Man

Near the end of my first year, I was asked by a few of the investigators to request an in-house reassignment to the investigation section. That was a great honor. Our investigators were some of the best in the business. Westminster had the largest ID section of all the barracks.

When an opening became available, I was asked specifically by TFC Dave Williams, to put in for it. When it was learned I was being considered, there was some grumbling from those troopers who were there before me, and had their requests in first. Nothing personal, that's just the way it was. An assignment to the ID section was coveted, and they all felt they were better suited; especially knowing I came from a "traffic" barrack.

With the retirement of the previous barrack commander Lieutenant Robert Weisenmiller, in 1981, the newly promoted commander, First Lieutenant Neil Bechtol, called me into his office one afternoon. Lieutenant Bechtol had been the assistant barrack commander as the second lieutenant when I first arrived. Lieutenant Bechtol informed me the ID section's commander, Detective Sergeant Paul Utz, requested I be reassigned from patrol to fill their vacancy.

Based on what he knew of my work habits, and with the recommendations from some of the investigators, he concurred. The lieutenant looked straight at me, and said a lot of people wouldn't be happy, but it was his decision to make. Lieutenant Bechtol asked me if this was what I wanted. I said, "Yes sir!" The Lieutenant said he believed I could do well, so don't let him down.

My reassignment apparently troubled one uniformed corporal in particular. He was overheard saying the section got their "token Black." I was told of his remarks by someone I trusted, who actually heard what the corporal said. Later that day, I passed Corporal Earl Breedenburg, in the hallway. He congratulated me on my reassignment. I told Corporal Breedenburg about what that corporal allegedly said about my reassignment.

I asked Corporal Breedenburg if I should go have a constructive word with that corporal in private. Corporal Breedenburg took me aside, and told me some people weren't worth getting upset over. He said I was given the position for one reason, and that was because Lieutenant Bechtol believed I could do the job.

As time went on, I saw for myself just how universally disliked that corporal was. He was an extremely polarizing individual, whose purpose in life, only made sense to himself. Before Corporal Breedenburg retired, he achieved the rank of captain. Like so many others I came to admire, he too possessed the leadership quality of being the adult in the room.

Being a trooper at Westminster was extremely satisfying. I couldn't imagine working anywhere else as a uniformed patrol trooper. As if things couldn't get better, the barrack soon received a new assistant barrack commander, Second Lieutenant Robert McAfee. Lieutenant McAfee was someone who like Lieutenant Bechtol, I grew to greatly admire and appreciate. Without a doubt, the leadership of these two men set the standard that epitomized what the MSP was all about.

Even in only my sixth year with the department, their examples of holding employees accountable, while treating them like they mattered, resonated most positively. It was obvious both lieutenants were gentlemen of integrity. They didn't demand respect, they earned it. I am most honored that over the years, we have become dear friends. Like many others I speak of, they personally made a profound difference in my career I won't forget.

My time in the section was very fruitful. I was very busy, learning a lot on the fly. I started out working a few days with Corporal Jim Leete, one of the section's veteran investigators, who was very helpful and encouraging. One day, I ran into Corporal Bernie Balog while at headquarters in Pikesville. Corporal Balog was a legend in his own rights as an investigator, and was well respected throughout the department. Greeting the corporal in passing, I asked him if he could name one trait you should have as a new investigator, what it was he'd suggest. Without hesitation, Corporal Balog replied, "Perseverance." He went on to elaborate saying that whenever possible, you should never give up on a case until you have checked all available leads.

Corporal Balog said there were others, but as a new investigator, he encouraged me to be perseverant in my efforts. That brief moment with Corporal Balog served as another reminder of why I loved being a trooper. After his own personal perseverance fighting a lengthy illness, retired Corporal Balog passed in 2018. The corporal was a quiet gentleman, and let his skill, and professionalism do the talking. His reputation and mentorship, are indelible to me, and to those who admired him.

As fortunes would have it, in just a little over three months, my time in the section would end. The sudden resignation of a uniformed trooper, necessitated his position be backfilled to maintain the barrack's required number of troopers for patrol duties. Rightly, I was the one selected to fill the patrol vacancy.

The section's immediate supervisor Sergeant Jack Kondisko, who was another excellent example of supportive supervision, expressed his approval of my performance in a detailed report to Lieutenant Bechtol. After breaking the news to me in his office, Lieutenant Bechtol gave me a copy of the detailed report written by Sergeant Kondisko. Lieutenant Bechtol said he was very proud to hear about the level of my performance, especially in light of the short time I was in the section.

Lieutenant Bechtol assured me that after the sitting academy class graduated, and the barrack received its allotment of graduating recruits, he would personally see that I went back to the ID section. Understandably, I was a bit disappointed, but happy I didn't let those who supported me down; especially Lieutenant Bechtol. Besides, it was just a matter of time before I'd be back in the section.

Chapter 16
This is Why I Loved Working at Westminster Barrack

I will never forget my time at Westminster Barrack. Those troopers really exemplified a sense of barrack pride. There was one very special trooper at the barrack who made a great difference in my career. TFC William (Bill) Burke was assigned to the crime lab (Crime Laboratory Division). He was an important part of my growth in the department as well as anyone.

Initially, I had no idea who he was. I would see him around the barrack, or sitting in his vehicle on the side of the road near the barrack. Our sworn crime lab crime scene techs didn't wear the standard patrol uniform. They wore a utility uniform of a light green shirt, and dark green khaki pants. I remember the troops referring to it as the "janitor in a drum uniform." The inference was they looked more like custodians than troopers.

The first time I really had any interaction with TFC Burke, came when I responded to a call for an assault. The location was a residence that doubled as an animal kennel business, situated on a large single property, well off the roadway. As I was heading to the call, I heard TFC Burke say over the radio he would back me up.

As I drove down the lengthy driveway, the male suspect saw me approaching, and started running away. I jumped out and ran after him. When I closed in and grabbed the suspect, we lost our balance on the driveway's slick gravel surface. While we were struggling on the ground, TFC Burke came speeding down the driveway.

It was now dusk outside. From his vantage point, TFC Burke thought the suspect and I were fighting. Thinking I was in trouble, he hurried to my rescue. With his flashlight in hand, TFC Burke quickly ran towards me yelling, "Hold on I'm coming!" As he got closer, TFC Burke could see I had control of the suspect. I thought that was so great. Bill didn't know it at the time, but he had just made a friend for life.

Afterwards, Bill and I went on to be known for having epic arm-wrestling matches in the troopers' room. Bill was just naturally strong, and I couldn't match his technique or strength. I gave him a run for his money a few times though.

In the days to come, as we became closer, Bill gave me guidance, especially at those times, when I mistakenly thought I had life at Wesminster all figured out. TFC Burke retired as a sergeant in 1996. He and I remain in contact, and he is my very dear friend, as was his late wife Susan.

One evening, I was standing in the hallway at the barrack with a prisoner I had just arrested. Obviously agitated over being arrested, he suddenly began spewing a rather intense barrage of racial epithets at me. Although his insults didn't particularly phase me. His comments nevertheless were overheard by the duty officer Corporal Dennis Murphey. Appearing like a flash from the radio room, he came to my defense, vigorously reminding the prisoner I was a trooper, and he was not to refer to me otherwise.

Corporal Murphey really scared the wits out of the prisoner; especially when Denny got in his face, asking the arrested man did he make himself clear. Denny retired as a Captain, in command of the Training Division. I told that story when I spoke at his retirement party. I wanted his family to know what that meant to me personally. Even to this day, his leadership, and sense of right are indelible to me. Denny and I became friends in the ensuing years of our careers, and we remain so today.

Once in a while, you had to fill in on another group if there was a shortage. One morning just before securing from night patrol with another group, I had to respond to a call on Route 27, for livestock on the roadway. When I arrived, there were three to four cows milling about on the road. The PCO asked me to identify their breed. Apparently the barrack could tell who they belonged to by their breed. Being from the city, I had no idea; so I did the next best thing, and began describing the cows by their different colors over the air. Immediately there was the sound of mics clicking over the air on the radio.

Back then when someone said something odd over the radio, the other troopers would start rapidly keying their mics. Pressing the button on the mics that way, made a clicking sound over the air. If that wasn't bad enough, I got the bright idea of turning on my siren to scare the cows off the road. Although using the siren worked, unfortunately for me, it got them off the road, and onto the properties of nearby homes. Those property owners apparently didn't appreciate my cow-wrangling technics.

Later that night when I went 10-41, I was told to 10-25 the barrack. When I arrived, there was good ole' Sergeant Dominic Dattilio standing at the back door. The sarge had a rather large book under his arm. The book was about farm animals. He told me to go upstairs to the troopers' room, and don't come out until I finished reading it.

One morning when I was assigned to work with Sergeant Dittilio's group, I was told to report to the barrack, and contact a complainant in the lobby. The complainant was the victim of a theft from his property. Seated at the small table in the lobby, the complainant began describing the nature of his complaint as I filled out the Criminal Investigation Report (CIR). When I asked him what was stolen, the complainant advised that a "cord of wood" had been taken off his property.

I asked, "A what?"

The complainant repeated, "A cord of wood."

As I had no idea what that was, other than something made of wood, naturally I had no clue of its value. Having to put a value on the CIR, I asked the gentleman if the item was about five dollars or something. He gave me a puzzled look, and asked me if I was kidding. Sticking his head out of the sliding glass window facing the lobby, Sergeant Dattilio said, "Sir don't pay any attention to him, he's from the city."

The man started laughing. The joke was on me. I had just received another lesson in rural living. I was told that a cord of wood cost more like $75 to $100 dollars. I told Sergeant Dittillo that where I was from, we used thermostats to heat the house.

Sergeant Dittilio retired in 1983. When the sarge passed in 2011, I attended his viewing. I shared those stories with his wife Jayne, and their daughter Karen. In his obituary, I read that Sergeant Dattilio was an active member of the Carroll County Farm Museum. No wonder he knew a thing or two about cows.

One afternoon, I was investigating an accident near Manchester. The operator had been transported to the hospital in Hanover, Pennsylvania. As I mentioned earlier, the Manchester area bordered the state's line into Pennsylvania. While I was en route to the hospital, I stopped for a red light in Hanover's downtown shopping district. To my left on the curb across the intersection, was one of the barrack's investigators, TFC Ronnie Hinkel and his family. When we made eye contact, I saluted him. With shopping bags in hand, he came running frantically towards me. Excitedly, he asked me what I was doing.

Pulling his leg, I casually said, "I'm on patrol."

TFC Hinkel said, "Fool don't you know where you are?"

I said, "You mean this ain't part of my patrol?"

I began laughing, and told him to get out of the street before he got run over. I then explained why I was in Hanover.

One particular late patrol, I was told as there were no field trainers available, a new trooper named Jerry Beason would be assigned to ride with me that evening. Our first call was for a hit and run accident involving damage to a utility pole in Hampstead. Utility poles are very expensive, and utility companies required an official police report for insurance purposes, even if the responsible party was unknown at the time of the accident.

While looking around the scene, I discovered part of a chrome nameplate belonging to a Dodge Charger on the ground. There was also a bit of blue paint on the pole. Shortly after we arrived, Hampstead police chief, Durwood Sites stopped by.

Chief Sites was a retired MSP sergeant, who was assigned to Westminster at one time during his career. The chief was a tremendous resource, and knew just about everybody in the town of Hampstead. If you gave him a kid's name he could tell you who the parents were, and vice versa.

Chief Sites embraced the role of community policing even before it would become a national occurrence. When I showed him the partial Charger nameplate, and the blue paint on the pole, he told us to follow him. Chief Sites led us to a residence in the area. When we arrived, the chief told us that a young man who drove a blue Charger, lived there with his parents.

Chief Sites said he had experienced problems with the young man before. By this time, the young man's father came outside. When I explained why we were on his property, the father became less than agreeable. He wanted to know what proof we had to accuse his son for being responsible for the accident. Before I answered the father's question, I asked him to get his son.

When I questioned the son, he flatly denied hitting the pole. I asked him where his Charger was. With the telltale sign of a sick look on his face, the son said it was in their garage. I then showed them the partial chrome nameplate. I then asked the father if he knew how many blue Chargers were in the immediate area.

The father looked at his son, and went to the garage in the rear of their property. Naturally, the father's attitude changed when he returned. Unfortunately for the young man, he became the object of his father's anger. Having all the proof he needed, the father was more cooperative now.

I told Trooper Beason afterwards that staying on course with your control of the situation usually works in your favor. When the facts are on your side, you have the last word. This was a great example for Jerry to see and learn. Checking the scene thoroughly, good observations, and having a mutual working relationship with allied departments can make all the difference, I said.

Chapter 17
Wrestling with the Truth

As the saying goes nothing good lasts forever. Corporal Crawford had been promoted to sergeant, and was transferred to the North East Barrack. By early 1983, Lieutenant Bechtol was transferred to command the Frederick Barrack. Second Lieutenant McAfee was also transferred. Eventually, Second Lieutenant McAfee was promoted to first lieutenant, and became commander of the Rockville Barrack.

A new barrack commander soon arrived, and it became very obvious, he was nothing like Lieutenants Bechtol and McAfee. With this change came another lesson in reality: Your personal issues weren't on everybody's list of immediate concerns.

Although I had never met the new barrack commander before, I was familiar with his name. During our first meeting, the lieutenant was very candid, and left no room for doubt about his management preferences. After reviewing my personnel file on his desk, the lieutenant paused to tell me about a conversation he had with Lieutenant Bechtol. He said it was Lieutenant Bechtol's intention to reassign me to the ID section, after the barrack's allotment of graduating recruits arrived from the academy.

The lieutenant looked straight at me and said, "But I'm not Lieutenant Bechtol. Now if you go out and write me some tickets, I might consider it." When he asked if I had any questions, I replied "No sir." I could see this man had zero inter-personnel skills. It was obviously his way or no way.

When I look back at that moment, my indignation over the lieutenant's management style was not my most constructive reaction. I couldn't see the correlation between the skills needed to be a good criminal investigator, and traffic enforcement. Besides, the lieutenant struck me as the type of person who wouldn't necessarily keep his word, even if I excelled at issuing citations. Brooding for the subsequent monthly period, I let my traffic production slip feeling sorry for myself.

I mentioned my personal revolt against what I considered unfair to TFC Burke one afternoon. Without mincing words, he told me I was wrong. With concern for me and my career, TFC Burke wisely challenged my attitude. Bill asked who I thought would be hurt in the end. He continued by asking me, "Do you think you're the only one to be disappointed around here?"

After going home and thinking about it, I knew Bill was right. He had beaten me every time we arm wrestled, and now he beat me so I could win in the end. Needless to say, my next period was much more representative of the pride I talked about being a trooper.

Thankfully, such attitudes would never negatively affect my work again. That was a lesson I would use in my own mentoring of others later in my career. I learned to understand the importance of being viewed as an excellent worker, regardless of the situation. If you aren't known to put forth the effort where you are, your reputation will precede you… and not in a good way.

Over the years, I have recounted that story to Bill. He refuses to take any credit for saying the right things, or seeing it as pertinent to any future success I had. He'd just say, "You would have figured it out eventually had I not spoken to you." That was true, but he kept me from digging myself an unnecessary hole. I came to learn that effective leadership was not just reserved for noncommissioned, and commissioned officers. It started with you holding yourself accountable; even at the lowest position in the rank structure.

One afternoon, the barrack advised me to telephone Lieutenant John Cook, Commander of the Special Services Division's (SSD) Intelligence Section. Lieutenant Cook advised that my earlier transfer to the SSD's Criminal Enforcement Section had been approved. Having gained valuable experience at Westminster, I felt ready to take on my longtime desire to work as a covert investigator, as the next step in my career.

It wasn't until I reported for late patrol a few weeks later, that I knew the transfer list had come out. Before going on patrol, I went to get gas at the barrack. Gassing up his vehicle ahead of me, was Major William Gerwig, Assistant Chief of FOB. After maneuvering my vehicle to go next, I got out and greeted the major with a salute.

Returning the salute, Major Gerwig looked at my name plate, and took note of my name.

"So TFC Russell, you want to be an SSD man huh?"

I said, "Yes sir."

The major said, "Well congratulations the list is out; you're now an undercover man. Do a good job trooper!" Excitedly, I thanked the major, and hurried to the barrack. There it was posted on the main hallway's bulletin board in all its glory. The bulletin board was just outside the lieutenant's office. He came out, and saw me studying the list.

"So, you got away huh?" He asked.

I said, "Yes sir. I'm going to miss you."

In just a few more weeks, I would be in another world of policing with all new challenges and people. Those two and a half years at Westminster seemed so much longer. That's what can happen when you stay as busy as the barrack was. There were a lot of good people in the county, and they were served by some of the best troopers in the department.

For me personally, police work wasn't the only thing I learned there. I had to take a step up in the maturation department. Growth in maturity, is one of the most vital necessities moving forward for new police officers. Such growth would be very important in my new assignment. After only six years on the department, I had probably experienced as many highs, and lows as anyone that early in their career.

Working at Westminster gave me the chance to meet some very nice people in the neighborhoods, and business communities on my patrol areas of two and three in Hampstead and Manchester. When I was moved to the lower part of the county on patrols seven, eight and nine, Eldersburg, Sykesville and Mt. Airy, I met a wonderful lady named Elaine Immler in Eldersburg. Elaine was a very caring person, who respected the job we did as police officers. I was sad to learn of her passing in 2007. She was a very special and kind person, and became a dear friend.

There was a young trooper at the barrack named James (J.W.) Long. I first met Trooper Long when he was a cadet in the Truck Enforcement Division, before I left JFK. After he graduated, Trooper Long was assigned to Westminster, and placed in my group.

Trooper Long's spirit, and love for the MSP, is second to none. Humorous and kind in nature, J.W. had a unique way of relating to everyone he met, especially those he dealt with in the performance of his duties. Many consider his off-duty activities during various charity, and other events around the county, as a staple of goodwill representing the best of the MSP. He retired as a sergeant, and is still a wonderful ambassador for the MSP, and an old friend.

It was my intent to stay out of trouble, and remain free from any unnecessary controversy prior to my transfer. During one of the days of my final shift (night patrol), I was 30 minutes away from securing for the day. I was on patrol in the lower part of the county, in an area known as the "Watershed."

Situating my vehicle off the road back amongst some trees, I was finishing my paperwork. A few minutes later, I saw one of our marked patrol vehicles go by at a high rate of speed from my left to the right on Deer Park Road. I hadn't heard any calls from the barrack, or seen anyone else go speeding by.

Quickly moving forward towards the roadway, I picked up my mic and called, "G-4 to the unit on Deer Park Road, are you looking for someone?" The vehicle came to an abrupt stop several yards up the road, and began backing up towards my location. By the tag number, I could see it was my friend the unhappy corporal, who was happy that the ID section had its "token Black" investigator.

Apparently he was up to his old tricks. I was told the corporal decided he would come out early, hoping to catch me leaving the county before the official end of my shift. Deer Park Road runs through Carroll and Baltimore Counties. At the end of my shift, I would have taken Deer Park Road as my route home. I'm afraid the corporal remained unhappy. I was still on patrol as required. Embarrassed I'm sure, he advised me to "10-22" (disregard), and went about his merry way... no doubt contemplating his next brainless waste of time.

Chapter 18
So You Want to Be an SSD Man Huh?

On December 12, 1977, Trooper Gregg Presbury, was shot several times during a traffic stop on Maryland Route 3, in Anne Arundel County. Sadly, he died from those wounds five days later. The suspect David Pfeiffer, was the subject of a massive search in the area. After his capture and subsequent trial, Pfeiffer was convicted in the murder of Trooper Presbury.

The day of Pfeiffer's capture, a number of troopers reported to Glen Burnie, prepared to help in any way possible. I was riding with another trooper in my group at the JFK Highway Barrack, named George A. Butler. George was an MSP cadet before entering the academy. He and Gregg were classmates in the 75th class.

Trooper Butler was driving me home after our shift, as we both resided in Baltimore City. Trooper Butler said he was heading to the Glen Burnie area to help search for Pfeiffer after he dropped me off. I also knew Trooper Presbury before we both became troopers, and I wanted to help too. Gregg and I met in 1974, when I had a part time job at the defunct Sears and Roebuck Department Store, on North Avenue in Baltimore City. I worked as a "Runner" in catalog pickup, and Gregg was a salesman in the hardware department.

One day during a break, we were both sitting on the loading dock just talking in general. Coincidentally, he mentioned that he had applied to become a trooper with the Maryland State Police. I happily told him I too wanted to become a trooper. Little did I know he would be in the 75th graduating class of 1976; and I would follow him right behind, in the 76th class of 1977. Regrettably, there was not much time for us to get together after we graduated before his tragic and untimely death.

When George and I arrived in the area, all units were told to respond to Ritchie Highway and Second Avenue in Glen Burnie. By the time we arrived, Pfeiffer had been located inside a residence, and eventually brought out without incident. At that time, I saw Pfeiffer being led by men who weren't in uniform, and didn't look like detectives either. I asked Trooper Butler who those guys were. George said they were our "undercover troopers." The sight of those troopers taking charge, and not looking like the police, captivated my attention.

Knowing I had no chance of getting a transfer into such a unit at that stage of my career, didn't deter my desire to seek a transfer at some point later on. So doing the next best thing, I found out where their office was, and went to see them for myself when I was off duty. At that time, the unit was called the Investigative Assistance Unit (IAU). The unit occupied a satellite office building in the Pikesville area.

These were seasoned troopers with superior investigative skills who could look and act streetwise. The first person I met at their office, was Corporal Al (Big Al) Hranicka. I remembered Corporal Hranicka as one of the troopers who had custody of Pfeiffer. The next member of the unit I met, was Detective Sergeant Paul Gillian, the section's commander.

They were both very generous with their time, but realistically advised me to learn all I could as a road trooper, and perhaps at some point I would be qualified for consideration. That time came six years later in 1983. After Corporal Hranicka was promoted to sergeant, he was no longer in the unit. Sergeant Hranicka was transferred to the Criminal Investigation Division at headquarters in Pikesville. Detective Sergeant Gillian was promoted to lieutenant, and became commander of SSD's Criminal Enforcement Section (CES). The Investigative Assistance Unit was no longer in existence.

The SSD was headquartered in the renovated old Waterloo Barrack in Jessup, Howard County. In addition to the CES, the division also included the Narcotics Section, and the Intelligence Unit. The division's personnel not only conducted our own statewide cases, but also assisted other Maryland, and out of state allied law enforcement agencies with their cases. The division also investigated criminal matters for the counties' State's Attorneys' Offices, the Office of the State Prosecutor, and the Maryland Attorney General's Office, upon request. Because of our statewide jurisdiction, we also engaged in joint operations with other local allied agencies.

Along with this new opportunity, came learning new terminology and technology. Terms like minimization orders, surreptitious, and "trash runs," were just to name a few. As for technology, there were pen registers, and eavesdropping equipment like wiretaps and body wires.

One of the most important methods of working covertly, is understanding how to keep your target from knowing they are under surveillance, whether you are driving, on foot, or watching them from a stationary position. You had to develop the patients to sit at a single location during a surveillance for hours at a time if necessary.

In time you learned how to become streetwise, while ensuring your safety in the process. Your basic report writing skills had to be elevated as well. The division's reports which were more on the level of a detailed report, were referred to as "Confidential Memorandums."

Very soon, I would begin working with several other covert investigators across the state. I learned that some of the brightest, and most resourceful people in law enforcement, were members of the various covert units I worked with. Equally, they were some of the most unique characters I have ever met.

Many of the activities performed by these special men and women, are constant reminders of their extraordinary dedication to public safety that go unheralded, due to the confidential nature of their investigations. Many of the friends and colleagues I have today, were made during the four years I was assigned to the division.

Trooper Butler would go on to make sergeant. For most of his career, George would work as a narc. Sadly, while I was writing this book, George would pass in 2020. Several of our retirees got to visit with him at his hospice care facility.

Two days before George passed, myself, my academy classmate retired Lieutenant Nick Plazio, and retired Sergeant Pat Byrnes, got to spend some time with him. I reminded George of the time we went to help look for David Pfeiffer in Glen Burnie. While we were driving southbound on I-95, a few miles north of the Harbor Tunnel, he was driving around 80 miles per hour trying to get there.

While I was looking out the passenger window watching the mile markers go blurring by, George suddenly said, "Take the wheel." I looked over, and he was trying to put his gun belt back on while we flying down the road. It was very scary having to steer the wheel from the passenger seat at those speeds. I told him it was funny now, but he scared the living daylights out of me back then.

Once, George and I were a part of a team from SSD, jointly working a wiretap case in St. Mary's County, with the Office of the State Prosecutor. Our set up was in a tiny apartment belonging to a retired trooper, situated above a furniture store. Inside the apartment's fairly empty refrigerator, was a packet of spoiled ground beef. One of the investigators, TFC Donny Newcomer, had candy he was saving for later. Despite Donny's warnings not to eat it, the always mischievous George, ate it anyway when Donny wasn't around. Donny was not one to let a transgression go unavenged. On the last day of the operation, Donny took the spoiled ground beef, and placed it under the driver's seat of George's unlocked vehicle.

As we were driving north heading home, it was hilarious watching the unsuspecting George looking around, trying to figure out where that awful, rancid smell was coming from. George found out the hard way, you didn't trifle with "Mr. Newcomer."

George remembered those times. I told George I mentioned him in the book I was writing. He was pleased to hear it, and asked that I say something funny about him. That was a promise I could keep. George was growing tired, and we decided to let him rest. As we were leaving the room George said, "Love you guys." We told him we loved him too. Rest in peace George, it was a pleasure my friend.

Chapter 19
For Pete's Sake!

My first CES supervisor was Sergeant Peter Fairchild (Pete) Edge. Sergeant Edge was a Coast Guard veteran, and a legend across the state. It seemed anyone who had been on the job for a while, knew who he was. In short order, it would be apparent to me Pete was no ordinary individual. He was certainly one of the funniest people you'd ever meet. Everything about him was unique as a person could get.

Equal to his unique brand of humor, was his prowess as a covert investigator. Pete had done just about everything you could do in those days working undercover. After retiring as a Detective Sergeant, his career would continue as our museum's civilian curator, before he fully retired from state service. Pete Edge was an MSP institution.

In 2002, as the commander of the Inspection Support Services Unit, I was honored to present Pete with a Commander's Ribbon in recognition of his efforts to beautify the landscaping around the headquarters' quadrangle, in time for our annual Fallen Heroes Memorial Service. Because there was no extra money in the Facilities Management Division's (FMD) budget, Pete got a local business, and volunteers to donate material and time to help with the effort.

The day before the ceremony, it was a particularly hot afternoon. I looked out of my office window, and saw Pete toiling away with a garden tiller around the quadrangle. I went to check on him. I told Pete he needed to take a break. He said he was pressed for time, as the event was the next morning. Since I was dressed down that day, I offered to take over for him while he rested for a bit.

When he asked if I ever used a tiller before, I just looked at him and asked, "Really?" After Pete showed me how to use it, I decided to give it a try anyway. My initial attempt to operate the tiller made it fairly obvious I was in over my head. Even when I thought I got the hang of the contraption, it still wasn't a pretty sight.

A short time later, two women entered the compound through the Reisterstown Road archway entrance. They walked over to where I was tilling a small tree mound. I stopped to see what they needed. The women were from New York, and looking for local directions. After I gave them directions, they walked back towards the entrance. Pete was coming out of the museum. The women stopped, and began having a conversation with him looking back at me.

When Pete came over to me, he couldn't stop laughing. I asked him what was so funny. He said the two women thought I was the gardener. But the real joke was when they said the area must be really bad if the gardener needed to wear a gun. I was wearing my shoulder holster, and forgot to take it off while I was tilling.

Pete was also an avid supporter of the department's Special Olympics "Polar Bear Plunge" events. He was not only the MSP's goodwill ambassador, he was the bridge that linked generations of troopers. The MSP's best friend, "Petey Boy" left this world he loved in 2015. We lost the original: A one-of-a-kind soul. I was honored to join Donny Newcomer as the other scheduled speaker at Pete's services. When I was interviewed about Pete for his obituary in the "Baltimore Sun" newspaper, I said Pete was the earthly version of Halley's Comet: "Something you only see once in your lifetime."

Sergeant Edge was not the only one to have a constructive influence on my start in the division. The CES had a cast of characters who were knowledgeable, talented and humorous in their own rights as well. These were a bunch of investigators, who all distinguished themselves as hard working, hard playing people, who in the end got the job done. I learned so much from all of them. I would go on to work for three different supervisors in the section, and be guided by other supervisors outside my group.

Thanks to my other CES supervisors Sergeants Thomas (TM) Moore and August (Augie) Stern, and the other CES supervisors like Ray (Uncle Ray) Leard, Doug (Gator Brown) Delever, assistant commander Detective Sergeant William (Bill) Vogel, and Lieutenant Gillian, I learned critical habits from each one of them that would not only ensure my safety, but provide me with vital skills moving forward. Many of the things I learned from all of them, played an important role in some of my most crucial cases.

From Sergeants Moore and Stern, I learned the art of better report writing (especially the importance of taking copious notes). From Pete and Sergeant Leard, I learned what to do, and what not to, when attempting to gain the confidence of your target, and the importance of having your story straight at all times. Any variance in your initial story could be disastrous to your case, and your safety. All through my initial training it was stressed to always watch your back, and have an exit plan in the event you felt uncomfortable.

I learned how to prepare, and obtain search and seizure warrants, and other required court orders from watching and assisting the senior investigators in the section. I also learned how to conduct surveillances, and the technical, and legal aspects of using eavesdropping, and surveillance monitoring equipment.

Corporals Larry Morse, Mark Snyder, Charlie Poole, Frank Walters, Ted Polinsky and Vince Milo; and TFCs Donny Newcomer, Gary Morgan, and Sherrie Bosley (who was transferred in with me), were the investigators I had the privilege of working with in the section. Corporal Terry Katz of the Intelligence Unit, also helped me with my transition into the division.

For the most part back then, you were on your own. So you were expected to be where you should, and taking care of your business. Reliability, perseverance, and integrity, were essential if you had hopes of staying in the division.

One of the things I really looked forward to, was being assigned a cool undercover vehicle. Back then ironically enough, the division's vehicles were actually referred to as "cool cars" by the department. So on my first day, I couldn't wait to see what type of vehicle I was being assigned.

Along with the three other newly assigned troopers, I saw all kinds of nice vehicles on our parking lot, as we were being led to our assigned vehicles. Some were purchased as fleet vehicles by the department, and others were obtained through court ordered vehicle forfeitures. One vehicle in particular caught my immediate attention. It was a white Chevrolet Corvette. I soon learned it was assigned to Sergeant Bill Reynolds, who was in the Narcotics Section.

When we arrived to the vehicles that were to be ours, it didn't take long for me to come crashing back to earth. My first undercover vehicle was an old blue, Chevrolet Citation two-door hatchback, with a round magnetic based antenna on the roof. The color was what I called "insurance man silver-blue." "Oh well, at least no one will suspect I'm the police," I jokingly thought to myself.

I began getting my feet wet by assisting others with their cases. I was required to do "trash runs" (where you looked for evidence in the target's discarded bags of trash). I also began meeting other covert investigators, especially those with the Baltimore City police: particularly Howard Caplan, and the late Ed Glaken, who passed in 2002.

In July 1983, I was a part of one of the more innovated drug raids we participated in. The lead investigator, TFC Renee B. Wartman, skillfully made hand-to-hand buys from a heroin drug organization, set up in the defunct Flag House high-rise housing projects in Baltimore City. The raid was facilitated with the cooperation of the city's housing authority administration.

In the dark early morning hours before the raid was to commence, a total of 18 Black male and female state police and city officers, were gradually filtered inside a vacant apartment within the high-rise facility. We had to go in two at a time during different intervals, as there were posted lookouts keeping watch for suspicious, or police activities. I was paired with the city's Sergeant Barry Powell, of the Southeast District. Later in his distinguished career, Barry would go on to become a deputy commissioner in their department. Like me, he started out as a cadet at the Central Records Division's "Hot Desk."

We were crammed inside a vacant roach-infested apartment. Seated on the floor, we waited for the designated time for the raid to begin. Later that morning as it became light outside, large trucks secreting at least 50 state and city officers, including city K-9 units, pulled in front of the high-rise buildings. At the appointed time, we exited the vacant apartment. Running upstairs and down hallways with keys in hand, we quickly made our way to the identified units on the third, sixth, seventh, eighth, ninth and 10th floors.

Without injury to the police, innocent residents, or the targets, the operation successfully culminated in the arrest of 16 people, for related heroin violations. Additionally, we seized an estimated $5,000.00 worth of packaged heroin, and recovered five guns.

TFC Wartman went on to become the first Black female in the history of the MSP to be promoted to the rank of corporal. Later, Renee would reach the rank of detective sergeant, and supervise the ID section at the College Park Barrack. Before she retired, we got to work together again in the Inspection Support Services Unit.

In the 1980s, illegal gambling such as lottery, and sports betting, was still prevalent in some parts of Maryland. I eventually began my own cases starting off with a "numbers" (illegal lottery) investigation or two. With the division's command feeling I was progressing well enough, I was assigned my first major case in September 1983.

A nineteen-year-old woman from Baltimore City, named Joann Charlton, was a student at Frostburg State College. Her body was found in the campus arboretum after she was reported missing. Ms. Charlton had been brutally stabbed to death. This senseless attack upon Ms. Charlton started a firestorm of rumors as to who was responsible for her murder.

A state police investigative task force was initiated, and reported to the area. The students were reluctant to come forth with any information. It was considered that if the students knew anything about what happened, they were probably sharing it amongst themselves. The decision was made to place someone in the college covertly posing as a student. Hopefully, the undercover would hear something that would help develop leads for the task force to follow-up on.

This matter was assigned to the CES. As the youngest in the section, I was selected to work with the task force. With the assistance of the college's administration, I posed as an enrolled student for the following two and a half months.

The crime scene photos showed an odd placement of rocks and sticks near Ms. Charlton's body. This prompted the lead investigator Sergeant Al Hranicka, to consider the possibility this case may involve some type of occult, or ritualistic sacrificial motive.

This type of murder was unheard of in Maryland. Sergeant Hranicka contacted a professor in California, who specialized in the occult and their activities. One of the particular occult ideologies known as "Santeria," fit the profile according to the professor. Although it was a theory worthwhile considering, further inquiries along those lines failed to provide any leads, and the task force moved on to other possibilities.

It's not for a lack of effort on the part of everyone involved, that this case remains unsolved. The department expended countless investigative hours, and utilized the technical resources available at that time, all regrettably to no avail.

This was one of the few regrets I had during my time in the department. With the MSP's director of Media Communications, retired Major Greg Shipley, I recently gave an interview to a local television station in Hagerstown, during their report on the anniversary of Ms. Charlton's murder. Obviously, the impact of her death is still felt today by so many.

Greg and I have shared a longtime friendship, and mutual respect. Director Shipley has been the department's media communications officer, and director, as both sworn and now as a civilian employee. Greg who started out as an MSP cadet, has been the consummate professional throughout his career.

Greg is also a leading advocate for the Special Olympics in Maryland. By organizing the MSP's annual "Polar Bear Plunge" event, Greg has been a great friend, and supporter to hundreds of special Olympians. He certainly personifies Andrew Gifford's quote: "You can't change the world, you can change a person's world. The more people you help, the more worlds you've changed."

As serious as covert investigations can be, there were instances that show the humorous side of undercover police work. There was an investigation on a target, in the areas of Cumberland, Maryland and West Virginia, taking bets on organized sporting events.

The section set up a mobile surveillance to gather evidence on the target's activities. At some point, one of our investigators tailing the target lost sight of him. The investigator radioed he lost the target. When the target unexpectedly passed my fixed location, I radioed my observation to the other investigators. The new CES Commander, Lieutenant Fred Davis, directed me to pick up the tail, but give the target space. Lieutenant Davis was previously the commander of the Narcotics Section.

After trailing the target through the town of Cumberland, he eventually drove into West Virginia. I radioed to the others that the target was heading into West Virginia. Lieutenant Davis authorized

inue following the target, and identify any possible pick-
-off locations.

e just a few miles into West Virginia, when the target
pulled into the parking lot of a diner. After reporting my location,
Lieutenant Davis advised me to follow the target inside. The
lieutenant said he was familiar with the diner, and would be on his
way to take over the surveillance.

Being determined not to let the target out of my sight, I gave no
thought to where I was, and quickly entered the diner. That's when
reality sank in. I was in a diner occupied by all White customers in
West Virginia. After I abruptly entered, everyone in the diner
stopped what they were doing, and focused their attention on me.

Acting nonchalant as I could, I had a seat at the lunch counter to
my left. I sat next to an elderly gentleman who was eating soup. His
hand began noticeably shaking after I sat next to him. Although the
diner wasn't too crowded, there was an uneasy atmosphere. The
target walked through the diner, and into an employee-only area.
When I could no longer see the target, I decided it was best to leave
without being more conspicuous than I had already been. The man
behind the counter asked what I wanted. After I ordered a sandwich,
he asked, "To go… right?"

I paid for the sandwich, and returned to my vehicle. I observed
that Lieutenant Davis was parked in a lot across the road from the
diner. Over the radio, Lieutenant Davis told me he would take over
the surveillance. The lieutenant directed me to return to the
Cumberland area, and stand by in case the target made him. I was
told by another supervisor, to take a fixed position on a ramp that
that led back to Cumberland.

We started around four in the afternoon. It was now around 8:00
p.m. I hadn't heard any radio transmissions for a while, so I tried
raising someone on our special channel to no avail. Switching to the
Cumberland Barrack's channel, I ask the PCO if he had heard from
any of the SSD investigators. The PCO advised they had cleared two
hours ago. Apparently unbeknownst to me, the surveillance was
called off.

I must have stepped out of my vehicle to get something out of my
trunk, when the order to terminate, and secure from the surveillance
was given over the radio. I thought, "Oh great, they forgot I was
sitting on this ramp." I had a nice lonely three hour drive home to

Baltimore. I was told to stay on that ramp, and that is exactly what I did. There was one consolation though. Appreciating my explicit following of directions, Lieutenant Davis authorized three hours of overtime for me.

The other case involved targets local to the Hagerstown City area, who ran a sports betting operation from their homes. Although I was not a part of the initial investigation, I was assigned to lead one of the raiding teams. The raid was to commence at exactly 1:00 p.m., during the start of that Sunday's televised National Football League games. Combined teams of MSP, and Hagerstown City police officers armed with search and seizure warrants, would raid the identified locations, hoping to catch the targets in action, and retrieve evidence of their illegal activities.

The intelligence on my location was that the targets conducted their activities in the basement of the residence. Our point of entry would be through the rear basement door from the alley. I had some of my team watching the front to keep anyone from escaping. Two Hagerstown officers and I would enter from the rear.

Just prior to the starting time, we snuck up to the back door, and crouched down. The upper half of the wooden door was made up of squared glass panes. We were able to peer through an opening in the curtains. There were two males present watching television. At 1:00 p.m., we began banging on the door announcing our presence: "Police open the door!"

Anticipating we may have to forcibly enter the dwelling, a sledge hammer was included in our raid kits. The targets quickly started gathering up the incriminating evidence around them. Using the sledge hammer, I attempted to break the door's lock. On my second attempt, I swung the hammer so hard, it slipped from my grip, and went through the panes of glass.

Reaching through the broken glass, I unlocked the deadbolt. We quickly moved through the room as both targets could be heard running up the basement stairs. As we reached the stairway, we heard the door at the top slam shut. The target who owned the house, made his way up the short flight of stairs to the door first. He slammed the door shut on his buddy, and knocked him backwards where he fell at our feet. I told one of the Hagerstown officers to cuff him, while I went after the other target.

When I tried opening the door, it appeared locked. I assumed the target had locked it. I tried kicking it in two or three times before I realized I had just failed the "pull, don't push the door open rule." After almost spraining my ankle, I twisted and pulled the door knob towards me, and wouldn't you know it… the door opened.

Making my way quickly through the kitchen, and into the living room, I saw that the living room door was closed. I open the door, and checked with the officers out front to see if they saw any sign of the target. They hadn't seen him, so he still had to be somewhere in the house. We searched the rest of the house, and found the target hiding under the bed in one of the bedrooms. Using the hallway for cover, we ordered him to come out. The target surrendered without incident, thankfully putting an end to my comedy of errors.

Even though Maryland's state-run lottery system began in 1973, there was still some semblance of illegal lottery (numbers) activity in the Baltimore area during the early 1980s. Historically established in mostly working-class, or low-income neighborhoods, number writers could be found at the local bars, social clubs, barber shops and lunch counters. Usually, the winning numbers they used were derived from race track results.

For many years, the winning numbers in the illegal lottery, came from the last three digits of the amount [track bettors] placed on the featured races at major racetracks. The results were published in racing journals, and major newspapers the following day.[1] Viewed as a victimless crime by many, including some judges, one benefit of the illegal game for bettors, was you could wager on different variations of numbers at higher, or lower paying odds to match what you could afford to spend; Plus if you won big, you didn't have to worry about paying taxes.

In one particular lottery case, I used a uniformed trooper to pull over a numbers writer I had been investigating for several days. I had just observed the target take several numbers at a bar in Baltimore County. I too had placed several bets with him in the bar. I made arrangements for the Valley Barrack to have a uniformed trooper in the area, ready to stop the target's vehicle on my signal.

When TFC William Starvis (an academy classmate) pulled over the target several miles from the bar, everything was fine until I approached the driver's window, and identified myself.

1 Wikipedia 10/4/2020

The target reached up to the sun visor, and grabbed his papers containing the bets. The target started cramming the papers in his mouth, trying to swallow the evidence. Reaching inside the driver's window, I had to pinch his nose until he spit the papers out. While the court commissioner was reviewing my statement of charges, even he had to laugh at that desperate attempt to destroy evidence.

Then there was the time I outsmarted myself during one of my investigations dealing with another numbers writer. The target lived on a small one-way street in Baltimore County. I wanted to get his discarded trash hoping to find evidence of his illegal activities. I planned on taking his discarded trash bag after midnight. I waited close by where I could inconspicuously observe the target's house.

After the lights went out, I moved my vehicle to the end of the block, and walked back to the top of the block. Getting a running start, I reached down to grab the trash bag. What I thought would be a lightweight bag of trash, was heavier than I anticipated. The weight of the bag pulled me backwards. I almost pulled my arm out of its socket. Grabbing the bag with two hands, I continued running till I reached my vehicle. As I was now in the clear, I drove to a safe area where I could check the bag's contents for any evidence.

Opening the bag, I embarrassingly discovered it actually contained wet grass clippings. If the target had been looking out of his window, he would have laughed himself silly I'm sure. I later found out that he was smarter than I thought. He took his trash with any discarded illegal materials to his job, and dumped it there. I did eventually preferred charges against the target, after I made hand-to-hand bets with him at a neighborhood social club.

In a matter challenging to my lack of life's inexperience, an informant had to be witnessed making contact with the target in a drug case. The connection was to take place inside a strip bar, in Baltimore City. I had never been to a strip bar before. I was assigned to go with Sergeant Doug (Gator Brown) Delever; who let's just say… was more sophisticated than I was in these matters.

While sitting at the bar, I was approached by one of the dancers, asking if I wanted her company. As I was supposed to be a high-rolling customer, I asked her if I could buy her a drink. She said she'd like a champagne cocktail. As a non-consumer of alcoholic beverages, I didn't know what that was. I just thought it was a fancy name for an exotic drink, and must cost about five dollars.

When I ordered it, I gave the barmaid a $10.00 bill. Giggling amusingly, the barmaid said, "Honey that will be $50.00." I was sick to my stomach, but I had to play it off quickly, saying, "Oh I thought that was a 50." Sergeant Delever who was seated nearby, later told me he was trying not to laugh, when he saw what happened.

Investigators in SSD, received what was known as a "Bank," in the amount of $100.00. It was a ready working fund for you to use in order to make buys, or facilitate other related activities during your investigations. After you spent any amount, you were responsible for providing receipts, or other forms of justification for your approved expenditures, before your "Bank" would be reimbursed by the Finance Division.

Our administrative officer at that time was Lieutenant Bob Graham. I found myself sitting in his office, thinking how I was going to justify spending half of my "Bank" on one drink. Seated before the lieutenant, I could see my undercover career coming to an end. I was unaware that Sergeant Delever had already advised the lieutenant of the circumstances I found myself in. I was ready to replace the money out of my own pocket.

Lieutenant Graham decided to pretend he was angry, but couldn't hold back his laughter, imagining the look on my face, when the barmaid told me the drink was $50.00. The lieutenant understood my predicament, and approved the expenditure. He knew this was a learning experience, and advised me to be more aware of my circumstances, before I committed to spending money in the future.

Joining the MSP in 1973, Doug was one of the earlier Black members on the department. Doug would retire from the MSP as a lieutenant. In the following years, he was appointed by two different governors to head the Department of Natural Resources Police, and the Transit Authority Administration Police, respectively. He is now fully retired from law enforcement.

Chapter 20
Always Take Copious Notes

During my four years in the SSD, I was assigned cases that required full integration within a particular environment in order to witness an alleged criminal act. The Annapolis City Police Department's (APD) Vice and Narcotics Unit supervised by Sergeant Russell Hall, requested our assistance with their investigation into the illegal activities of a particular narcotics, and numbers operation.

Through Sergeant Hall's connections, I got a job driving a cab in the city to become a familiar fixture in the neighborhood. After a week or two of hand-to-hand drug buys, and placing illegal number wages with the identified targets, enough evidence was developed to obtain search and seizure warrants. This joint operation led to the subsequent arrests of those involved. I did have one hairy moment that had nothing to do with the case though.

One evening a fare tried to pretend he had already paid me, and started arguing the point. I turned towards the fare and asked him how he could have paid me before we reached his destination. I thought he was setting me up for a robbery. When he acted like he was going reach across the seat from the rear, with my gun in hand I told him I knew he wasn't trying to cheat a brother, so cough up the fare or else. He took out a wad of bills, and told me to take what I wanted. I told the fare all that wasn't necessary, and to hand over the right amount, and get out. Fortunately, I never saw him again during the investigation.

In another county, information was received by the barrack about a suspect plotting a contract murder-for-hire scheme. The CES was contacted, and brought up to speed with the intelligence developed by their investigation section. I was assigned the case by my new supervisor, Sergeant Auggie Stern. First, I had to establish a casual contact with the target, in order to make my sudden appearance seem coincidental. That still didn't mean the target would confide his alleged desire to have someone murdered to a stranger. Although I didn't drink, it was necessary to frequent a local bar, where the target was known to frequent.

The informant casually pointed out the target to me. The informant was told to hang around for a few minutes, and then quietly leave. I was able to innocently start a conversation with the target, by joining in on the ongoing conversations about sports. I bought a round of drinks for the informant, and a small group of patrons. (Thankfully, there were no $50.00 champagne cocktails, or dancers in this case.)

I had to be careful not to appear unnecessarily friendly, causing the target to become suspicious or uncomfortable with my sudden attention. I also had to be mindful that we didn't want to lose control of the intended victim's safety, by having the target decide to solicit someone else.

After the second day of showing up at "Happy Hour," the target said he wanted to ask me a question. He said I looked like a "good guy," and revealed his plan to me. The target asked if I knew anyone that would take out somebody for money. I asked him how much money he was talking about. He told me he could pay $400.00.

I told the target I believed I knew a guy who would. We agreed to meet the next day at a different location for my answer. Although $400.00 sounds very low even back then, if I balked, or asked for more, we stood the chance of losing control, and possibly endangering the intended victim's life.

When we met the next day, I was wearing a body wire, intended to intercept and record any incriminating conversation spoken by the target in my presence. Solicitation to commit murder, is one of the enumerated crimes in Maryland, making it permissible to intercept verbal communications without the knowledge of the other party. Sergeant Stern and Corporal Ted Polinsky, were nearby in our surveillance vehicle, videotaping and monitoring the recorded conversation between me and the target.

The target was informed since I needed the money, I decided to do the job myself. I convinced the target that the less people who knew his business the better. We then discussed the particulars, and the identity of the intended victim. The target gladly offered suggestions on how to best carryout our plans. The target gave me the first down payment of $200.00. We agreed to meet again later, and conclude our planning. At that time, he would pay me the remaining $200.00 balance.

After the target left the parking lot, I drove to another location to meet with Sergeant Stern and Corporal Polinsky. Sergeant Stern suggested that I not wait till the next day to prepare my notes. He said I should take "copious notes" now, and not rely on recall later. Honestly, I didn't know the meaning of the word "copious" at first. But when Auggie explained what it meant, I followed his advice. That would later prove to be a crucial suggestion on Auggie's part.

The next day, when we reviewed the video in the technical equipment room, we were surprised when the video had no audio. The audio of the incriminating conversation was missing. The tape recording equipment apparently malfunctioned. If the target had decided to back out, we may not have had a strong enough case to arrest and charge him.

Although there was video showing an exchange of money, the target could have said it was for something unrelated. With no audio, a defense attorney could try and discredit my retention, questioning my motives to make up for the loss of any corroborating audio evidence. Having taken my notes contemporaneous to the act, I could testify if necessary, that my notes were not prepared with a lack of retention after the fact. Before the target arrived for our next meeting, the audio equipment was checked, and found to function properly.

The motive for this crime was the age-old sin of lust. The people involved, were a struggling young couple staying with the target at his home. He was an older man, and became infatuated with his intended victim's wife. The target figured with the husband dead, the wife would be so desperate to be taken care of, she would most certainly turn to him for love and support.

The intended victim didn't drive. As a routine, the target drove and dropped him off at a nearby location at 4:00 a.m. There the intended victim would wait to be picked up by coworkers, and driven to work. At that location, I was to be secreted behind nearby shrubbery. Once the intended victim was dropped off, and the target drove away, I would accost, and shoot the victim, before fleeing the scene.

To further convince the target of my bad intentions, I displayed a handgun with an obliterated serial number, borrowed from the division's seized weapons storage area. I also showed him a set of another state's registration plates that I said were stolen. The plates were actually gratis from that state, for official law enforcement use only. The target was very impressed, and gladly gave me the remaining $200.00 as we closed the deal.

On the scheduled morning, the target's vehicle pulled up to the location on time. The intended victim stepped out, unaware of what his planned fate was to be. Once the target pulled off, he would be under surveillance by barrack troopers.

Sergeant Stern and I approached the intended victim. After we identified ourselves using our flashlights, Sergeant Stern asked the gentleman his name. He was verified as the intended victim. The gentleman asked what was going on. Sergeant Stern informed the gentleman of the target's plan to have him killed. In disbelief, the gentleman momentarily lost his bearing, and had to be seated on the curb. Asked what if any conversation he had with the target in the vehicle, the gentleman said, "Not much, he just told me to have a nice day as I got out of the car."

Sergeant Stern radioed the go-ahead to stop and arrest the target. Once the target was stopped, he was told he was being arrested in connection with a suspicious shooting that had just occurred. The target vehemently denied any knowledge of any shooting incident. The target was placed in a trooper's vehicle, and transported to the barrack.

In an attempt to see if we could get the target to come clean, we staged a fictitious broadcast that the target could hear while being transported to the barrack. The broadcast was intended to convince him that a Black male driving a blue mustang, was the subject of a pursuit. The Black male who was now in custody, was under arrest in connection for a shooting that just occurred.

To further this ruse, I was taken to the barrack, and put in the cell with the target. Predictably, he acted as if we had never seen each other before. Even after telling him I wasn't going down alone, he just sat on his bed staring ahead, saying he didn't know what I was talking about.

After about twenty minutes, it was apparent the target wasn't going to take the bait, and acknowledge his involvement; so the ploy was ended. I subsequently completed a statement of charges, and applied for an arrest warrant at the court commissioner's office, charging the target with solicitation, and conspiracy to commit murder.

Before he retired Ted would make sergeant. Long after Ted and I retired, we stayed in contact. In the later years, he and his wife Deb would meet with my family, and have dinner. Sadly, Ted passed after his bout with cancer in 2017. I was able to visit with him a few times in the hospital before he left us. We relived the happy days of our careers, sharing laughs, and performing the made-up handshake we always gave each other in the old CES days. Teddy really loved being in the MSP, and we miss him, and his rugby shirts and matching pants!

Chapter 21
The Honest Prisoner

One of the most unique types of cases the SSD took on back then, was to have a trooper pose as an inmate, in order to get evidence on an existing crime; or one that was being planned. During the preparation for such cases, the covert investigator was only afforded minimum information about the case's details. This would eliminate any possible later suggestions, that the incarcerated investigator was pre-warned of any incriminating facts. In the event any pertinent information about the case was uncovered, it would have to come from the target, or those with knowledge of the crime.

On four different occasions, I was assigned to conduct such investigations in three different detention centers in Maryland, and one in West Virginia. In each case, we required the cooperation of the administrator of those centers, and the local State's Attorney's Offices to ensure my seamless incarceration into those facilities.

In the first investigation, the target was an incarcerated inmate awaiting trial for his involvement in the attempted murder of an off-duty police officer. After a local police detective secured a confession from the target, he began having second thoughts about his decision to confess. The target allegedly wanted to have the detective murdered, keeping the detective from testifying against him in court. When that intelligence was received by the local police department, they reached out for assistance from the SSD. With the cooperation of the State's Attorney's Office, the necessary charging documents were prepared by the local barrack's criminal section supervisor, Sergeant Rob Garber.

After being put through the preliminary admission required by the correctional staff, I was placed in my cell. Rather than put me in the same cellblock with the target, it was decided it would be less obvious for me to make contact during a general recreational period. As this was my first time being incarcerated in a detention facility, I didn't know what to expect. While I anxiously waited for my chance to meet the target, I had to remind myself to calm down. It was essential to gain the target's confidence as quickly as possible, but do so cautiously.

It was a very hot Friday evening. As I lay on the steel bed that was bolted to the wall in my cell, I began sweating profusely, and took off my shirt to rest under my head. There was a big oscillating fan in the corridor between the cells, just blowing hot air. As it was going to be a while before it was my turn to go to the recreation area, I decided to take a nap. After a few minutes the temperature increased, and I really began to sweat. I opened my eyes, and what I thought was sweat, was actually three roaches crawling across my chest and stomach. That was it for naps.

After what seemed like two hours, I asked one of the passing officers when I was going to get out for recreation period. The officer said I would have to ask the shift supervisor. The supervising sergeant came to my cell, and said I wouldn't be allowed out of my cell. The sergeant gave me no reason, and just grinned at me afterwards.

I didn't want to overreact, but I felt uneasy with this development. As time was of the essences, I decided not to wait and figure out what went wrong. Concerned by the sergeant's behavior, I felt my identity may have been compromised. The backup plan was to get word to the barrack, by informing the detention center officials I was ready to confess to Sergeant Garber. Sergeant Garber would then immediately respond, as though he was going to take my statement.

My first request was ignored. In order to get them to notify the barrack, I had to make so much noise and became such a disruption, they finally asked me what my problem was. I was only aware they complied with my request, when Sergeant Garber arrived and secured my release from the cell. Afterwards I told Rob what happened.

Rather than push the issue further, we decided to have me removed from the facility. We could only surmise that my identity was compromised, and perhaps the officers thought I was there to investigate one of them. There wasn't enough evidence to prove the detention center's sergeant knowingly interfered, but I had my doubts.

When a murder-for-hire case is compromised, or the target may become suspicious and backs out of a planned act, we subsequently confront the target. The target is then officially notified of our suspicions. The target is told to cease and desist. They are warned that if any harm befell the intended victim, they would be sought for the crime. The intended victim would also be notified and offered various means of protection, until it was determined the threat reasonably no longer existed.

In this case, the target failed to realize, that any previous (relevant), testimony given as evidence under oath during the preliminary hearing by the detective (which included his voluntary confession), would be admissible at the subsequent trial; even if the detective succumbed to natural causes prior to the trial. The target was later convicted on his original charge: Attempted murder of a police officer.

In my second case, I was incarcerated in the Jefferson County Detention Center in Charles Town, West Virginia. The operation was limited to no more than five days. I was assigned to gain the confidence of an inmate, who was awaiting trial for sexual assault and attempted murder. This inmate was also a possible suspect in three unsolved sex-related murders in Washington and Frederick Counties in Maryland.

I was placed in the maximum security cell with the inmate. In order to help gain his confidence, there were similar (fictitious) charges to that of the inmate's, placed against me as a fugitive from Maryland. After my second day, the target was comfortable enough that he began speaking freely about some of his alleged exploits. After listening to his preoccupation with the bizarre, sexual nature of his self-alleged acts, I felt they were the product of a deranged mind, in my opinion. For my purposes, I had to appear interested in these ramblings, even though I was thoroughly disgusted with him.

On my final day, Detective Sergeant Vogel, had arranged for my release, and I was transported back to Maryland. I was debriefed by the investigators connected with the ongoing Maryland cases. I advised them that after hearing the inmate's contrived nonsense, I thought he was out of his mind. I repeated some of the things I heard the target say. The investigators determined there was nothing he said that had any possible connections to their cases. I told them the target was just trying to impress me, thinking I was a fellow sexual predator.

However warped the target may have been, he was also devious. When members of a prison ministry visited the detention center, he would go up to the door's opening, and join them in singing hymns, and receiving prayer. As soon as the ministry left, he would start laughing. He told me he was using them. He only wanted to appear accepting of their gospel, thinking this would help him seem remorseful in the eyes of the authorities. Like I said, he was one vile individual.

Chapter 22
The Parting Gift that Kept on Giving

When informant information revealed that a correctional officer was smuggling marijuana into a county detention center, SSD was asked to help uncover evidence against the suspected officer, and the inmate receiving the contraband. According to the informant, the suspected inmate was supplying the marijuana to other inmates in the facility.

Once again, I was processed for arrest on an approved fictitious statement of charges. This time by the local barrack investigator, TFC Roger Layton. I was placed in general population where I could casually meet the target inmate. After playing outside basketball during a recreation period, my cellmate wasted no time in pumping me for personal information. Even though he became at ease with my story, at some point I had to ask him was he writing a book.

The next step, was to get my unsuspecting cellmate to introduce me to the target inmate. I was well prepared to convince the target of my story as well, thanks to Sergeants Edge and Leard. Both who had experience in these types of investigations, and taught me why it was important to have your story straight.

However, at some point, you can't appear too willing to tell your whole life's story. That could be considered suspicious, and work against you as well. It's a fine line between not appearing too timid, or becoming over confident. Sometimes working undercover, you had to wing it and pray.

My cellmate introduced me to the target inmate my second day. After the obligatory round of seemingly innocent questions from the target, it appeared I was in good with him too. Later that night, I confirmed the identity of the officer in question, when he was pointed out to me by my cellmate. The target had gained trustee status, and could move about freely, distributing the marijuana. To my amazement, the information was true. Some of the inmates were actually having pot parties in our wing of the cells after lights out.

As a covert investigator, you were authorized by the department to reasonably consume alcoholic beverages without getting inebriated, or losing control of yourself. However, ingesting controlled dangerous substances was prohibited. In extreme circumstances, common sense had to prevail if your cover was at stake, causing a threat to your life. If such an instance occurred where you were forced to indulge, as soon as possible, you had to notify supervision, and be treated medically.

When the marijuana joints were being passed around, it was noticed I wasn't participating. I didn't know this was going to happen so quickly. If pressed as to why I wasn't smoking, I was prepared to offer some medical reason as an explanation. Thankfully, they waited till it was dark enough, and I could put it up to my lips pretending to ingest it, before passing it to my cellmate.

Part of our plan, was to have Corporal Hank Howland (a narcotic section supervisor), pose as my attorney, and meet with me on the third day to determine my progress. By that time, I also learned the identity of the outside source supplying the marijuana, that was being brought in by the correctional officer. That information was a plus, especially as I had no physical evidence, only what I had overheard, and observed.

There was enough information gathered to justify initiating subsequent surveillances on the officer, to further supplement the case. After my contact with Corporal Howland, it was determined that my time was up, and I would be removed the next day. As I had to go through the standard release protocol, it took some time before I was to be released on a fictitious bail order.

My cellmate was out on his recreation period. In an unexpected turn of events, I was visited at my cell by the target inmate. He told me he heard I was leaving, and wanted me to have something as a going away present. Unbelievably, he handed me a marijuana joint through the opening of my cell. Unknowingly, the target just handed me the physical evidence to go with my observations. Although just one joint, based on the circumstances of this investigation, he could be charged with possession with the intent to distribute under Maryland's felony law.

Underneath my calm exterior, I was very excited. But there was a problem I had to consider. If it were discovered I had that joint in my possession during the time I was being searched for release, the entire case could embarrassingly backfire. I didn't have a lot of time to decide whether to keep it or not. We wanted to pursue follow-up attempted buys from the outside source. So the last thing I wanted to do, was to have the investigation prematurely exposed.

As it was summertime, I was dressed in shorts, tennis shoes, a tank top, and thick knee-high sweat socks. Taking a chance, I decided to keep the marijuana joint. As the joint was pliable, I made sure my socks were pulled all the way up, just under my knees. Outwardly folding over the tops of both socks, I hid the joint under the partially folded top of one sock, hoping it wouldn't be noticeable.

When it was time to be released, I acted nonchalant while being searched. They checked inside my shoes, and patted me up and down. As I was lightly dressed, I guess they figured I couldn't hide anything noticeably. I was able to get away with it, and immediately driven to the barrack by Corporal Howland. The evidence was processed, and in the following days, our drug task force was able to make contact with the outside source. They solidified the case by making hand-to-hand buys from the outside source.

After wrapping up the investigation, I returned to the detention center with arrest warrants for the target inmate, and the officer. When the inmate was brought into an office and confronted, he obviously recognized me. He pretended he had no knowledge of what I was talking about. When it was apparent his denial wasn't going to help him, he inexplicably uttered he knew I was a cop. The correction officer who was off duty, was arrested at his residence by other troopers.

Chapter 23
The Styrofoam Cups Were More Useful Than the Food

In my final incarceration case, we were requested to assist in an ongoing homicide investigation. The case was being jointly investigated, by the Hagerstown Barrack, and the Washington County Sheriff's Department (WCSD). My incarceration inside the county's detention center, was facilitated with the cooperation of the Federal Bureau of Investigation (FBI). I was charged with unlawful flight to avoid confinement on the charge of murder.

The plan was to place me in a cell, between the two cells occupied by the charged co-conspirators. This would hopefully allow me to overhear any ensuing incriminating conversations between them. Detective Sergeant Vogel, was acting as my attorney. He accompanied me along with an allied investigator to the detention center.

Detective Sergeant Vogel brought along some reading material, toiletries, and a notepad and pen for me to take notes with. These items were left at the processing station, with the understanding I would receive them once I was placed in my cell.

The cells were concrete wall cubicles. The doors were solid steel with slots at the bottom for your meals to be slid to you, and windows at eye level, allowing the officers to look inside. When I asked the officer escorting me to my cell for the things left by my attorney, he said I wasn't allowed to have them.

Not wanting to compromise the investigation, I just accepted it. The next day, I could hear chatter between the two target inmates. They were joking, and saying things I felt may be pertinent. Although they spoke in terms of slang, I figured out what they meant. Sometimes they couldn't hear each other, so I voluntarily passed the message on. I tried relying on retention, but there was just too much being said. I wanted to be sure to take note of what seemed important, and disregard any superfluous chatter.

Later that day, I was issued a plastic bag with a small comb, a plastic shaving razor with a recessed blade (safe enough not to be used as a weapon), and other needed toiletries. The terrible food was served in styrofoam cups and on styrofoam plates. Concerned I was going to forget something important, in desperation I started using the comb's edge to inscribe abbreviations on the outside of styrofoam cups as notes. That way I didn't have to totally rely on retention of the things I felt were vital. I flattened the cups, and put them underneath my sweater.

After three days, Detective Sergeant Vogel came to the detention center to learn of any progress. I quickly wrote down my notes on the notepad he gave me. My notes consisted of somethings from memory, and some translated from the inscriptions written on the styrofoam cups. My notes coupled with the initial evidence in the case, led investigators to conclude my incarceration. I was released to the custody of an allied investigator, and transported to the Hagerstown Barrack for debriefing.

A few weeks later, I received a letter of appreciation, and my "mugshot" photo from the case investigator, Sergeant Doug Mullendore, WCSD. The letter stated that the main suspect in the case was found guilty of felony murder, and received a life sentence. He also promised to do something about the terrible food for any future visits on my part. In 2006, (now a lieutenant), Doug was elected as sheriff in Washington County. He is still honorably serving the county and its citizens as their sheriff.

I was not required to be incarcerated in another plot, where an inmate wanted to have his victim murdered prior to trial. SSD was contacted by a local police department for assistance. Information from an inmate turned informant, was that he had been approached by an inmate awaiting trial on a rape charge.

The suspected inmate, allegedly offered to pay the inmate/informant $500.00 to arrange it so the victim didn't make it to court. Once again assisted by Detective Sergeant Vogel, it was arranged for me to meet with the informant to work out the details. We planned to have the informant tell the suspect he knew someone who needed the money, and would do the job. The informant was told to have the suspect put my fictitious name on his visitors list. We wanted to remove the informant from the picture, and take full control of the plot.

Before we could move forward with the plan, the suspect apparently had second thoughts, no money, or became fearful he was being set up. The suspect never made any further attempts to contact the informant after that. Without that connection, we were unable to proceed as planned.

A few weeks later, Detective Sergeant Vogel and I received a letter of update, and thanks from the chief who requested our assistance. The letter said that the suspect was tried in circuit court, and found guilty of first-degree rape, and attempted solicitation to have the victim murdered. He received a sentence of life imprisonment.

Chapter 24
He's No Narc

While working on a wiretap case in Hagerstown with Corporal Frank Walters and Detective Sergeant Vogel, I was asked to assist with an ongoing drug investigation. The request came from Washington County Assistant State's Attorney, Andrew Norman. ASA Norman, wanted me to start making a few drug buys from suspects in a particular part of the city. I told him he needed to ask my detective sergeant, but I wouldn't mind, if the narcotics section had no objections.

ASA Norman said he was told that the narcotics section didn't have anyone immediately available, so he wanted to know if I would help him. I had the utmost respect for Andrew, and was happy to do anything I could to help him. He was the best prosecutor I have ever worked with.

When he told the narcotic section I agreed to help him, the person on the line remarked that I was no narc, and had no real experience in the drug culture. ASA Norman informed him that I had already made several hand-to-hand buys, and was in good with the dealers. ASA Norman later told me that once my foot was in the door, the narcotic section wanted to assume the investigation. ASA Norman told them they were no longer needed, as I was working in conjunction with the Washington County Narcotic Task Force (WCNTF), and all of my buys were being processed, and stored as evidence locally.

There was a new form of cocaine surfacing in the area, referred to as "crack." One of the problems I initially encountered, came when trying to identify the individuals involved. No one was in the habit of using their real names around there. Everybody had nicknames. Thankfully, the Hagerstown City Police (HCPD) had extensive arrest-photo identification books, and their investigators were familiar with most of what I refer to as the "frequent flyers," in the area.

For those whose pictures I couldn't find in the books, I had to rely on my personal recollections. As a backup, we also had surveillance photos of my activities taken by a member of the SSD, Corporal Jimmy Schroyer. Jimmy was secreted in a nearby building overlooking the area.

Interestingly, the amount of actual cocaine found in my initial buys, began decreasing substantially in my subsequent purchases. My first piece was analyzed at 66% purity. Subsequent pieces were down to 41%. The purpose was to get you quickly hooked on the high potency in the early stages.

In a method referred to as "stepped on," drug operations gradually decreased the percentage of actual cocaine, replacing the drug with other fillers. Users would feel less of the desired effect on subsequent buys, and would need much more to get the sensation they initially experienced. The "slab-like" pieces were getting smaller as well.

In this particular housing unit, there was a blatant "open-air" of drug activity going on. By now, I was assigned a nice black Chevrolet Camaro, and had the task force's funds to back up my cover. I had two or three dealers approaching me, arguing over my business. In order to obtain evidence on more than one dealer, I would vary my times, and dealers. I could see the frightened faces of some of the residents, especially the elderly. My part of the combined investigation lasted for two months.

The day of the raid on the housing development, was a sight to behold. Already on the scene prior to the raid, I had to wear an item that alerted officers I was the undercover. My identity was unknown to most of the raiding officers. All they were told at the briefing, was to be careful of the undercover wearing the standout item.

Using a "Trojan Horse" method, several trucks, and vans surrounded the development. At the designated time, our helicopter began hovering above the target area. That was the signal for the officers who were secreted inside these trucks and vans, to jump out, and overtake the scene. Using flex-cuffs, the officers secured everyone in the immediate area. I had to make a personal identification of those who were the dealers, and those who were in illegal possession as buyers at that time. Those who were detained, but innocent of any illegal activities were immediately released.

Borrowing a quote from a resident, the local newspaper's headline read, "They came in like gangbusters!" This tremendous effort culminated in two separate arrest operations for those who were responsible. Based on my hand-to-hand buys, 12 suspects were arrested, and approximately $15,000.00 was seized. Subsequently, a second group of 14 more suspects were arrested on related charges.

There were four additional warrants on suspects that could not be immediately served. This was due to their unknown status in the United States. I could only identify them on the arrest warrants, as "John Doe." On my statement of charges, I listed their descriptions, and stated I could personally identify them.

The two main suspects each received 40 year sentences in circuit court, thanks to the aggressive prosecution of ASA Norman. The combined efforts of the WCNTF, the HCPD, the Washington County Sheriff's Department, the Immigration and Naturalization Services and the MSP, ensured the total success of this major undertaking.

Sergeant Ronnie Graves of the HCPD, and the members of the WCNTF: Bill Baker, Craig Bakner, Doug Mullendore, Nelson Sheppard, ASA Andrew Norman, and our chemist Jeff Kerchavel, were some of the most knowledgeable, dedicated people I have ever known. They were the kind of law enforcement officials I was privileged to work alongside of: The kind who made public safety a priority in the communities they served.

Chapter 25
They Don't Make Them Like That Anymore

After three years in the SSD, 1986, was a very productive year for me professionally, and a very satisfying one personally. My immediate supervisor Sergeant Stern, was kind enough to submit an extensive detailed account of my overall performance, nominating me for the department's "Trooper of the Year Award," representing the SSD.

With the division commander's concurrence, this in turn led to my nomination for the "Police Officer of the Year Award," presented by Baltimore's "Evening Sun" newspaper. The new superintendent Colonel George Brosan, approved my recommendation as the department's nominee for the 21st Annual "Parade Magazine/International Chief of Police Service Award."

Although I didn't win any of the three awards, I was most honored, and proud to be considered. Just to be recognized for my efforts was good enough for me. I received a very special personal letter of recognition from United States' Congresswoman Barbara Mikulski, who represented the State's 3rd District. Congresswoman Mikulski's kindness was very much appreciated. A month later in June, I received my first supervisory promotion to the rank of corporal. Like I said, it was a very satisfying year.

A few months later, the division was disbanded. I was reassigned to the newly expanded Drug Enforcement Division. The remaining members of the Criminal Enforcement Section, were reassigned to the Criminal Investigation Division (CID), and relocated to another facility.

I would not get to work directly with any of my group again. After the reassignments, our paths went in different directions. Several of them retired a few years later. I cannot say enough about my feelings towards them. They had such a positive influence on me. Thanks to each of them, the state police unquestionably stood out, as a valued ally to our law enforcement partners, and the criminal justice agencies we assisted.

SSD's commander was Captain Wilford (Will) Lawrence. Captain Lawrence was the perfect leader for our collection of investigators, who possessed various talents and personalities, in a field not suited for everyone. When acknowledging a request for our assistance from other agencies, Captain Lawrence would close his letters with the phrase, "You may be assured of our continued cooperation, in all matters of mutual concern." I liked that; and adopted the captain's phrase for myself, when closing my own letters addressing departmental matters, later in my career.

Sadly, in the last few years, we have lost those who I personally owe so much. For those whose passing was not already mentioned, in tribute, I recognize the following as well with admiration, and the utmost respect: They don't make them like that anymore.

Sergeant Al (Big Al) Hranicka, 2010.
Colonel George Brosan, 2014.
Sergeant Ray (Uncle Ray) Leard, 2015.
Lieutenant Paul Gillian, 2016.
Corporal Larry Morse, 2016.
TFC Donny (Hummer) Newcomer, 2017.
Captain Will Lawrence, 2020.

Chapter 26
The One Minute Narc Supervisor

Although I wasn't given a choice, I found myself reassigned to the newly created Drug Enforcement Division (DED). When the new captain came in, he immediately made it clear what his preferred management style was based upon. The captain said he prescribed to the principles featured in the book entitled, "The One Minute Manager."

The division's new administration, decided to initiate a strategy using hit-and-run tactics, aimed at local street activities in certain parts of the state. They formed groups referred to as "Selective Enforcement Teams" (S.E.T). It was hoped these teams could make a dent in local drug activities, while developing a new network of informants to go after the higher level dealers. In order to facilitate the needed personnel for this expansion, the department transferred a number of troopers from the field into the division.

A seminar was held at the Pikesville National Guard Armory, to quickly acclimate these troopers into their new world. At that time "Miami Vice," which premiered on television in 1984, had glamorized the role of the undercover narcotic detective. Several of the veteran narcs found it lighthearted, when some of these troopers showed up looking as if they were attending a "Miami Vice" convention: Badges on chains around their necks, shoes with no socks, fresh stubble growth on some faces, and to complete the look, earrings in their ears.

My team was assigned to the Eastern Shore, and included four of the newly assigned troopers, TFCs Bill Bonnell, George (Mickey) Forsythe, Phil Nolan and Donald Wiggins. The day we got started, the group reported to our office in the old K-9 building behind the Easton Barrack. TFC Nolan came dressed in a short-sleeved dress shirt, a tie with an attached handcuffs tie-tack, and patent leather uniform shoes.

The rest of us looked at each other. We were all dressed down in jeans, etc. I asked Phil who he planned on buying drugs from dressed like that. I told him that was a novel approach, because nobody would ever think he was a narc. Despite that unusual start, I tried easing them into their development with an organized game plan. I was very pleased with their efforts once we got started. It's not an easy transition to go from uniform to undercover.

In my opinion, no one at the top of the division, gave the development of this S.E.T operation much thought. I think in order to justify someone's lofty ambition, all of this was more of a "Let's just go out there and wing it" decision. From where I stood, there was no real planning, support, or available resources to speak of. It wasn't for a lack of effort on the troopers' part that I had issues with the new command's expectations.

As I was once a new covert investigator, I knew it was important to gradually ease new investigators into this type of work. Instead of placing four new narcs in one group with one supervisor, they should have been mixed in groups with other veteran investigators, allowing them to learn under observation. This was not like transferring from one barrack to another. It's a completely different set of circumstances.

If this was an example of the new command's principles, I shuttered to think how the division's fortunes were going to end up, when it was all said and done. Once again, I felt my days were numbered. I wasn't considered a "drug guy," coming from another part of the disbanded Special Services Division. And that was fine with me. I did my job as expected, despite my concerns.

As TFC Forsythe was soon to discover, there is nothing like the excitement of your first drug buy. George developed a relationship with a suspected dealer who agreed to sell him cocaine. Traveling from Hagerstown after a day of court appearances, I went to act as backup for George. After the buy, we went to another location, and conducted a field test using a reagent kit for cocaine. A positive test for cocaine would yield a reaction turning the suspected substance pink, and blue during the sequential breaking of the vials.

The substance TFC Forsythe purchased turned pink in a split second, meaning there was very little cocaine, and plenty of who knows what used as a cutting agent. George was so angry with the dealer; I tried not to laugh. We went back to the area where he made the buy. We observed the dealer coming out of a local convenience store carrying a bag of groceries. The dealer was approached, and arrested without incident, for possession of suspected CDS, with the intent to distribute.

The dealer wanted to know what he could do about his groceries. TFC Forsythe personally saw they wound up in the parking lot dumpster. The lesson here I told George, is that he wasn't the first narc to get bamboozled, and he wouldn't be the last. Along with what George recovered from the suspect pursuant to the arrest, he still had enough to make a criminal case against the suspect. I said the lab would be able to determine what the percentages were of any cocaine present in the samples he submitted for analysis.

In January 1987, the MSP was part of the law enforcement response to the fatal crash of an Amtrak train in Chase, Baltimore County. When I stopped by the Waterloo Barrack to get gas, I saw one of my former CES lieutenants, Charlie Mazzone. He was now a captain, and the new commander of CID. The captain was gassing up the department's command vehicle to be transported to the scene of the crash.

Captain Mazzone told me he was starting a new unit in CID, out of headquarters in Pikesville. The unit was being created to specifically find and arrest wanted fugitives, and repeat offenders, by using covert methods. The captain wanted to know if I would be interested in a transfer to this new unit.

Feeling fate was telling me it was time to move on, I accepted his offer. A few days later, I went to pick up some paperwork at DED. When I attempted to gain access through the rear door, I found the combination had been changed. After ringing the bell, I was told I had to wait. I was asked for the keys to my nice "cool car," and received the keys to a not-so-nice, "uncool sub-compact car." That was the end of my career as a "One Minute" narc supervisor. Despite my misgivings, my group worked well together, and we had some fun in the process, albeit brief. Those guys made the best out of the cards we were dealt.

Although we would never work together again, Bill, George and I became dear friends in the following years. Bill went on to make corporal before he retired, and later became a deputy sheriff out of state where he relocated. Bill was proud to have his son Brian follow him on the MSP. Brian is currently a sergeant with the department. Becoming a sergeant before he retired, George investigated a few murder-for-hire cases, proving he was an excellent covert investigator in his own rights.

Two of the team members are no longer with us. Phil Nolan retired as a sergeant. In 2013, early one morning, Phil was asleep on a cot, inside his garage-like structure. The garage was situated close to the road. Phil was tragically killed after the operator of a speeding vehicle lost control, and crashed the vehicle into the structure, striking Phil in his sleep. In 2012, Donald Wiggins lost his battle with health issues after he resigned from the department.

Although I was able to attend Phil's memorial services, I was unaware that Donald had passed until after the fact. May God bless them, and keep their memories in our hearts.

Chapter 27
"Come on Down Bunk... We'll Help You!"

The Fugitive Unit was a new concept to the MSP. Generally warrants and summonses were served by the barrack troopers, or assigned to barrack or CID investigators. Our unit served the more serious warrants in state, and when necessary, we also traveled out of state to return wanted fugitives back to Maryland. The unit also assisted the barracks, by locating, and apprehending their defendants in other parts of the state upon request.

Soon after, it was revealed that individuals wanted on Division of Correction (DOC) "Retake Warrants" for violations of their parole or probation, weren't actively being sought. This was attributed to personnel resource limitations at DOC. Eventually, we were mandated to begin serving those DOC warrants in addition to our own.

In 1987, we were working in a task force, searching for the suspect wanted for the attempted murder of a United States Park police officer. During that time, I met Detective Kenny Dyson, of the Baltimore City Police Department's Escape and Apprehension Unit (EAU). I told him about the influx of warrants with city addresses I had to serve. Detective Dyson told his supervisor Sergeant Bob Sharp, who said, "Come on down Bunk... we'll help you!"

These detectives were a great union of resources, expertise, and camaraderie. Sergeant Sharp was the perfect supervisor to lead this cast of outgoing characters, who distinguished themselves locating fugitives on a daily bases. Baltimore City Sheriff's Detective George Cunningham, was temporarily detailed to the MSP for administrative purposes. As Deputy Cunningham had worked with the EAU before, he joined our impromptu task force. Like the EAU's detectives, George was a solid investigator who knew how to locate fugitives.

Any jurisdictional limitations were eliminated by this joint effort. If any of the EAU's warrants needed to be addressed outside

Baltimore City, I would accompany them as the lead, or take members of our fugitive unit to search for, and capture EAU's wanted fugitive. As the majority of the DOC retake warrants had Baltimore City addresses, they would reciprocate helping me in the city.

Due to their other shift obligations, there were times when the detectives weren't available to assist me. Sergeant Sharp assigned me a unit number, and one of their portable radios to call for assistance, when I was in the city on my own. That had never been done before, and showed their concern for my safety.

When responding uniformed officers arrived to my calls for assistance, they were obviously expecting one of their own detectives. They were puzzled to find out I was a state trooper. After a brief explanation resolved their questions, it was on to business as usual.

Needless to say we worked some outstanding cases together. Our collaboration resulted in the capture of fugitives wanted for arson, assaults on law enforcement officers, narcotics violations, escapes from the Division of Corrections and the Baltimore City Jail, fugitives from other states, homicide and sex offenses, and other crimes both in Baltimore City, and other counties. That's how things got done in those days. No red tape, just officers respecting one another, and working together for the public's safety.

Besides Sergeant Sharp and Detective Dyson, I want to recognize the other members of the city's EAU. They were Detectives Fred Ballard, Teddy Black, Danny Gunter, the late David Hollingsworth who passed in 2017, James Shields, Byron Williams, the late Paul Wingate who passed in 2017, and Richard Young.

Those detectives were truly some of the best in our business. Our joint efforts would be the precursor to what is now recognized as the official warrant task force established between the MSP, Baltimore City Police Department and Sheriff's Office, Baltimore County Police Department and the U.S. Marshals' Service.

Chapter 28
"Mac" Was No Ordinary Joe

Despite everyone working cohesively and effectively, I would have to endure the unwarranted behavior of a supervisor, who failed to read the warning label. Our immediate supervisor was a sergeant who had supervised the department's Repeat Offender Unit (ROPE), operating in Prince George's County. He was reassigned to head the everyday operations of the new Fugitive Unit, out of headquarters in Pikesville.

As I mentioned earlier, there was an attempted murder of a U.S. Park Police (USPP) officer in 1987. A task force of fugitive investigators was assembled which included the MSP and Baltimore City. A collective search culminated in the suspect's eventual capture. In order to show their appreciation, the USPP hosted an absolutely wonderful gathering in Southeast Baltimore City, inviting all of the allied departments involved. The USPP also sent out letters of appreciation for each member of the task force who participated.

When their letter acknowledging our participation was received, each member of the unit received a copy for our personnel files. However, there was one problem. The letter only listed the name of the sergeant, and referred to the rest of us as the "other members."

The sergeant saw to it, that his name was the only one mentioned. One of the unit members TFC Mike Smith, started referring to us as the "Other Members." Even today in retirement when we occasionally meet, we still greet each other as the "Other Members."

Unexpectedly one afternoon, the sergeant scheduled me to meet with him the next morning, and help serve a warrant for the Montgomery County Sheriff's Office. I assumed he wanted to judge for himself how I was progressing. Before we began looking for the defendant, the sergeant stopped by the apartment of a sheriff's deputy he knew. While we were there, the sergeant and deputy began socializing. The deputy showed the sergeant some of his personal rifles, and then unbelievably, they started watching porn movies on VHS tapes.

Eventually we left, and began our attempt to serve the warrant. We went to an apartment complex listed as the defendant's address. The apartment was on the third floor. As the defendant was a Black male, the sergeant who is a White male, decided that I should knock on the door, and ask for the defendant. This was not an unusual tactic under the circumstances.

The sergeant said he'd remain out of sight, while watching from the stairwell, a floor below. An elderly woman answered the door. I asked for the defendant by his first name, and pretended I had money to give him. I pulled some bills out of my pocket to convince her.

The woman left the door ajar, and called out to the defendant. I could hear her tell the defendant there was some guy at the door who owed him money. I didn't want to vocally alert the sergeant, so I snapped my fingers trying to get his attention instead.

Keeping an eye through the door, I could see a male appear from another part of the apartment. When he reached the door, he peered through, and realized he didn't know me. When he tried to close the door on me, I was able to get my shoulder in, and knocked him backwards with the door. I identified myself, and told the defendant he was under arrest. The defendant tried to escape, and a brief struggle ensued. There was no sign of the sergeant, who I expected to be on my heels by now.

Once I was able to get control of the defendant, the sergeant finally entered the apartment, and helped me handcuff him. The sergeant said he didn't know I had gotten inside. Thankfully no one was hurt. I explained to the woman who turned out to be the defendant's grandmother, why I had to deceive her, and apologized for doing so. She was assured her grandson would not be mistreated.

Although I wasn't happy about the sergeant's lack of attention regarding my safety, I just dismissed it as one of those times miscommunications can happen. We then transported the defendant to the sheriff's department. Once inside, the sergeant immediately took control of the defendant from me, and told me to have a seat in the lobby. After several minutes went by, I wondered what was taking so long just to hand over the defendant. Identifying myself at the front glass window, I asked for the sergeant. After I was buzzed in, I found him in an office kidding around with a couple of deputies.

When I appeared at the door, naturally they wanted to know who I was. The sergeant told them I was with him. The deputies joked out loud, saying they thought I was turning myself in. I presumed the sergeant had taken credit for the arrest, since they had no idea I was even in the building. Again, I just passed it off as no big deal. I already knew he was a credit-grabbing clown.

Two days later, the sergeant asked me to meet him at the office around 6:30 a.m. He said he wanted to get an early start serving warrants. I arrived at the office on time, but there was no sign of the sergeant. I started checking some of my own paperwork thinking he was running a little late. The sergeant didn't arrive until 8:00 a.m. I asked him if we were still going out. The sergeant told me to wait in my office, and he would come get me when he was ready.

A short time later, the sergeant stuck his head in the door, and told me to follow him. He led me to the office of the unit's commander, Detective Sergeant Joe McLeary. The sergeant told me to have a seat, and sat opposite me. The sergeant handed me and Detective Sergeant McLeary, copies of a Form 17. A Form 17 is a written form of communication. It is used to inform, or to initiate some type of request, or action for various reasons. Initially, I thought I was about to receive some sort of compliment from the sergeant; especially since I arrested his defendant in Montgomery County, just two days before.

The sergeant began this impromptu meeting by exclaiming how he was dissatisfied with my overall performance, and requested I be removed from the unit. The sergeant continued his verbal assault by adding, that in his experience as a fugitive investigator, I was the worst he had ever seen. I couldn't believe that garbage was coming out of the sergeant's mouth. Fortunately for me, Detective Sergeant McLeary was a very fair supervisor. Detective Sergeant McLeary looked over at me and said, "Russ this is your time to speak up."

As I hadn't looked at the Form 17, I asked for permission to read it first. After doing so, I told Detective Sergeant McLeary I was ready to respond. The sergeant's narrative was bulleted, listing his so-called observations of my performance since I had been in the unit. Addressing each bullet in order, I went down his list, and factually dismantled each point as either fabricated or inaccurate.

Additionally, I told Detective Sergeant McLeary about the sergeant's activities in Montgomery County. I spared no details, including how the sergeant was watching porn videos, and carousing with his deputy buddy on state time. I accused him of cowardice conduct. I described how he unnecessarily endanger my safety by being inattentive, and hiding in the stairwell while I struggled with a defendant. I also told Detective Sergeant McLeary how the sergeant left me in the lobby of the sheriff's department, while he took credit for my arrest.

Finally, I told Detective Sergeant McLeary the sergeant was a poor excuse for a supervisor. I said the sergeant's feeble attempt to discredit me, was his way of getting his buddy (a trooper from the ROPE Unit) to replace me. I asked Detective Sergeant McLeary to grant my immediate transfer out, because I couldn't work for anyone that disgusting. Detective Sergeant McLeary looked over at the mortified sergeant and said, "I think he's got you."

In an attempt to recover from his misjudgment of my nature, the sergeant said he was willing to forget the matter, telling me he was the reason I was in the unit. I had to stop the sergeant, and inform him that he had nothing to do with it. I told the sergeant it was Captain Mazzone who asked me to join the unit. Detective Sergeant Mc Leary said he was going to lunch, and would continue the discussion afterwards.

When we returned, Detective Sergeant McLeary asked me to reconsider. He said the sergeant had no say in the matter. Detective Sergeant McLeary said he wanted me to stay. I was happy that the D/Sarge wanted me to stay; and so I did.

Not before too long, the sergeant was sent packing to another unit in the division. Eventually, he was transferred out of CID, and returned to uniformed duty at a barrack. Once again still early in my career, I had to endure someone's personal attack on my creditability. But thanks to Detective Sergeant McLeary's leadership and fairness, things worked out as they should have.

Detective Sergeant McLeary was an Army military police veteran, who began his civilian law enforcement career with the Baltimore City police. He eventually became a motorcycle officer there, before joining the MSP. I first met him when he was one of our associate instructors in the academy.

As a sergeant, Joe taught classes on criminal investigations. One of his lessons highlighted incidents involving the mild deviant sexual behavior of others. His visual aids were slides, and personal homemade films that were seized as evidence from real cases. I can tell you no one was sleeping during his classes. Some of us couldn't believe our eyes. Self-sheltered as I was, not only couldn't I believe my eyes, I didn't even understand what they were seeing.

"Mac" as he was affectionately called, had earned a sincere respect from all the troopers he supervised, and I was at the top of that list. In the years that followed, we became very dear friends. Mac was always one of my biggest supporters, even after he retired.

Sadly, Mac passed in 2014. I had my final moments with him in his hospital room. Mac will always have a place in my heart. The D/Sarge will be fondly remembered for his love of the MSP, his wife Maggie, and their pet Bull Terriers. Mac was quite a guy. And he was certainly no ordinary Joe!

Chapter 29
What's in Your Attic?

There were two particular cases that highlighted the value of my relationship with the city's EAU. In April 1988, a warrant was issued by the BCPD, for a defendant wanted for assault by maiming one of their officers. Although initial information indicated the defendant frequented the Anne Arundel County area, EAU's detectives developed additional intelligence that the defendant had family in Cecil County.

This subsequent information led us to believe the defendant was most likely being harbored in one of two residences there. After coordinating with my supervisor Sergeant Fred Morton, the next morning at 4:00 a.m., we responded to the area identified by the EAU. One of the locations was a trailer home, and the other was a standard dwelling. Both structures were on the same property, but several yards apart.

We approached the trailer first. An elderly woman peered through curtains from her bedroom window. I identified myself, and told her who we were looking for. I informed her that this was very serious, and we didn't want to see anyone get hurt. Reluctantly, she nodded over to the house. I thanked her, and gave her my word, I wouldn't let on she told us.

Quickly, we moved towards the house quietly. After the house was surrounded, I knocked on the door. After a few minutes, a light came on, and a robed young adult female appeared slightly from behind the door. After identifying ourselves, I asked if she knew the defendant. The woman said he was her brother. I asked if we could come inside where we could speak further. I showed her the arrest warrant in our possession, charging her brother with assaulting a Baltimore City police officer. Coming to her brother's defense, she became very upset, and requested we leave.

I informed the woman that her brother was considered dangerous, and it violated Maryland law to harbor a person wanted on felony charges. While the woman continued speaking to Sergeant Al Rehn three small children came into the living room. With their mother's back turned to me, I quietly asked one of the children, if her uncle was home. The little girl said yes.

The defendant's sister was told we would get a search warrant if necessary, but the troopers would remain there until I returned; If her brother was there, he wouldn't be able to escape. I promised her I would arrest her, and have the county's child protective services take custody of her children, if she was harboring her brother. I cautioned the sister, that the choice was hers.

Apparently confident we wouldn't find her brother, she relented, allowing us to search without a warrant. We conducted a search of the premises to no avail. The only place we didn't check, was the attic in the ceiling located in the main hallway. Unlike some attics with doors that you pull down, this one had a hatch that you pushed upwards. As it was my case, it was my responsibility to go up there, and look for the defendant.

Receiving a boost up, I pushed open the hatch door, and slid it aside. I began checking the attic with my flashlight. Not seeing anything obvious, I was boosted further up inside the attic. Using my flashlight, I systematically scanned the cluttered surroundings. I noticed a horizontal partition towards one end of the attic. With my weapon in hand, I made my way on an angle, trying not to expose my silhouette from the beam of my flashlight.

Moving outward and to my right, I could eventually see the legs of a figure from behind the partition. I pretended to end the search, and called out there was no sign of anyone. As I was stepping backwards away from the partition, I noticed it moved slightly. Unaware if the subject behind the partition was armed, I forcefully pushed the partition forward with my foot, onto the subject. Struggling to keep the partition on top of the subject, I dropped my flashlight in the excitement.

In the commotion, my partners thought I was in grave danger, and began calling out to me. Fortunately I retrieved my flashlight, and gained control again. I ordered the subject to put his hands out from underneath the partition were I could see them. Shining my flashlight, I immediately recognized the man as our defendant, as he emerged from underneath the partition. Thank goodness he was unarmed. At gunpoint, I made him walk ahead of me to the attic's opening. The defendant was helped down by my relieved partners.

Sergeant Rehn was so beside himself, he heatedly voiced his displeasure at the defendant's sister. Once I was down from the attic, he hugged me in great relief. I was grateful for his concern, and assured him I was fine. The defendant's sister wanted to file a complaint against Sergeant Rehn for his conduct. The sister become even more agitated, when she expressed her belief that we were going to hurt her brother in retaliation. I asked Sergeant Rehn if he would leave her to me, and take the handcuffed defendant outside.

After the house was clear, I told the woman that as Sergeant Rehn was my supervisor, I would have the Internal Affairs Unit contact her at the county detention center, after I charged her for harboring her brother. Predictably she had a change of heart. I advised her to be absolutely sure that was her decision.

Asking if she would accept my apology for my sergeant's reactions, I explained how he was merely concerned that her intentional failure to reveal her brother's whereabouts, could have ended in tragic consequences. She clearly appreciated the gravity of the situation afterwards, and accepted my explanation, and apology. Using my discretion, I decided to give her the benefit of doubt. We shook hands, and I reassured her that no harm would come to her brother, while he was in police custody.

Once we cleared the scene, the defendant was taken to the Valley Barrack. Afraid of retaliation, the defendant insisted I take a picture of him before the city detectives arrived. I told him he had nothing to worry about, but I would take his picture to satisfy him. At that time, the department used Polaroid cameras that instantly gave you your pictures. The defendant was turned over to Sergeant Sharp and Detective Dyson, and returned to Baltimore City to face his pending charges. Predictably, there was no retaliation against the defendant.

Critiquing the situation from a best case scenario, pretending that the defendant wasn't in the attic was the right move. After withdrawing from the attic, we could then order him down. However, as I would come to find out, sometimes you have to adjust on the fly. I was blessed that day, and throughout my career on more than one occasion, that things worked out the way they did.

Chapter 30
A Master of Deception on the Loose

In July 1988, Roy Cantler, who had been convicted on murder charges, escaped from a work-release program while serving time at the Baltimore City Correctional Center. While at large, he committed bank robberies in Harrisburg, Pennsylvania, Wilmington, Delaware, and Alexandria, Virginia respectively. In February 1989, a warrant was issued by the Alexandria, Virginia Magistrate, charging Cantler with armed bank robbery.

During the robbery, in addition to wielding a handgun and a grenade, Cantler handcuffed a briefcase to the bank manager's wrist. Cantler claimed the briefcase contained explosives. After stealing approximately $148,000.00, Cantler left the briefcase attached to the manager's wrist, and made good his escape.

Based on the belief that the briefcase contained some type of an explosive, the responding Alexandria authorities contacted the local military ordinance unit to assist them. An x-ray machine revealed the presence of what appeared to be sticks of dynamite bound together inside the briefcase. The briefcase was carefully removed from the manager's wrist, and taken to a safe location where it was detonated. Fortunately for all concerned, it was road flares, not dynamite, connected to a 7.5 lantern battery inside the briefcase.

Subsequently, Cantler's abandoned van was recovered in the parking lot of a nearby shopping center. Forensic technicians, uncovered latent evidence that positively identified Cantler as their perpetrator. After discovering Cantler was a wanted escapee from Baltimore, Alexandria detectives requested assistance in locating Cantler from the EAU. Assisted by Deputy George Cunningham, the unit tracked down several address possibilities around Havre de Grace, in Harford County. Having done so, Sergeant Sharp and Detective Dyson requested my assistance in locating Cantler.

Joining our search, were uniformed members of the Bel Air Barrack "D," Sergeant James Ballard, TFC Bill Harden and TFC

Ronald Troutman. They were also members of the department's Special Tactical Assault Team Element ("STATE," our version of "SWAT"). Surrounding the identified residence around 4:00 a.m., we made contact with a male subject who was not Cantler. He was the homeowner. I immediately recognized the gentleman as an MDOT employee from my days at the JFK Highway Barrack.

After looking at Cantler's photo, the gentleman recognized him, but by the name of "Dennis Carter." He told us that Carter (Cantler) was his border, renting the nearby dwelling on the property. As the van belonging to Cantler was parked there, the gentleman believed Cantler was at home.

Because there was a chance Cantler could be armed, I decided to telephone him to see if I could negotiate his surrender. I obtained Cantler's telephone number from the property owner. With his dwelling surrounded at a safe distance, I telephoned Cantler from the property owner's home.

Someone picked up the phone, but didn't answer. I just began speaking, and trying to reason with the person on the line. I advised the listener that the house was surrounded by the police. I said as I was responsible for everyone's safety, I didn't want to see anyone get hurt; so please surrender. When the person didn't answer, and ended the call, we assumed the worse.

With everyone safely in position at the residence occupied by Cantler, I used the loud speaker on my vehicle's radio, asking Cantler to surrender. A few anxious moments later, the front door opened. Over the loud speaker, I instructed him on how to exit safely. He complied by stepping outside with his hands up, awaiting our safe approach.

After taking control of Cantler, the residence was carefully checked to ensure there were no other people secreted inside. When we discovered there was evidence of his criminal activities all throughout the house, a search and seizure warrant for the premises was required. The residence was secured while the warrant was applied for.

With the assistance of the Bel Air Barrack's criminal section supervisor, Sergeant Paul Banes, a search warrant was obtained. A systematic, photographed and documented search was conducted. After they were notified, we were eventually joined by the lead investigator from the Alexandria Police Department, Detective Dave

Hoffmaster, and Detectives Dyson and Wingate from Baltimore City's EAU.

Some of the recovered items that immediately stood out, included a tin box containing $74,000.00 in cash found by Corporal Paul Svoboda, a cache of firearms, and a non-lethal hand grenade. When he wasn't robbing banks, Cantler was obviously very busy stealing several high-priced electronic, and photography devices from retail businesses. We located equipment that he used to create laminated fictitious Maryland drivers' licenses, and generic birth certificates.

To help facilitate his nefarious activities, Cantler made a fictitious identification card, indicating he was "duly" appointed by the governor, as a member of our "Special Tactical Division Undercover Narcotics." Cantler assumed the identity of Sergeant Dennis R. Carter. Although there was no such unit in the MSP, to the unfamiliar eye, it could have passed for an authentic laminated form of police ID. Cantler certainly had a vivid imagination, and he was very bold.

When asked how he was able to steal so many of the recovered items from retail businesses, Cantler calmly replied, "I just put them on a platform cart, and walked out the door as though they were paid for." I was told later, that Cantler informed investigators he had contemplated suicide after being confronted with arrest. However, he reconsidered after hearing me say I didn't want to see anyone get hurt.

Happily things had gone well up to that point… that is until we discovered a briefcase in an upright wardrobe cabinet. Detective Hoffmaster alerted us about a similar looking briefcase that was used in their bank robbery. Among Cantler's other bad habits, was his knowledge of what an explosive device would consist of. The briefcase Cantler used during the robbery, even had a blinking red light on the top of the briefcase. Cantler held a plunger device, and threatened to detonate the briefcase, if the bank manager refused to cooperate with him.

Not taking any chances with our briefcase (which also had a small plastic red light affixed on top), we used a landline telephone instead of the police radio to request assistance from the State Fire Marshal's Office. As we didn't know if this was a real device or not, the use of any transmitting radio equipment, was not advisable in the presence of a suspected explosive device. Radio Frequency

Identification (RFI) emissions, can serve as a trigger mechanism for detonating some explosive devices.

The fire marshals arrived, and set up their x-ray machine. As it was in Detective Hoffmaster's robbery case, the image inside of our briefcase, also showed what looked like sticks of dynamite bound together, connected to a lantern battery. The fire marshals decided to remove the briefcase, so it could be detonated at a safe distance.

In order to proceed carefully, a clothesline and pulley system was rigged. The fire marshals' clothesline setup went from the bedroom, through the kitchen, to the outside. The briefcase was hooked onto the clothesline, and would be slowly maneuvered by the fire marshal through the rooms until it reached the outside. When the fire marshal was ready to start sliding the briefcase along the clotheslines, we were supposed to move to a predetermined safe location.

As the briefcase slowly made its way inside the kitchen, its weight caused it to start bouncing on the clothesline. The marshal was unaware of this. He also thought the immediate area was clear. When he moved the clothesline forward a bit more, the briefcase popped opened unexpectedly before we were totally clear of the back porch. Fortunately the briefcase was another fake setup, and not loaded with dynamite. Imagining how we must have looked scrambling off the back porch has its humorous side now, but we all had to go home, and change our underwear after that near mishap.

Upon his conviction, Cantler received a sentence of life, plus 65 years in Virginia. As it has been in many instances for me, working good cases, and making good friends as a result, go hand-in-hand. Dave Hoffmaster, and I have remained friends, long after we've both retired.

Even in a serious and dangerous law enforcement function such as searching for fugitives, there is an occasional moment of humor. One day, Detective Dyson and I were looking through a basement in a vacant house. Ahead of us near an above ground window, was a swarm of some type of insects. Before we knew it, the swarm started towards us. We immediately headed for the stairs. The swarm was on our heels as we ran up the stairs through the kitchen, and out the front door, quickly shutting it behind us.

We looked at each other laughing in relief. Driving back to city headquarters, I saw a tiny insect on the leg of my pants. I hit it with the palm of my hand, but it just kept on moving. I hit it again to no avail. It turns out these insects were fleas, and our clothes had been infested by them just that quick. The city police had a designated area at their headquarters where they addressed these types of conditions experienced by their officers. Our clothes had to be placed in plastic bags and sprayed. The inside of Detective Dyson's agency vehicle had to be treated as well.

While assisting one of the unit's newest members TFC Gloria Wilson in her attempts to locate a fugitive, we had to use a trick to flush out the defendant. You may not get too many chances to find fugitives once they know you're hot on their heels. Fugitives aren't easy to find for a reason.

Figuring the defendant wouldn't be overly suspicious of a female, I had TFC Wilson knock on the door, and ask for the defendant while I stood off to the side. When the defendant saw TFC Wilson, he was more than happy to step outside. That's when we grabbed him, and placed him under arrest.

Gloria was an excellent trooper, a heck of a softball player, and funny as well. She retired as a sergeant, and is one of the many friends I made in the MSP family, who remain so today.

Chapter 31
His Hypocrisy Had No Bounds

When Detective Sergeant McLeary was reassigned to command another CID unit, I was personally sad to see him leave, but that was life in the MSP. Our new detective sergeant was someone I knew, but not well. One day while on his way to, or from Pikesville, the new detective sergeant drove by my neighborhood, and apparently observed my assigned vehicle parked outside of my residence. Based on the time of day, the detective sergeant assumed I went home before the end of my shift.

Normally our shifts ran 8:00 a.m. to 4:00 p.m. The detective sergeant confronted me with his suspicions soon after. The detective sergeant asked me where I was on that particular day and time. I learned a long time ago with certain people (and evidently he was one of them), who ask you a question, nine times out of 10 they already know the answer. Not wanting to play his game, I told the detective sergeant I had no idea, and asked him to tell me what was on his mind. That's when he told me he saw my vehicle parked outside my residence on a specific date, about 2:00 p.m.

The EAU's standard shift was 5:00 a.m. to 1:00 p.m. When I scheduled myself to work with them, that was my shift for that day too, I said. I told the detective sergeant he should've knocked on my door, or paged me, if he had any concerns. Back then the department had no cell phones. In order to reach you in different parts of the state, the department issued you a pager, or as I did, use my own instead. I lived about two miles from headquarters. Even if I wasn't with the city that day, I could have temporarily stopped home for any number of legitimate reasons, I said.

It soon became apparent the detective sergeant had a personal dislike regarding my relationship with the Baltimore City police. He unnecessarily reminded me that I was with the state police. Inaccurately, he felt I was neglecting my warrants in favor of their cases. I assured him that wasn't true. I told the detective sergeant, they were helping me with my cases that generated in their jurisdiction as well.

Coincidentally, at that time, I was working with the city, looking for the suspect who was wanted for murdering two children in Anne Arundel County. The suspect was in active violation of his parole, when he allegedly committed this heinous act. That particular case precipitated the department's mandate to begin serving DOC's Parole and Retake Warrants. It was the notoriety of this particular case that revealed their inability to keep up with the increasing number of issued warrants.

Later that evening, the suspect was confronted in the Pimlico area of the city by a uniformed city officer. Wielding a butcher's knife, the suspect approached the officer ignoring commands to stop. The suspect was fired upon by the officer, and fatally wounded.

Apparently, I failed to convince the detective sergeant that I was working my entire shift as required. He was determined to catch me red-handed. A few days later, Sergeants Morton and Rehn came by my desk, and handed me a piece of paper. They said the paper was a present for me.

The piece of paper had a hand-drawn map, displaying the route from Pikesville to my home. The detective sergeant drew the map. He told the two sergeants to drive by my house, and document the number of times my assigned vehicle was observed there, before the end of my scheduled shift.

As my immediate supervisors, Sergeants Morton and Rehn, had no issues with me. They were personally aware of my work productivity, and my creditability. They told me not to worry about it. With a wry smile on his face, Fred said he and Al were too busy going home early before the end of their shifts, to be bothered checking on me.

Fred and Al were very close friends to each other. They referred to themselves as MSP's "Batman and Robin." Before they were transferred into the unit, they had been assigned to the Executive Protection Unit. After being replaced with troopers favored by the newly elected governor, they wound up as "Other Members" in the Fugitive Unit. I can honestly say that under their immediate supervision, the unit became much closer as a functioning group.

I know I won't soon forget our mutual respect, and their unwillingness to go along with the baseless suspicions of a superior.

Al passed in 2005, and Fred in 2017, both after their retirements. I will always remember them for their humor, and being more than just coworkers or supervisors…they were my friends.

The postscript of this chapter ends ironically, with the detective sergeant's own conduct being called into question. The detective sergeant was suspected of using his computerized access to the Motor Vehicle Administration's (MVA) classified information, in connection with his part-time job. The Criminal Justice Information System (CJIS) confirmed the allegation through an off-line search, attributed to his logon ID number. His queries were not made for official law enforcement, or criminal justice information purposes as required. As you can imagine, this was not only against departmental policy, but it also violated criminal law.

The State's Attorney for Baltimore County, issued a declination not to prosecute him, in lieu of allowing the department to address this matter internally. With the revelation of the detective sergeant's own misconduct, I think we should have been the ones drawing maps…to his "glass house."

Chapter 32
The Dilemma Involving the Police, Loving Parents, and Their Fugitive Sons

One of the things I saw as a fugitive investigator, was what some parents would go through to protect their children. In one case, even if it meant going to jail to protect their son from being legally captured. Both cases occurred in Baltimore City. Early one morning, teamed with the EAU, I attempted to serve a warrant at the last known address for a defendant wanted in connection for an attempted murder in Prince George's County.

Our knocks at the front door were answered by the defendant's parents. After explaining our 5:00 a.m. presence, we asked for permission to search for their son. The parents vehemently refused, telling us to get the hell out of their house. I tried reasoning with them, explaining how they could help ensure their son's safety by cooperating with us. I told them I didn't know if he was guilty or not, but hiding him wasn't going to solve the matter.

I asked them again to consider that he was wanted for attempted murder, and might do something foolish, causing the police to use deadly force in response. Still they ordered us off their premises telling us they weren't cooperating with us. Doing as they demanded, I gave them a warning. The parents were told that knowingly harboring a fugitive wanted on a felony charge was against the law. I promised them that if I found out they were harboring their son, I would arrest them as well.

They slammed the door in our faces, and that was that. I gave the uniformed officers who were with us my business card. I asked them to notify me if they came across the defendant. A copy of the arrest warrant was provided to the Western District.

Two days later, I received a telephone call from an officer, advising me they apprehended the defendant. The officer said one of the neighbors alerted the police, after the defendant was observed entering his parents' residence. I asked if the parents were home when he was arrested. The officer said they were both home at the time. I thanked the officer, and told her I would be there the next morning at 5:00 a.m., with warrants for both of the parents, charging them with harboring a fugitive. The officer said she would alert the officers on that shift for me.

The next morning, I arrived at the Western District with my arrest warrants. Accompanied by two of their uniformed officers, both parents who now wanted to rationally discuss the situation, were placed under arrest. I didn't want to appear callous, but they were warned. They not only could have put an officer's life in danger, but that of their son's as well. The parents weren't known people of bad character, but they disregarded the law, despite being warned.

Some people who have heard this story, felt I was being too harsh. They would say the parents were only trying to protect their child. Even as an adult, he is still their child, people would say to me. I did understand, but they put their son in more danger than I did.

They were given the facts, and knew the consequences. Instead of sitting down with us to discuss how they could best help their son as I was willing to do, they slammed the door in our faces. We didn't enter their home using profanity, or initiating physical contact with them. We were trying to do our job the right way. They made their decision, and I made mine.

Even after reading my statement of charges, the district court commissioner wanted to issue summonses for court appearances, instead of arrest warrants. I had to insist he issue warrants, as the facts met the criteria to issue warrants. When I never received a summons to testify in court at the parents subsequent trials, I was sure some deal was made with the State's Attorney's Office, based on the parents' previous non-criminal histories, and standing in the community. Perhaps the judicial system took into account the position they found themselves in as parents.

The other case involved a defendant wanted for violation of his parole. When I arrived at the address listed on the warrant, the knock at the door was answered by the defendant's mother. She was holding a low-lit-battery-operated candle. As it was still dark outside, I asked her to please turn on the lights, so we could speak with her more safely.

The mother apologized, telling us that her electricity had been cut off, due to her inability to pay her utility bill. Unbelievably, she was employed by the local utilities company. She told me after paying her son's legal fees, and other expenses trying to keep him out of jail, she didn't have enough left to pay her utility bill.

Fortunately, it was the summer season, and not cold outside. I asked was there anyone else at home. She said just her daughter, who eventually came down the stairs, also holding a battery-operated candle. I could plainly see the young woman was expecting. The mother wanted to fully cooperate, even allowing us to search the premises for her son. I really felt bad for her. She was employed by the utility company, and couldn't afford to have electricity, all because of her loving son. She certainly deserved better than that.

Chapter 33
Not All Supervisors Are Created Evil

During my time in the Fugitive Unit, there were three different sworn administrators of the warrant section, Corporal Gordon Titsworth, Sergeant Lenny (Commander) Armstrong, and Sergeant John Davis. They along with Charlotte Lippy, and other civilian administrative aids, ensured the warrants were entered, and removed from our data base as needed. Sergeant Armstrong and I, would go on to become barrack commanders in the Washington-Metro Troop later in our careers.

Sergeant Davis was known as a solid drug, and criminal investigator in his time. He became a mentor, and a great example of leadership for me personally. While I was preparing for the sergeant's examine one day during my lunch break, Sergeant Davis noticed I was updating my manuals with the current revised pages.

Sergeant Davis told me to give him my manuals. Using a red marker, he wrote an "88," indicating the year, on some of the pages. He referred to those pages as the ones I should concentrate on, based on his experience as a sergeant. That was something I would never forget. It made a difference in my preparation to take the test.

My third, and last commanding detective sergeant in the Fugitive Unit, was Detective Sergeant Henry Black. We had never met before. Considering the job was getting done, I figured what was there to be concerned about.

Detective Sergeant Black called everyone in his office individually, for an introductory meeting. After Detective Sergeant McLeary's excellent example of leadership compared to my last, map drawing detective sergeant, or the sergeant who tried to have me transferred, I had great examples of leadership to follow, and those to avoid if you valued your reputation.

Any questions I had about Detective Sergeant Black, were answered very shortly. Leaning backwards in his high-back swivel chair, he first complimented me on what he heard about my work.

But when asked me to do him a favor, that's what sealed my immediate respect, and appreciation for him. He started by saying it would never be his intent to bother us with crazy things, but there would be times he would have to relay directives from above him. The favor he asked us to do in those instances was to "Just say ok Henry."

I asked, "That's it?"

He said, "That's it."

Smiling, we shook hands, and I said, "Ok Henry!"

That moment of being humble enough to ask for the unit's help to keep the brass happy, was indicative of what I came to know, and always respect about his leadership. Like Detective Sergeant McLeary, Sergeant Davis, and Sergeant Armstrong, he was someone you would never want to disappoint. As it was with the others I would come to admire, and respect in the MSP, they gave you the courtesy of treating you like an adult. They were upfront, truthful, and truly cared about you, and what you thought.

One day Detective Sergeant Black asked if I had any plans that evening. I thought he had an assignment for me. He actually invited me to go with him, to see his son play in a high school football game in Westminster.

I was surprised, and gladly accepted his invitation. After the game, he introduced me to his son Brent. I didn't know it at the time, but I was shaking hands with a future MSP trooper. Brent would go on to have an excellent career, and retire at the rank of captain. I know Henry was proud to have Brent follow in his footsteps. Like his father, Brent "knew what to do."

When the promotion and transfer list came out in November 1989, I was on vacation. Detective Sergeant Black telephoned my home. He said, "Hey Stewart this is Henry, how come you want to leave me?" I told him I hadn't requested a transfer out of the unit; I loved working for him. Henry started laughing, telling me he was joking. He told me I had just been promoted to sergeant, and was being transferred to the Valley Barrack, as their criminal section's supervisor.

Although I was certainly happy to get promoted, it was a little hard to move on from the people, and type of work I enjoyed. But now I was moving to the next rung on the department's ladder. From here out it wouldn't get easier. It would be a harder transition than I imagined, and a most humbling experience at times.

Chapter 34
Valley Barrack "R"

After a six year absence, I was back where I started… in the Field Operations Bureau (FOB). The Valley Barrack "R," was located in Baltimore County. The barrack had been operational inside a section of the State Highway Administration's (SHA) building on Joppa Road at Falls Road, since the late 1960s. My duties would be as the barrack's criminal section supervisor. Criminal sections at barracks commonly referred to as "traffic" barracks were generally led by sergeants. Criminal sections at barracks referred to as "full-service" barracks, were headed by those at the rank of detective sergeant.

Valley Barrack troopers enforced traffic, and criminal laws, and investigated accidents and other public safety related matters. Troopers patrolled the eastern half of the Baltimore Beltway I-695, while troopers at the Security Barrack "K," patrolled the western half of the beltway.

Valley also patrolled parts of Interstate 95, from the White Marsh area, to the Harbor Tunnel Throughway, and Interstate 83, from the Baltimore City line, to the Pennsylvania State line. The barrack shared joint jurisdiction with the Baltimore County Police Department, and along a portion of the tunnel throughway, with the Maryland Transportation Authority Police.

Unique to the barrack was the responsibility of investigating calls for service at the Department of Juvenile Services' Charles Hickey School. Dealing with juveniles certainly presented challenges for the barrack and school officials alike. Troopers investigated calls for escaped juveniles, and assault complaints stemming from juveniles, security officers and the staff. Troopers also investigated burglaries, thefts, property damage and industrial accidents, occurring at state-owned properties located in the barrack's geographical area.

One of my vital responsibilities, would be reviewing, and signing off on all reports regarding criminal matters. That required learning how to properly classify the reports using the FBI's Uniformed Crime Reporting (UCR) codes. These codes are used by the FBI to keep track of the various crimes being committed across the United States. By state, these annual reports containing statistical information from reported crimes, are provided by local law enforcement to the state police or a designated agency, who in turn, forwards the data to the FBI. The FBI will then provide the formulated data to all law enforcement throughout the country.

UCR reports provide information on crime trends, as well as the race, age and gender breakdowns of the victims and perpetrators, in addition to other relative information. This data can assist law enforcement officials when planning future crime reduction activities in their communities. The data will also help the federal government provide local law enforcement with grants that help facilitate these initiatives.

A major function of all barrack supervisors, is the administration of the decentralized line inspection program administered by the department's Staff Inspection Unit (SIU). SIU conducts audits to ensure administrative programs are appropriately maintained as required by MSP policy, Maryland's Code of Regulations (COMAR), Maryland, and federal laws, and any other delineated regulations. The criminal section supervisor is responsible for those programs tied to the barrack's criminal investigative activities.

Becoming the criminal section supervisor also meant I was designated as the property officer. The property officer is responsible for administration of the property room, and its contents. The property room is where seized evidence is stored by the troopers, and released to them for court appearances when needed. The property room is also where lost and found property is kept, until it can be returned to its rightful owner or destroyed. Should any property of value go unclaimed, it is eventually recovered by the state, and sold during a public auction facilitated by the department's Property Section.

The change in the barrack's property officer, necessitated I meet with my soon-to-be predecessor, Sergeant Ron Gallant. A formal transition of the property room from his custody to mine was required. An inventory ensuring that all the property, and evidence recorded in the property ledger (MSP Form 99) was accounted for, and had to be acknowledged before I accepted control.

Although I was still on vacation, I decided to go in to complete the changeover, and get other advice from Sergeant Gallant regarding my new duties, while he was still available. These duties were far more than I had experienced up to that point as a corporal. I personally knew Sergeant Gallant, who was happy to walk me through my new duties and responsibilities.

With just a few days left on my vacation until the list became effective, I continued going in on my own time, after Sergeant Gallant was no longer there. I started checking reports, and figuring out how to properly code them. This was also a good time to become acquainted with my two investigators, the barrack commander Lieutenant Wayne Saunders, and the other assigned personnel.

One particular morning while checking reports at my desk, the first sergeant came in the investigators' area. Looking over my partition, the first sergeant asked me what was I doing in the barrack. I thought, "Do I need permission to be here?" I explained to the first sergeant as I was new to this position, I wanted to get a head start so I wouldn't be totally lost when I officially reported.

The first sergeant asked, "Aren't you on vacation?"

I said, "Yes sir."

The first sergeant said I wouldn't receive overtime. I told him I wasn't doing it for overtime. He responded, "Well that's dumb." I didn't expect flowers, but his empty-headed response to a subordinate's initiative, showed whose actions were the dumber by far.

First sergeants assigned to barracks were now considered the assistant barrack commander, as there would be no more promotions to second lieutenant. I was familiar with this first sergeant, but it was my first personal interaction with him. I was happy for both of us that any future interactions were only as members of the department.

The two investigators assigned to the section were TFCs Efrain Rosario and Doug Zeller. They were excellent investigators, and we got along very well from the start. We were so closely situated in a sectioned-off part of the barrack's limited space, we were literately on top of each other. It was a good thing we enjoyed each other's company during the day.

These two guys were also some of the biggest pranksters I ever worked with. I had to be careful of their well-planned pranks; especially if they got to the office first. I started referring to them as

"Whitey and Larry," from the 1950s "Leave it to Beaver" television sitcom; mainly because TFC Zeller resembled Beaver's friend Whitey; especially with his really light blonde hair. As there were two of them, TFC Rosario naturally became Larry.

Before he retired, TFC Zeller would go on to make lieutenant, and command the Bel Air Barrack. Doug and I would have a reunion, when I requested his transfer to my bureau, where he would command the warrant unit at CID's headquarters in Columbia.

We lost Doug after his long battle with an illness in 2015. Doug's memory lives on in the MSP through his son Brian, who followed in his dad's footsteps. Doug lived to see Brian graduate from the academy, and proudly pinned on his son's badge during the ceremony.

In 1992, TFC Rosario was transferred to the FBI's "Safe Street" initiative. In 2001, he became a member of the state's domestic terrorist watch group. After his retirement in 2007, he returned as a civilian, acting as the coordinator for Maryland's Department of Corrections Prison Intelligence Section, located at the Maryland Coordination and Analysis Center (MCAC). Rosie is now fully retired after serving the MSP as both a trooper, and a civilian.

Chapter 35
The Infamous Plastic Bag

On March 29, 1990, at 4:20 a.m., an off-duty Washington Metropolitan police officer, found Corporal Ted Wolf of the Waterloo Barrack "A," slumped over the steering wheel of his patrol vehicle, with its emergency lights activated. Corporal Wolf died after he was shot during a traffic stop, on Northbound I-95, near Route 175, in Howard County.

Subsequently, there was an immediate search launched for the suspect(s), and their reported vehicle, in Maryland, Delaware and Virginia. The department initiated a task force that included the FBI, and brought in our investigators from all over the state.

I personally knew Ted, having played pickup basketball games with him at our academy's gymnasium. We were also teammates on the MSP's flag-football team that participated in charity games against other local police departments, known as the "Copper Bowl." He was an outgoing, rugged, and competitive individual.

As it was after the murder of TFC Gregg Presbury, I wanted to get involved; especially since the Baltimore area was being checked. As I was from Baltimore, I thought I would be able to navigate the area better than many of the investigators from other parts of the state. Initially, all I could do was make myself, and my two investigators available if needed.

A few days into the investigation, I was still in the office checking reports on a Friday evening past my shift. Sergeant Pete Edge called the barrack looking for me. The task force had a telephone tip-line system set up, and someone reported they thought the suspect(s) could be located in an apartment complex in Woodlawn, Baltimore County.

As the complex was in a predominately Black community, Sergeant Edge asked if could front for them at the apartment identified by the tip. After meeting with Sergeants Edge and Stern and TFC Newcomer, I received relative information regarding the tip. I knocked on the apartment door, and identified myself to the female occupant explaining why we were there.

The woman was very cooperative, and all though this was a random tip, she gave us permission to search the apartment. We thanked her for being understanding. As we were leaving, she sincerely wished us luck in trying to find the suspect(s). After we met back at the nearby Security Square Mall parking lot, I told them I would love to help, and let them know my two investigators and I were available if needed.

Later that evening, I received a call at home from Lieutenant Joel Underwood, Commander of the Security Barrack. Lieutenant Underwood was the acting troop commander that weekend. In that capacity, he informed me I would be assigned to the task force starting the following Monday morning. That authority was from Captain Thomas Bosley, Commander of the Criminal Investigation Division. Sergeants Edge and Stern requested my assignment to the task force, and Captain Bosley approved it.

The command center for this operation was established at the Waterloo Barrack. I was assigned to remain at the barrack where at times I was manning the tip-line phone. Other times I was running computer checks on leads, or making follow-up telephone calls for the investigators. I thought I would be doing some other types of activities, such as checking leads on the streets. But since I asked to be included, I gladly accepted the assignments given, and considered everything contributed as vital.

The vehicle used by the suspect(s) was stolen from an apartment complex in Alexandria, Virginia. The vehicle had been abandoned, and recovered in the rear of a restaurant in the Lansdowne area of Baltimore County. The blue 1988 Chevrolet Nova, was being held at the crime lab's storage bay, where it was to undergo a detailed latent and forensic examination.

One afternoon, Sergeant Diane Kulp an investigator from the Prince Frederick Barrack, and I were assigned to report to the crime lab building, which was on Sudbrook Lane, across from headquarters at that time. We were told to check the vehicle for anything that may assist in the investigation. Although the inside of the vehicle was pretty cluttered, one item caught my attention.

I found a draw-stringed plastic bag. The bag was white and featured black stripes in a zebra patterns across it. Printed on the bag was the name of a clothing store: "Disco Boutique, Bronx New York." After checking out other items in the vehicle, that bag clearly seemed out of the ordinary for this Virginia registered vehicle.

After obtaining the name and telephone number of the owner/victim, I telephoned her apartment in Alexandria. The main question I asked was if she had been to New York recently. She replied she had not. I then asked if she let anyone use the vehicle who may have gone to New York. Again the reply was no. The bag was carefully removed, and turned over to lab personnel as a possible piece of evidence. A day or two later, I was told I was no longer needed. I returned to the barrack and resumed my normal duties.

It wasn't until several years later, that I learned the plastic bag was actually a vital clue that helped identify the suspected shooter, Eric Tirado. The bag had three fingerprints that were matched to Tirado. Tirado would eventually be charged, tried and convicted with the first-degree murder of Corporal Wolf.

Our latent-fingerprint expert Mr. James Sims, would later testify in court, that in addition to Tirado's fingerprints on the plastic bag, his fingerprint's ridge characteristics, were also found in a blood print taken from the armrest of the stolen vehicle.

Tirado's accomplice in this case was Francisco Rodriguez. Rodriguez's fingerprints were found on papers belonging to the vehicle's owner. Unbeknownst at that time, Sergeant Kulp and I played an important role in securing vital evidence in this case. Mr. Sims, who is a veteran latent technician, explained the method of his most incredible work on this case, when I contacted him while writing this book.

After using "Super Glue" on the plastic bag to lift latents, Mr. Sims discovered a #9, or ring-finger latent print. This particular print was described as having a "double-loop whorl" characteristic. Exhausting searches through the National Crime Information Center's (NCIC) database of fingerprints for a list of 25,000 possibilities, yielded no match. Mr. Sims turned his attention specifically to New York, reaching out to the New York City Police Department (NYPD). Mr. Sims spoke to a lieutenant in records, and asked for their assistance in a search for that particular fingerprint characteristic.

The lieutenant could only promise a limited effort, due to their own workload. Meanwhile, Mr. Sims and his colleagues acquired a software that isolated the search for that type of fingerprint characteristic. Performing 500 searches at a time, the NYPD got a match between number 500 and 1,000. Surprisingly, the match didn't come from a criminal data base. Tirado had been in the NYPD academy a few months, and resigned before he completed the academy. Tirado's prints were in the state's non-criminal data base.

At the extradition hearing for the second suspect Rodriguez, Mr. Sims' expert testimony along with that of the lead investigator Sergeant Tom Coppinger, secured Rodriguez's return to Maryland as the co-defendant in Corporal Wolf's murder. We were fortunate to have such innovative, and dedicated forensic science technicians in the department like Mr. Sims.

Before he retired, Sergeant Coppinger would eventually be appointed to lieutenant colonel, and became chief of the Homeland Security, Criminal Investigation Bureau. When he retired in 2008, I succeeded him as the bureau chief.

Chapter 36
Just Like Old Times

One May evening, I received a call from the duty officer advising me there was a citizen at the barrack, who wanted to report an alleged plot against a trooper assigned to the barrack. Information provided by the individual indicated that the target in this case, was stopped by the trooper in question. Reportedly, the trooper wrote the target several citations subsequent to that traffic stop. Apparently incensed by the trooper's actions, the target allegedly sought to hire someone to injure the trooper in retaliation.

I responded to the barrack, and questioned the citizen specifically about his information. After checking out his personal identifying information, I immediately notified the trooper of the alleged threat against him. Verifying the identity of the target from the trooper, I was satisfied that there was some validity to the citizen's story. The next day, we devised a plan to seize control of this case.

The introduction would take place at the nightclub where the target was employed. The plan was to have our acquired informant introduce me to the target, as someone he had just met randomly at the club during the evening. Once that was accomplished, the informant would be removed from the picture.

After a few visits to the club, the target started feeling comfortable with me. I became aware of this, when the target began unwittingly voicing his disdain for the trooper, in our seemingly innocent conversations. That was my opening to take control. I asked the target what he was going to do about it. He said he'd like to have the trooper messed up, but not killed. The target asked if I knew anyone who did that type of thing. I seized the opening, and offered to do it for him at the right price.

The target offered me $300.00. I accepted his offer, and received the money the next day. Now we had the control we needed to ensure the trooper's safety. After meeting with the trooper, I asked if he had something personal he didn't mind parting with. I planned on using it as proof that I had incapacitated him. The trooper had an expired driver's license in his wallet, with a former address and his picture on it. It was perfect for my intended use as a prop.

Ready to end the case, I met the target at the club later that evening. When I showed him the driver's license I supposedly took from the trooper, the target was so impressed, he immediately solicited me to injure a female who had recently angered him. After getting her information, I told him to let things cool down a few days, and we could discuss the matter then. We shook hands, and agreed to meet later. I gave him the old license as a souvenir.

The assembled arrest party waited on the parking lot for the target to leave, after the club closed for the night. Before he could enter his vehicle, he was accosted, and arrested without incident. The target was charged with solicitation to commit a crime. He was still in possession of the trooper's old driver's license, which we used as additional evidence against him.

During the Christmas shopping season a few years later, I was off duty at the defunct Best Products Company's catalog/showroom store on Route 40, in Golden Ring. As I was standing in a cashier's line, I felt a tap on my shoulder. When I turned around, I immediately recognized it was the target we arrested in the above case. Seeing the intense look on my face, he quickly put me at ease, by assuring me he meant no harm. He said he just wanted to say hello.

Not wanting the people in line hearing our business, I stepped out of line, and we walked to another area so we could speak in private. I asked him how he was doing since we last met. He said things were better for him now, and thanked me for how I treated him after he was arrested. He admitted he did a stupid thing, and was very fortunate that I was not a real criminal, who would have actually tried to carry out his plan to hurt the trooper.

He said he learned his lesson, and was trying to be a better person. I told him I appreciated hearing that, and I was happy for his life's change. He went on to say, he recognized me earlier, but he didn't want to rush up on me. I thanked him for that, and we shook hands. After wishing him continued luck with his life, we parted company wishing each other a happy holiday.

Although it was very gratifying to hear my arrest helped someone change their ways in life, that was a bit unsettling at first. I think that scenario in a negative aspect, is one of the most fearful concerns of a law enforcement officer. Fortunately it was a positive experience.

The ID section also participated in drug eradication efforts. The MSP's new Bureau of Drug Enforcement, in conjunction with the Baltimore County Police, and the Maryland Army National Guard, conducted joint marijuana eradication operations in our area. One major effort involved the discovery of marijuana plants in two different wooded fields off of I-83, near Belfast Road.

With directions from the helicopter's observer, Baltimore County Officer Don (Chopper) Coburn, the ground search party located 175 marijuana plants. With no one to charge criminally, the stalks were cut with machetes, and hauled away in a state highway dump truck. The stalks were seized, and eventually taken to a local incinerator to be destroyed. We had to personally witness the disposal of the plants, much to the chagrin of a few onlookers who worked at the incinerator.

One evening, an off-duty MSP corporal who had a disc-jockey business on the side, reported he was maliciously punched in the face by a drunken student athlete. The corporal was performing at a party for students at a nearby university. The assault came when the corporal asked the young man not to touch his electronic equipment. When the report reached my desk, I had one of the investigators contact the corporal. We weren't going to let this go unchallenged. An arrest warrant for the suspect was obtained. "Whitey and Larry" arrested the suspect the next day without incident. The defendant was very contrite and apologized for his actions.

One of the most difficult things we do as law enforcement officers, is when we have to make death notifications to family members of the deceased. There were two deaths that happened on I-83, which had nothing to do with a crime, or a traffic accident. It didn't make notifying family members any less difficult.

Early one morning, one of our troopers stopped to check on a SUV parked on the right shoulder southbound, just south of the Pennsylvania line. The trooper found the lone female occupant unresponsive to his knocks on the window. Opening the unlocked driver's door, the trooper found that the woman was deceased. It was discovered she was the victim of a gunshot wound to the head. After our investigation, it was determined that the cause of her death, resulted from a self-inflicted act. The young woman was terminally ill, and committed suicide.

There was evidence to support that determination, located in her vehicle. We located a receipt, indicating she had recently purchased the recovered handgun found inside the SUV. There was also a note to her family, saying that she had just paid for her own funeral arrangements, and had her hair done in anticipation of committing suicide. The medical examiner's office ruled the death a suicide as expected.

In another case, we received calls from motorists about a tractor-trailer parked on the right shoulder southbound, a few miles south of the Pennsylvania line. The callers reported seeing a person laying near the rig. Our troopers responded, and found the victim, who was deceased. They found no obvious signs of injury. After notifying his family, we learned the male victim had a history of heart disease. By the way his pants were situated, he apparently attempted to relieve himself, and suffered a heart attack. The cause of death was confirmed through an autopsy at the medical examiner's office.

In April 1991, functions at the Valley Barrack would cease. A new facility in Eastern Baltimore County, would be the location of the new Golden Ring Barrack. Meanwhile, on the other side of the beltway, rumors began circulating that Governor William Schaefer, was planning to close Security Barrack, and in Prince George's County, the College Park Barrack. This set off a firestorm of all kinds of dim possibilities throughout the department: Especially for those who would be the innocent casualties of political expediency.

Chapter 37
Golden Ring Barrack "R"…
A Most Humbling Experience

T he transition from investigator with no administrative responsibilities, to that of a full-time supervisor with all the administrative responsibilities, was not an easy one for me. In the beginning, it was difficult to separate myself from my past investigative functions as a corporal. Instinctively, I still wanted to go out and work with my two investigators. By spreading myself too thin trying to do both, I learned a valuable lesson: But not before suffering professional consequences, and personal humiliation down the road.

During an investigation into a most despicable allegation of misconduct against a trooper assigned to the Security Barrack, I received a request for assistance from the Internal Affairs Unit (IAU). I met with their investigators, and learned of a complaint from a citizen, who had been arrested for driving under the influence (DUI). The complainant reported that she had been contacted twice by the arresting trooper. With her upcoming trial date approaching, the complainant alleged that the trooper was soliciting her for sexual favors. In return, the trooper allegedly agreed not to appear in court, which would more than likely result in her case's dismissal. As these allegations also involved criminal implications, IAU required assistance with their inquiry. IAU could only deal with the administrative aspects of the case.

When I was first told of the circumstances, I have to admit I had my doubts. I couldn't imagine a trooper would be that stupid. I was only casually familiar with the trooper named in the complaint. Detective Sergeant Matt Lawrence and Sergeant Frank Ford were investigating the complaint. I knew both of them well. They were excellent troopers, who were experienced, and well-respected investigators. Detective Sergeant Lawrence is the son of the late

Captain Wilford Lawrence, the SSD commander who I mentioned earlier.

Later that evening, we responded to the complainant's residence. On record, the complainant alleged that the trooper who arrested her for DUI, telephoned her offering not to appear for the trial, in exchange for sexual favors. The complainant said that the trooper tried convincing her that his failure to appear for her trial, would result in the case being dismissed.

The complainant said she told the trooper she would think about it, in order to buy the time to report the trooper's actions. The complainant said the trooper gave her his pager number, and told her to page him when she made up her mind. She showed us the number. That by itself didn't prove the allegation of course. The complainant said the trooper telephoned her earlier that day, reminding her that her court date was fast approaching. That convinced the complainant she needed to report the trooper's conduct.

After our plan was devised, Detective Sergeant Lawrence had the complainant call the trooper's pager number. The trooper returned her call. We were monitoring the conversation on an extension phone as it was being tape recorded. The complainant revisited the trooper's previous conversation, pointing out where he solicited her favor, in return for failing to appear at her trial. The trooper never denied saying it. I now knew the sickening truth.

When the complainant agreed to meet the trooper, he started giggling childlike, and nervously. The trooper suggested the location and time they would meet. The complainant agreed. The trooper would be on night patrol beginning at midnight, when he planned to meet the complainant at the designated time. As it was predictable, something went wrong initially.

After following the complainant to the location where she was to meet the unsuspecting trooper, we established our positions in order to observe the trooper's actions, as well as protect the complainant. While monitoring the barrack's channel, we heard the trooper call out a vehicle stop for DUI. Naturally, we thought the investigation would be temporarily canceled. We had the complainant page the trooper from a nearby payphone to tell him she had arrived as planned. The trooper told her he was processing a violator, but still intended to meet her as soon as he could. He asked her to wait. The trooper hurriedly processed the violator, and then placed him in the cell, to be released to a friend. In short order, we heard him go "10-8" (in service) over the radio.

As we were back on, we had to move quickly. Improvising on the spot, Sergeant Ford sought the assistance of a business that was still open, in the small strip of shops where the meeting was to take place. Sergeant Ford was allowed to use an apron and cap worn by their employees, in order to inconspicuously monitor the situation. When the trooper arrived, Sergeant Ford eventually came out with a broom, and start sweeping in front of the business. The trooper was assigned an unmarked vehicle. In the dark, an unmarked vehicle would draw less attention, than a traditional marked vehicle.

Detective Sergeant Lawrence was in his vehicle on one side of the parking lot, and I was on the other side, peering from a reclined position in the driver's seat of Sergeant Ford's vehicle. The trooper pulled onto the medium-sized parking lot, and drove up next to the complainant's vehicle. With their windows down, they spoke briefly. Afterwards, the complainant got out, and walked around the front of her vehicle to the passenger side of the trooper's vehicle.

With his mind on other things, the trooper was unaware that we were quickly approaching them out of his view. Standing outside of the driver's window, I actually saw him start to put his arm around the complainant. I knocked on the window with my credentials in hand. Sergeant Ford was on the passenger side. He quickly removed, and escorted the complainant to her vehicle, and directed the complainant to leave.

Detective Sergeant Lawrence and I had the trooper step out of his vehicle. While Matt informed the trooper of the obvious, I removed the trooper's weapon. He was now under an emergency suspension order. Frank radioed the barrack requesting that a supervisor respond to our location, along with someone to drive the trooper's vehicle back to the barrack.

While we were waiting for the trooper's corporal, you could plainly see the trooper was visibly shaken. He began nervously wandering around the parking lot, tossing an object in the air, and then catching it. The trooper then started walking towards the roadway in front of the shops, and sat on the curb. Although he wasn't under arrest, and running away wasn't going to help him, I was concerned for his present state of mind. I feared he might do something rash like step in front a moving vehicle. Even during the midnight hours, there was light traffic moving along that frequently traveled roadway. I ordered him to come back, and sit by me.

When his corporal arrived and learned of the general particulars, he was in disbelief. The corporal felt there had to be some extenuating explanation. The corporal was assured there were none to be had. The trooper was told to sit in the front passenger seat of his corporal's vehicle, while I sat in the rear. It was obvious the trooper was feeling the reality of his circumstances closing in on him.

Although it was dark, and not really hot that time of the morning, the trooper began sweating profusely. I watched him turn on the vehicle's AM/FM radio, nervously moving the knob from one radio station to another. The corporal who was still not convinced of his trooper's guilt, glanced at me through the rearview mirror, as if he were saying: "Are you seeing this?" While we were heading for the barrack, I was watching for any instance of an emotional breakdown from the trooper.

It was somewhat humorous to see how the trooper's nervous fidgety, began affecting his supportive corporal. I could see how the corporal (who is left-handed) began uncomfortably leaning against the door panel, trying to keep his weapon away from the trooper as we drove along. Arriving at the barrack, we drove to the rear entrance. We parked in an open space with a posted sign that read: "Reserved for Trooper of the Month." This recognition was given to the trooper who led the barrack in statistical performance for the previous month. In what had to be the cruelest fate of irony, the designated space had just been awarded to that very same trooper: Someone who had just committed an exploitative act against a citizen, in betrayal of his oath, and the public's trust.

Late in September 1991, termination notices from Governor Schaefer went out to 1,700 state employees which also included 83 troopers. Some of the 83 were recruits still in the academy. The terminations would be effective two months later in November.

Necessary budget cuts was the purported reason given. After hearing news reports on a Friday, that cuts would take effect on that following Monday, I remember telling people Schaefer wouldn't dare do that to us. But the unthinkable happened. The governor used state employees as political pawns because he couldn't have his way.

Some of the troopers affected were in Iraq serving our country. They returned home only to find their jobs had been eliminated. Rightly, those troopers filed suit, and had their jobs reinstated. An eventual deal was made, and the unfortunate recruits in the academy had their Personnel Identification Numbers (PINS), and positions terminated. That eleventh hour deal, did save the jobs of those troopers who were vetted employees. The troopers who were reinstated, had to accept transfers wherever assignments in the department existed.

Although the College Park Barrack reopened in 1994, Security Barrack's facility would no longer function as a barrack. It was later used as an office location for other MSP functions. The Golden Ring Barrack had to assume all of the records, and administrative functions that were once administered by personnel at Security Barrack. With all the uncertainty surrounding the rumors of job eliminations and the barrack's closure, several of the administrative processes were left unattended, or incomplete. These problems were all now on Golden Ring's personnel to bring up to required standards.

Shortly after, Golden Ring was audited by the department's Staff Inspection Unit. This was my first departmental audit experience, and it was far from my finest hour. Some of the programs under my responsibility were heavily scrutinized by the auditors, and were found not up to standards.

Although staff inspection acknowledged some of the uncovered deficiencies were mainly inherited from Security Barrack, it was still my responsibility. I willingly accepted this, and wanted to cooperate. I did not excuse any failures on my part, or shirk my responsibilities for what took place during the audit. However in my opinion, the audit was more like an inquisition than an audit. I was made to feel like the biggest incompetent in recent years. This experience was very disheartening to say the least. After a time of having success in the recent past, this was a disastrous turn of events. One I admittedly contributed to.

In the meantime, on the morning of February 28, 1992, I received a telephone call from the barrack, reporting that a passing motorist entering the on-ramp to eastbound I-695, from northbound I-95, noticed the partially nude body of a White female lying in a ditch. I advised the PCO to contact the crime lab, and have "Whitey and

Larry" respond to the scene. I told the PCO to tell the initial responding troopers, to ensure they protected the integrity of the scene, until relieved.

By the time I arrived, there were several Baltimore County police personnel there as well. This was not unusual as we shared a mutual jurisdiction. After conferring with my two investigators, and the crime scene tech TFC Ray Leonard, I went to check the victim, and initiate the investigation. TFC Rosario walked over, and told me he overheard the county officers speaking as though they were handling the investigation, not us. I was soon to find out that was true. The barrack received a call from FOB Chief, Lieutenant Colonel "Sonny" Hayman. Lieutenant Colonel Hayman relayed the order advising me to turn the case over to the county.

I was aware, that the department was transitioning to relinquish some of our criminal responsibilities to county police departments in some parts of the state, but this was embarrassing. Later at the barrack, I was sitting in the kitchen wondering to myself, what next. First the audit was killing me, and now I had to be ordered to turn over a suspicious death investigation to the county police. The troop commander, Captain Ray Presley was in the area, and stopped by the barrack. Seeing I was in the kitchen, the captain sat next to me at the table.

I first met Captain Presley in 1983 (when he was the lieutenant at the Cumberland Barrack in Allegany County), during the investigation into the murder of Joann Charlton at Frostburg State College. Captain Presley noted that I was upset. When I voiced my objection to surrendering the case, the captain said that people knew what to expect from the department in Baltimore County. I responded telling the captain, "It's not about what the public expects, it's about what we expect of ourselves."

Reportedly, the victim was later identified as Judith Miller. Ms. Miller was last seen at a variety of bars, and dance clubs the night before her body was discovered. She had suffered upper body trauma. Unfortunately, this case still remains unsolved today.

Although by this time I had been on 15 years, I still hadn't been personally exposed to the "Third Floor's" reasoning for the things that were dictated to the field. The "Third Floor," or "Puzzle Palace" (as the executive building was jokingly referred to in the field), was where the superintendent, and the three bureau chiefs operated. This was where all the marching orders came from. That wasn't the level I operated on. You just followed orders. Your satisfaction was not guaranteed, or a part of the equation.

Eventually there would be the dawn of Memorandums of Understanding (MOU) between the MSP, and other county jurisdictions. Even in my most basic nativity, I felt the more responsibility we gave up, there was a greater chance we would never get it back. Politically, that ship had sailed. It was obvious to me that the sheriffs, chiefs, and their political representatives, couldn't wait to go before their respective budget committees, attempting to bolster their resources, in lieu of what we were surrendering to them.

Coincidentally, in October 1991, I attended a homicide seminar at the State's Medical Examiner's Office in Baltimore City. It was sponsored by the world-renowned Frances Glessner Lee Harvard Associates in Police Science, Inc. My attendance was courtesy of Captain Guy Guyton, who at the time was the association's president.

Captain Guyton, was a well-respected investigator in the department during his early years at the Annapolis Barrack. The captain was a world-class gentleman who I admired greatly, and considered an outstanding leader and friend. Very sadly, we lost Captain Guyton after his retirement, in 2016.

At the rate things were currently going for me personally, I needed to end my one-man outrage, and get back in line. Without malice, but to the point, Captain Presley said if I wasn't happy there, I could transfer. Apparently working in SSD, and CID for the previous six years, shielded me from the realities of life in FOB. I told the captain I appreciated his time.

There was a promotion/transfer list about to come out. I was told there would be an opening in IAU. I decided to put in a transfer request, for a reassignment there. As I had just assisted them earlier during my time at Golden Ring, I had hoped that staff inspection's audit results, and my personal outrages, wouldn't eliminate me from consideration. In the end, thankfully it didn't.

Although there were some issues with the items recorded in Security's property log, there were none with Golden Ring's. At least that was some solace for me. Even after moving on, and thoroughly immersing myself in my new assignment, I would never forget how that audit felt. You never know where you'll find yourself in the department. Sometimes in the MSP, you can come full-circle as I would experience a few years later.

Regardless, you have to care enough about your job, and try to keep positive. You can't lose faith in yourself. However, it is vital that you admit your failures, and work extremely hard to recover. There are people who will support you, as long as you put forth the effort. It was a matter of personal pride for me. Despite your rank, what is important is your reputation. So undaunted by this experience, I couldn't wait for this new start in IAU. I was grateful that some of my soundness gave me a second chance...one I didn't intend on squandering.

Chapter 38
Making A Difference Internally

I can honestly say I had never considered internal affairs as a choice for an assignment, but in the end, doing so turned out to be one of my better career affecting decisions. The first order of business came while sitting in front of Captain Mike C. Barnes (who sometimes referred to himself as "MCB").

Captain Barnes said although I came highly recommended by some of the outgoing investigators, the audit from Golden Ring Barrack didn't do me any good. I was embarrassed and certainly humbled, but glad he gave it to me straight. I felt most ready to close that door, and try very hard to regain my reputation as soon as possible.

IAU generally conducted the more serious breaches of departmental policy committed by our sworn personnel, whether by citizen complaint, or from allegations preferred internally. Other cases less considerable, regardless of origin, were generally investigated by barrack, or divisional personnel as designated by the respective commanders. When there were allegations of a criminal nature, IAU would be assisted by one of the department's criminal investigative units. Criminal and internal matters had to be investigated separately, as was the case when I assisted IAU earlier.

Upon request, and with the concurrence of the superintendent, the unit investigated internal complaints from allied agencies in matters considered conflicts of interest, or if the requesting agency lacked IAU resources. They were referred to as non-agency investigations, or "NAIs."

Up until 2021, when the state repealed the law, Maryland police officers were under the protection of the Law Enforcement Officer's Bill of Rights (LEOBR). Sort of a police officer's Miranda rights. LEOBR addressed the need for a uniform level of procedural protections, and safeguards against the potential harm to an officer's career. The law was enacted in 1974, by the Maryland General

Assembly. The protections of LEOBR, did not apply to law-enforcement officers who were on an entry-level probationary period, except in cases of allegations for brutality, committed in the performance of the officer's official duties.

Some officers may have a difficult time investigating their fellow officers. I took the position that the facts would properly address the outcome. So regardless, good or bad, I was just following the trail where it led me. I later found out it was not always that simple. The dispositions in IAU investigations concluded as "Sustained," "Non-Sustained," or "Unfounded." There were times when arriving at a non-sustained conclusion didn't end there. Sometimes you were required to expend a bit more effort, in order to clearly remove the officer under investigation from any light of uncertainty.

During my time in IAU, I seemed to draw the cases involving alleged racial overtones. As an example, there was a case where a White trooper was accused of unnecessary use of force, and uttering remarks considered racially motivated, during a traffic stop involving two Black males.

The main complainant was an off-duty Washington Metropolitan police officer, who alleged the trooper's inappropriate conduct arose after he and his cousin were stopped for a traffic violation. The encounter with the trooper, subsequently led to the arrest of his cousin for DUI. The complainant said they were unduly manhandled to the point of being injured, resulting from the excessive treatment by the arresting trooper.

The complainant also alleged that the trooper referred to his cousin as "Boy," suggesting this too was racially motivated. The trooper denied the allegations, and said he never used the word "boy," or any other inappropriate term towards the complainants during their encounter.

After interviewing the complainant and his cousin, I noted their versions of the details varied. That alone wasn't necessarily an indication they weren't being truthful. The only thing they said resembling any consistency to their respective versions, was about the trooper's alleged use of the word "boy," when referring to the cousin. Both complainants viewed the trooper's alleged misconduct during the entire incident, as being "racially motivated." Even though the main complainant was a police officer, I felt he was dubious about his own conduct at the scene.

According to the trooper, the complainant tried to interfere with his cousin's lawful arrest. The trooper said the complainant objected to his cousin's arrest, when he (the cousin) became emotionally distressed at the thought of being arrested and handcuffed. The trooper said that's when it became necessary to request backup.

During my interview with the cousin, I asked if he had ever been arrested before this incident. He replied, "No." After reviewing both interviews, I decided to make inquiries into the cousin's claim he hadn't been previously arrested. My inquiries revealed that three years earlier, the cousin had been arrested by the local sheriff's department for his involvement in an assault case. The deputy coded the case as a "race/hate crime."

Without provocation, the cousin and a group of other Black males, attacked an innocent White male coming out of a convenience store. The victim was kicked and punched for no apparent reason, other than he was White. When I confronted the cousin with this arrest, and the racial nature of his own actions, his only explanation was he forgot.

A combination of all the factors, which included a lack of medical attention sought for their alleged injuries, and the cousin's lacked forthcoming, called into question the creditability of the complainants. After summarizing the facts, I found no corroborating factors that gave credence to the complaint against the trooper's actions being racially motivated. To the contrary, I opined that the trooper's actions were consistent with departmental policy, governing arrest procedures. Accordingly, I recommend the allegations against the trooper be considered unfounded. The department agreed.

In a case totally opposite in nature, IAU received a complaint from a Black trooper, who objected to four other Black troopers allegedly using the "N-word" jokingly amongst themselves one afternoon, inside the troopers' room at the Waterloo Barrack. The department had its share of citizen and inter-departmental complaints against White troopers for this type of conduct; but to my knowledge this was a first.

During the complainant's interview, he recounted when he heard the so-called jovial banter between the four troopers. The nature of their remarks, were about their own interpretations, regarding the differences between the classifications of Black troopers on the job.

One of the troopers seemed to be more vocal than the others. In the complainant's opinion, this senior TFC was the ringleader of their alleged commentary. The complainant described the topic of their expressed sentiments as follows: If you were a Black trooper out in the field (meaning road patrol duties), you were a "Field Nigger"; But if you were a supervisor (a corporal, sergeant, etc.), you were a "House Nigger."

For those not familiar with these negative connotations, there is an accurate depiction of these characterizations in the 2012 film, "Django Unchained," featuring the actor Samuel L. Jackson's vivid portrayal as the cunning and evil house slave, employed by the plantation's equally cruel owner, portrayed by actor Leonardo DiCaprio. Mr. Jackson's character's treatment of the slaves on that plantation was just as inhumane if not more, than that of plantation's owner. (Thus explaining an irresponsible attempt at humor, through a generalized racial commentary.)

The complainant went on to say he told the troopers they were stupid, and said he was offended by their remarks. According to the complainant, he asked them to reframe from continuing their conduct.

A month later, the complainant crossed paths with the senior TFC on the barrack parking lot. Once more his comments featured the "N-word." This time he used the word to describe other Black troopers at the barrack, calling out those whose conduct he took issue with. This prompted the complainant to file his report of alleged misconduct against the TFC. The complainant's allegations were documented, and submitted to his barrack commander, who forwarded the complaint to IAU.

When I was asked by Captain Barnes about the subject matter, I explained the historical inferences to him. The captain then had me go over to the "Third Floor," and explain it to the chief of FOB. During my individual interrogations with three of the four troopers named in the complaint, they all admitted to the nature of the conversation. Although they discontinued their comments in front of the complainant, to a man, they all failed to see the problem, and defended their actions as harmless banter.

One of the troopers earnestly tried to excuse their behavior, comparing it to Richard Pryor's 1970s comedic routines, and the skits on the television series "Def Comedy Jam." I told him, and the others, they weren't on television; and as far as Richard Pryor's act went, they were state troopers not entertainers. I suggested that they be more sophisticated, and appreciate the ignorance of their actions, especially in the workplace.

I reminded them departmental rules and regulations, didn't exempt personnel who are Black from the penalties for such violations. To drive home my point, I posed the following scenario: What if an employee of another ethnicity standing outside the troopers' room overheard them, and joking or not, walked in and said, "I think all of you are a bunch of N's." I then challenged each of those three troopers to explain how they'd react.

Predictably, each one just sat there with a cheese-eating grin. I asked, "What would you do… on the whistle, draw your weapon, fire five rounds and holster?" Not being an option they could consider, I told them they'd just have to stand there with their collective mouths open, looking rather stupid. Imagine the irony.

As they were under the misapprehension they were covered by some unofficial ethnic exemption to use that word, or any associated with it, they had to be set straight. I told them you can't contribute to an issue of this nature by holding others accountable, while you engage in the same behavior, claiming exclusion along cultural lines. After my interrogation of the senior TFC named as the offender in the complaint, the allegations were investigated and accordingly sustained.

Amusingly enough, this same TFC was promoted to corporal just prior to the initiation of my investigation. It appeared that the shoe was on the new corporal's other foot. Once he became a supervisor, I had to sarcastically wonder if those would-be comedians felt their definition of a "House-N," now applied to their ringleader as well.

Even though I admittedly outsmarted myself at times, one of the satisfying aspects of an investigation, came when dealing with those who thought they were smarter than the police. I certainly encountered those situations on more than one occasion. However it was a bit more gratifying, when dealing with a citizen's complainant alleging misconduct not based on facts, or a genuine perception, but in a blatant attempt at retaliation against a trooper. This was the case, when a complainant who had allegedly assaulted one of our female troopers during his arrest for DUI, notified the barrack he was a victim of brutality, at the hands of the troopers responding as backup.

In his lengthy handwritten version of the incident, the complainant said the arresting female trooper radioed for backup, and two male troopers, one Black and one White responded. The complaint felt the methods deployed by the responding troopers to subdue him, were overbearing. The complainant insinuated that racism, not necessity precipitated the uncalled for physicality employed by the two backup troopers. Summarizing the detailed statements submitted by both of those troopers: They met force with the appropriate level of force.

Before personally assigning me certain cases, Captain Barnes would give me a brief synopsis of the allegations, and then ask for my initial thoughts. Evidently in this case, the barrack commander and one of his sergeants, prematurely injected their sense of sustainability regarding the allegations against the troopers. Captain Barnes and I agreed their assessment was not only premature, but also inappropriate at best. Especially since the matter had not been thoroughly investigated.

Telephoning the complainant at his home in Virginia, I scheduled an appointment to meet him at the barrack. The complainant insisted that I come to his home in Virginia instead. When I arrived, I found the complainant to be quite hospitable offering me dinner, or a beverage. With thanks, I declined. He then insisted I take a brief tour of his very nice home. The complainant even showed me the voice-activated calling system in his new Lincoln Continental before we got started with the interview. I really appreciated his congenial demeanor.

After reviewing the complainant's written account with him, I told the complainant I had previously highlighted some of his comments, and I would appreciate it, if he would expound upon them during the interview. Regarding his allegations of brutality, I asked if he required medical assistance, or subsequently sought medical attention for the injuries he claimed to have sustained. The complainant said, "No," to both questions.

The complainant also expressed how he felt it was unnecessary to be handcuffed to a steel ring affixed to the wall in the trooper's room. I explained that it was procedural, while the troopers were attending to their paperwork. I let the complainant know that the alternative, would have been to place him in one of our holding cells.

I said, I was sure he preferred being handcuffed to the steel ring instead.

Continuing with his allegations that concerned racism, I asked the complainant, if he could be more specific about a certain comment he made. The complainant wrote he was in fear of his safety, because of a news article he read in a local newspaper. In the complainant's written account, he stated that the article focused on the presence of "racist county cops" in the area where he was stopped by the trooper.

The complainant was asked if he had personally encountered any of these "racist county cops," before he read the article. He said, "No." I then asked if he personally knew of anyone, who suffered at the hands of any "racist county cops." Again the answer was "No."

Finally on this subject, I asked him if the article he read mentioned any similar complaints against the state police. He said he didn't think so. I then asked the complainant, if it was fair to say his fear wasn't based on anything he personally knew about, but was just his perception; One acquired by reading the news article he referred to. In response, the complainant said had he known he was going to be asked that question, he would have checked with some of his friends who traveled in that area, and may have been stopped by the police.

The next question was whether or not, any of the troopers said anything that could be construed as racist. Again, "No" was his reply. I concluded the interview by asking the complainant, if there was something he'd like to add to his statement. The complainant had nothing to add, but he wanted to know what would be the status of my investigation from that point. I advised the complainant I would be interrogating the three troopers before concluding my investigation. After the administrative review of my report, he would be notified by certified mail, whether or not the troopers were in violation of our policies. At that time, the disposition would be final.

In the end, the complainant's alleged concerns about racist county cops in the area, amounted to nothing but speculative commentary, not facts, or a genuine perception. In my opinion, it was his own alleged unlawful actions that precipitated his physical confrontation with the troopers. The troopers' use of force was consistent with departmental policy. Accordingly, the allegations were non-sustained against all three troopers. Fortunately for those three troopers, their case was investigated by IAU, and not their barrack commander or sergeant.

Chapter 39
Will the Real Sergeant Russell
Please Take the Stand

One afternoon, Captain Barnes called me into his office. As he sometimes would when he was about to discuss a case, the captain invited me to have a seat on the sofa in front of his desk. I listened as the captain began telling me the details of how Mr. Frank Mazzone, Deputy Commissioner, Maryland Department of Public Safety and Correctional Services (DPSCS), had just attended a court trial at the Essex District Court, in Baltimore County.

Before his appointment with DPSCS, Mr. Mazzone was a life-long member of the MSP. Retiring as a lieutenant colonel, he was also the deputy superintendent during his time as a bureau chief.

Mr. Mazzone was there to witness court proceedings involving a correctional officer charged with DUI. The officer had been arrested by the MSP, and processed at the Golden Ring Barrack. Apparently had a guilty verdict been adjudicated, Mr. Mazzone was prepared to terminate the correctional officer's employment immediately. Captain Barnes went on to say the case was dismissed, because the arresting trooper failed to appear for the trial.

I noticed that the captain was looking at me intently, and I began wondering why. Certainly this was no more than a case of a trooper failing to appear for court, and would normally be handled at the barrack level. I just assumed because a former lieutenant colonel, who was now a high-ranking state government official was involved, the "Third Floor" wanted IAU to conduct the investigation. Or perhaps there was some improper act that went beyond just the trooper's failure to appear.

As his story came to an end, Captain Barnes leaned forward asking if I knew anything about this. When I told him I didn't, he sternly divulged the trooper's identity as "Sergeant Russell." I told the captain my last DUI arrest was in 1983, before I left the

Westminster Barrack; nor had I been summonsed as a witness for anyone else's DUI case. I advised the captain there was a Sergeant Lloyd Russell, at Golden Ring. I said the sergeant was a uniformed patrol supervisor, and an intoximeter operator, who also happened to be my cousin.

Now awkwardly leaning back in the other direction, the captain picked up his telephone, and called over to someone on the "Third Floor." Captain Barnes informed the person on the other end that they had the wrong Sergeant Russell. The captain confidently said he knew it wasn't his man.

As I sat there while the captain was on the telephone, it occurred to me that he tried systematically undressing me, seeing if my body language revealed signs of guilt. Instead of just directly asking me if I forgot I had court that morning, the captain tried in vain to psychologically make me sweat. While halfway listening to his conversation, I just shook my head as he came to my defense.

The Golden Ring Barrack is directly across the street from the Essex District Courthouse. You'd think someone on the "Third Floor" would've checked there first. Any documents related to the correction officer's DUI arrest, would have been located in the barrack's DUI files. That certainly would have immediately identified the arresting trooper, and the intoximeter operator. I wondered if there was residue from that audit business still lingering in the back of somebody's mind.

So, with this newest case of "mistaken identity" settled, it was back to business as usual. As I said earlier, the MSP is full of ironies; and soon enough, I would experience another one related to my cousin.

Chapter 40
Getting the Band Back Together One Last Time

In February 1992, Dontay Carter terrorized Baltimore City, during a brazen crime spree, when he abducted three separate victims from two different parking garages. At gunpoint, Carter robbed and forced his victims into the trunks of their vehicles, as he rode around the streets of Baltimore, plotting their fates. Carter brutally murdered the second of these three helpless victims.

Carter's first victim was abducted on February 7. The victim was beaten, and left inside the trunk. After the vehicle was abandoned, the victim was able to manipulate the trunk's lock, and escape. Unfortunately Carter went undetected, and remained at large.

On February 11, Carter's second victim was beaten to death with a metal pipe, and left in an abandoned row-house dwelling. On February 14, after being abducted, Carter's third victim was able to disengage the trunk lock, while Carter was driving around in the city. After Carter had momentarily stopped in traffic, the gentleman escaped from the trunk. Fortunately there was a Baltimore City police officer nearby. The gentleman alerted the officer, and Carter was subsequently apprehended in the vicinity nearby.

In the aftermath of Carter's apprehension, it was revealed that unwitting MSP personnel confronted him on two separate occasions. The first took place at the Baltimore Washington International Airport. Employees at a rental-car station summonsed troopers (who back then, were regularly assigned to patrol the airport), when they were suspicious of Carter's use of a credit card. It was unknown at the time that the credit card belonged to the deceased second victim. Carter was able con his way out being detected, and allowed to leave.

The second incident came when Carter was stopped for a traffic violation. The information on Carter's fraudulent Maryland drivers' license was radioed to the PCO at Golden Ring Barrack for inquiry. Although the identifying name and information suspiciously matched that of the deceased victim (who by now had been reported missing), it went unheeded. Again, Carter bluffed his way out of being detained. The trooper wrote Carter a warning for the traffic violation, then permitted him to proceed on his way.

When it was discovered that these contacts, and inquires made by MSP personnel went unconnected to any of Carter's recent activities, this was troubling to the governor, who demanded action. The department reportedly disciplined those personnel involved for their lack of wherewithal in this matter. The only one I was aware of who was disciplined, was my cousin, Sergeant Lloyd Russell. He was the duty officer when the radio transmission regarding Carter, was relayed to the barrack from the trooper who initiated the traffic stop.

When these matters came to light, apparently someone's head had to wind up on a platter. I was told in confidence my cousin got a raw deal, but someone had to be sacrificed. I was actually in the barrack when the traffic stop took place. But no one decided to seek the ID section's guidance, despite the suspicious nature of the circumstances that should have been explored further.

On January 18, 1993, Carter was standing trial for the abduction of his first victim. Although in the custody of two DOC Pre-Trial Detention guards, Carter managed to escape during a break in the proceedings. Carter was allowed by the guards to use the bathroom in the judge's chambers. The bathroom was not checked prior to allowing an unshackled Carter to occupy it. Carter locked the door, and promptly escaped through the second-floor window of the Mitchell Court House, in downtown Baltimore City.

On January 19, I received a telephone call from Captain Barnes before I reported to the office. Apparently, the governor made it clear he wanted the state police involved in the search for Carter. The captain advised me that on the authority of the superintendent, I was to immediately report to Baltimore City Police Headquarters to join in the search for Carter. I reminded the captain it had been years since I worked fugitive cases. Captain Barnes said, "You've been specifically requested by the city."

When I got to the EAU's office on the sixth floor, there was an uneasy atmosphere about the room. The office was filled with several troopers, and a few MSP commissioned officers. I was extremely happy to see Sergeant Sharp, Detective Dyson, and Deputy Cunningham, and the other city detectives as well. I was approached by one of our commissioned officers who wanted to know why I was there. I told him I was directed there by the superintendent.

After a few minutes, the EAU's commanding lieutenant came into the office. The lieutenant didn't mince words. He asked, "Where is Russell?" I raised my hand. The lieutenant told everyone else from the state police they could leave. After a briefing, we got busy and started checking developed leads.

Intelligence gathered by Detective Cunningham and EAU's other sources eventually led us to focus our attention in Northeast Baltimore City. The search ended at the Goodnow Hill Apartments. Informant information said that Carter was hiding out inside a third-floor apartment unit at that complex.

With the cooperation of the apartment's management, we were able to have access to the vacant apartment directly below the one harboring Carter. I called Captain Barnes on my cell phone, and informed him that although we had located Carter, we were on standby, until a search warrant was obtained.

Unaware if Carter was armed, Sergeant Sharpe opted to maintain surveillance on the apartment. Sergeant Sharpe also requested their Quick Response Team (QRT) be assembled to serve the search warrant when it arrived. Notifications were made to all the concerned executive officials. Within an hour or so, the news media, and more responded to the scene. It was like a carnival. There was plenty of airtime, and photo ops to be had for all the responding officials.

After we systematically evacuated the building, with search warrant in hand, the QRT breeched the apartment's front door. Searching the apartment, they eventually located Carter hiding under a bed. Carter was recaptured without incident. We were gathered in the foyer on the first floor, as a handcuffed Carter was being escorted down the stairs. I called my cousin on my cell phone, and told him to watch the news. I said, "What's done is done… you've been vindicated."

In November 1992, Carter was convicted on first-degree murder, kidnapping, and other related charges in the death of his second victim. On January 8, 1993, Carter pled guilty to abducting his third victim.

This was a perfect four-year reunion for me and my friends. It was just like old times. The band got back together, came through one more time, and took its final curtain call. Thanks to their efforts, a dangerous murderer was again in custody.

During the following months, most of the department's personnel began turning their attention to the upcoming promotional testing cycle. As a unit, we decided to pull our resources, and work together creating study material in the form of a test document. Individually, we took designated chapters of both the administrative and patrol manuals, focusing on the sections prescribed by the Promotional Standards Testing Unit's (recently) developed publication of "KSAs" (Knowledge Skills and Abilities).

KSAs identify areas in the manuals you need to focus on, while studying for an upcoming promotional exam. Each rank testing from corporal to captain has its own set of KSAs. Any new changes in policy mandated through updates in the law, personnel matters, or other related topics, would most certainly be featured on any ensuing exams. This was a tremendous study resource, and it was provided to all participating personnel.

Our selected questions and answers, were given to Corporal Bruce Diehl, who formatted them into a multiple-choice study document. Corporal Diehl was a wizard when it came to the computer. At that time, not everyone's skillset with the early computers went beyond basic word processing for typing reports. I know mine didn't.

The promotion/transfer list came out in August 1993. I was promoted to detective sergeant, and transferred to the Criminal Investigation Division (CID). I would be in command the ID section at the Waldorf Barrack, in Charles County. I was thankful for my time in internal affairs. I learned a new skillset, dealing with a different, and exact form of investigation. I really appreciated Captain Barnes for accepting my transfer into his unit. Despite that missing court matter, we certainly enjoyed a pleasant, and respectful relationship throughout my time there.

As you would expect, the members of the unit were top-notch people. The assistant commander, Detective Sergeant Donald Lewis would eventually go on to become a major, and command the Aviation Command. After he retired Donny became the civilian director of our Human Resources Division (HRD). In 1993, Sergeant

Bruce Speck would retire from the MSP, and become chief of the Elkton Police Department in Cecil County.

Sergeant Dennis Murphey would become a lieutenant, and eventually succeed me as commander of the Rockville Barrack "N." After being promoted to captain, Denny would become the commander of the Training Division, before retiring. After being promoted to lieutenant, Corporal Bruce Diehl commanded the North East Barrack "F." After being promoted to captain, Bruce would become commander of the Personnel Section in HRD. When he retired, Bruce returned as the civilian director of HRD.

After he retired, Corporal Vince Maas joined the Carroll County Sheriff's Department. Ms. Lori Brewer, our civilian administrative aide, and I, would work together again in a different unit in 1999. Captain Barnes was promoted to major, and became a FOB's command staff before he retired.

The IAU's hallmark was its investigative thoroughness, and unbiased professionalism. In the end, arriving at the truth is what mattered most. What I learned in internal affairs, would serve me time and again in the years to come.

Chapter 41
Waldorf Barrack "H", CID

The nature of my new assignment was a return to the same type of duties I had at Valley/Golden Ring, but at the next rank. I knew there would be no abject repeat of my first audit failures when it came to the department's decentralized inspection programs. My own internal message that I was an administrator first, and investigator only when necessary, was much clearer this time around.

Waldorf was a "full-service" barrack, and had a sufficient, experienced civilian support staff in place. Mrs. Robin Guy was the section's designated administrative aide, and my human safety net. She was as competent as they came.

The barrack was very fortunate to have other competent aides like Mrs. Inez Early and Mrs. Theresa Jenkins as well. They all worked closely, and I can say without a doubt, they truly acted like family. They were excellent examples of the type of dedicated civilian support we had in the department; and they were an absolute pleasure to work with. The criminal section's immediate supervisor was Sergeant Willem Van Der Heyden, who was one of my academy classmates. The three investigators were TFCs Chip Ewing, Rob Mignogna, and Ted Jones. I had no previous experience with them prior to this assignment.

The first thing I wanted to do, was assure them it was not my intent to come in, and make a lot of unnecessary changes. If the job was getting done correctly, that's what I cared about. I also let the investigators know their thoughts, and ideas mattered. I always found it wise to give people the necessary autonomy to handle their business, and as the supervisor, be there as a resource when needed. All I expected from them was that they do their best, keep me informed of what I needed to know, and be where they were supposed to be at the appropriate times.

I was not an unreasonable clock-watching supervisor. I knew first hand, the amount of hours most investigators worked that went uncompensated; So I wasn't about to nickel-and-dime them about their exact hours. In return, I expected them to reciprocate when it came to asking for overtime. Overtime usage, was always on the "Third Floor's" list of budgetary concerns. I assured them when warranted, they would have no worries about receiving overtime.

Finally, I made sure the investigators knew they were accountable to me, and the department. Before they saw this as a one-sided deal, I quickly added, "But the department and I, are accountable to you as well." I saw their faces light up after that. I really enjoyed fostering a family environment. For the most part, I found it very effective for morale. My general attitude was people didn't work for me, they worked with me.

However sometimes, even the most sincere intentions are unwelcome, or abused. Happily, there were only a few instances where I had to recognize subordinates as backstabbers, or cunningly ambitious, throughout the following years of my command experiences. When appropriate, I was known to inject some sort of humor to ease the tension whenever possible. There were a lot of demands being placed upon the employees' shoulders, especially our civilians.

There was a popular corporate slogan going around that state officials and politicians liked directing at state employees: "Employees should learn to do more with less." Based on budget cuts, and so-called fiscal oversight by our friends in Annapolis, that was a fine slogan. Too bad many of those same officials and politicians didn't think that slogan applied to them. Unfortunately the eventual reality became: "Do everything with nothing."

In order to address concerns at any given time, I came up with a few slogans of my own. I wanted to get a point across, while giving my folks an insight to things at my level. This was my way of preparing them for their future supervisory, and command experiences.

The first: "Let's not bleed before we're cut." That meant don't overreact before we get the facts. The second: "An informed superintendent is a happy superintendent, and a happy superintendent, tends to worry about somebody else." I think that speaks for itself.

I also had something I called my "85-15 rule." Eighty-five percent of the time, you got to run your business your way, as long as it reasonably got the job done. Occasionally, 15% of the time, they had to allow an interruption of their routine if I need something important, even if it was at the last minute.

That meant if there was an occasional, or last minute mandate from the "Third Floor," the governor's office, or some other outside influence that may have caused a sudden halt in their routine, they had to acquiesce, and move forward without drama. Sort of a longer version of Detective Sergeant Henry Black's "Just say ok Henry," from my Fugitive Unit days.

I ended by telling them we may not always agree with an order from above, but as long as it was a legal one, we could cry about it on one another's shoulders. But when the tears dried up, we had to move on, and follow through. I said we had to consider it just another day at the office.

Those pearls of wisdom, would be a reoccurring message for all of the sworn and civilian personnel, I would command at some point throughout my career. I wanted to give them the benefit of the leadership qualities I had been fortunate enough to experience. I treated my folks like adults, extending them the courtesy of giving it to them straight, while trusting they were capable of appreciating the circumstances, and moving forward with the task at hand.

Chapter 42
I Wasn't There Five Minutes Before…

TFC Ewing and two detective sergeants from neighboring barracks within the southern troop, were conducting a surveillance on a cold-case homicide. In order to appear inconspicuous, they had need of an innocuous vehicle. I was temporarily assigned a minivan, until my regularly assigned unmarked sedan was ready. TFC Ewing and I switched vehicles. Some of my personal things from IAU were in boxes, situated in the storage area of the van. TFC Ewing asked if I wanted to remove the boxes. I told him there was nothing important inside them, just some stuff I brought with me from IAU. I said the boxes could remain in the van.

At some point during their surveillance, TFC Ewing decided to check inside the boxes to see if there were any reading materials to help pass the time. While looking through the boxes, he came across my study material for the last promotional exam. Unknowingly, he considered the document may have been something he shouldn't concern himself with, and abruptly put it back in the box.

TFC Ewing's reaction apparently didn't escape the notice of one of the detective sergeants, who asked TFC Ewing what was wrong. TFC Ewing's response that it was nothing to bother with, evidently only heightened that detective sergeant's inquisitive nature. I was later told that on a pretense, the detective sergeant later secured the keys to the van. He then took the liberty of going through the boxes, and found my study material.

The detective sergeant thought he had discovered evidence of skullduggery on my part. Erroneously, he thought he found an illicitly obtained official answer key to the promotional test questions. The detective sergeant smuggled his discovery, and immediately reported his suspicions to the very place I was promoted from…IAU. When I radioed 10-7 the barrack, the recently promoted barrack commander, Lieutenant Harold Hart (who was also at one time in IAU), met me at the barrack's rear entrance. Lieutenant Hart had a radio monitor in his office, and heard my radio transmission.

Lieutenant Hart had already been made aware of my alleged misconduct. The lieutenant was very concerned, and wanted to break the bad news to me first. When I arrived at the back door, he asked me to follow him to his office. Lieutenant Hart asked me to have a seat. As he looked very uncomfortable, I asked if he was all right.

Lieutenant Hart said, "Stewart, they found the test!"

I asked, "What test are you talking about?"

The lieutenant said, "The one in your box, inside the van."

I asked, "Are talking about my study materials we made up at IAU?"

Suddenly with a deep sigh of relief, the lieutenant's whole demeanor changed, thankful that this wasn't what it appeared to be. I asked how he knew about my study materials. The lieutenant then told me of the circumstances, and assumptions that turned out to be incredibly embarrassing for that inquisitive detective sergeant.

Understandably, the department was obliged to have the Promotional Testing Unit make a comparison of my study materials to that of their official test for first/detective sergeant. Telephoning IAU, I asked to speak with Captain Barnes. Knowing I was on the line, he started by saying, "Now Stewart I know you are upset." I told him he had no idea. The captain assured me that the matter had been put to rest, and he told the detective sergeant who initiated the inquiry the same thing.

I thanked the captain, and hastily got off the telephone, so I could give that detective sergeant a piece of my mind. We both knew each other in passing, so he was no stranger. When he answered, and knew I was on the line, he told me he was going to call me. I was in no mood to be charitable. I asked the detective sergeant who told him he could go through my things. True to his nature, the detective sergeant put the blame on TFC Ewing's suspicious reaction to what he (TFC Ewing) saw in the box. I reminded the detective sergeant that was hardly probable cause to go through my things.

When he said he felt obligated to report his findings as the study material appeared authentic, I had to concede that point, thanks to Corporal Diehl's computer skillset. I let the detective sergeant know I was not at all happy with him. Now that I had my say, it was time to let it go. I was thankful once more to survive an allegation of misconduct. I just didn't think it would come again so soon.

After I spoke to TFC Ewing about it, he apologized profusely. As I was his new detective sergeant, he said he didn't want to get off on the wrong foot with me. I assured him everything was fine between us. I said you never know when your integrity will be challenged. Jokingly, I told Chip that I wasn't there five minutes, and from IAU no less, before some nut case tried to get me fired.

Unfortunately, we would lose Lieutenant Hart at such a young age, after his battle with an illness in 1997. In November 2000, the Waldorf Barrack was replaced by the newly constructed LaPlata Barrack. The staff at LaPlata, held an event in celebration of his memory. I had the honor of being asked to emcee the event. Members of Harold's family were also in attendance.

Harold left his brief, but positive imprint on the department, and those who knew him. I know I'll never forget his concern for me in the case of the "Stolen Promotional Test Mysteries," or his fixation on having all the venetian blinds in the barrack, at a uniform level.

I'm not kidding about that uniform blinds thing. During the event, I made a joke about it. I recalled the evening when I heard him complain about the uneven height of the window blinds. After he left the room, I asked the administrative aide Mrs. Early (who also heard him) was he kidding. She assured me he was quite serious. Even his family had to laugh when I joked about it. They knew firsthand he was serious about those blinds.

Chapter 43
Quit Dancing in the Street Before You Get Hit

In the eleven months I was at Waldorf, I found the investigators to be a very competent group. As it was with most of the investigators I worked with in the past, they too liked having fun, and kidding each other. They worked long hours, and dedicated themselves to solving their assigned cases when they could as well. In a sprawling rural, but growing area considered a District of Columbia suburb, there were bound to be all types of calls for service.

The barrack shared public safety responsibilities with the Charles County Sheriff's Department. Having less personnel than the sheriff's department, didn't stop the barrack from handling its share of the calls for service. The ID section ably investigated, and solved cases involving thefts of farm equipment, burglaries, sex offenses, armed robberies, and theft by fraud.

TFC Jones even investigated a bank robbery prior to my arrival. The unidentified suspect in the case, was arrested in Baltimore City on an unrelated charge. Informant information received by the arresting officer, revealed his arrestee had supposedly robbed a bank somewhere in the Maryland/Washington, D.C. area. That information was passed on to the local law enforcement officials in Southern Maryland.

Thanks to an organized gathering of information sharing within the region, TFC Jones was able to establish a possible connection to his case and the arrestee. I accompanied TFC Jones to Baltimore, where he questioned his suspect at the city jail. Naturally, the suspect initially denied his involvement. When he was confronted with the existence of surveillance video clearly putting him at the scene during the robbery, the suspect was compelled to confess.

One late afternoon while riding with TFC Jones, a call was broadcasted over the police radio, reporting the robbery of a gas station on Route 301. The robbery had occurred just minutes before the broadcast. A patrol trooper's timely response to the area, enabled him to observe, and pursue the reported getaway van used by the suspects. The pursuit continued north on 301, onto Mattawoman Beantown Road, not far from the barrack. It ended when the suspects' van lost control, and ended up in a ditch alongside a wooded area.

The suspects were successfully apprehend without incident by troopers on the scene. With the suspects in custody, an immediate search for the stolen money was conducted. The trooper involved in the pursuit, thought he saw something being thrown out from the passenger window. We thought this was an effort to discard the stolen money.

After a search in that area, we found no money. We believed the trooper saw something else being discarded, and assumed it was the stolen money. Our attention then turned to where the pursuit ended. We thought that the money could have been discarded somewhere close by, even perhaps in the adjoining woods, which was just a few feet from where the van ended up in the ditch.

As the loss of daylight became a concern, the local fire department was kind enough to let us use their bank of overhead lights to illuminate the woods and surrounding area. With nothing to show for our efforts, and night fall setting in, we ended the search. A trooper was posted through the night, until we could start again in the morning. Subsequent interrogation of both suspects by TFC Jones, revealed that the money had been stashed in an undetected, hidden compartment inside the van. The money was recovered at the tow company's storage lot.

On one of my days off, I received a telephone call from TFC Jones. He seemed rather happy to hear we were getting a new regional commander. CID's regional commanders were at the rank of lieutenant. I asked TFC Jones for the lieutenant's name. When I heard it, I told him to quit dancing in the street before he got hit by a truck. I gave TFC Jones the benefit of my experience with this lieutenant, telling him the lieutenant was not necessarily a bad guy, but he was different.

TFC Jones said, "So he's not like you huh?"

I said, "Everybody's different Ted."

I told Ted we'll just do our jobs and see what happens. I said I would leave it up to him to form his own opinion. It can be a very different dynamic working for someone you know. It is up to both people to respect the other's role, and conduct business as business first. Generally, I was fortunate enough to have excellent working relationships with those I knew personally, when they were assigned to units I commanded. There were only a few exceptions, and those individuals were most treacherous.

It didn't take long for TFC Jones to see what I meant about the new lieutenant. Although everyone did their jobs accordingly, the lieutenant found it necessary to regard his opinions on most things, as the one that mattered in the end. Even as the section commander with my own level of experience, I was not immune from the lieutenant's undesirable micromanagement preferences.

As the results of the current promotional exams had been announced, it was time for supervisors to make promotional recommendations for their subordinates. Supervisors had to provide a list of their eligible sworn personnel on an MSP Form 17, indicating whether or not, the employee would be recommended for promotion.

The only supporting documentation required to accompany the list of names, was for those who were "non-recommended." Attachments documenting the employee's "failure to meet expectations" during the previous performance appraisal period was mandated. The employee had the right to review any negative documentation for dispute, general comment, or simply refuse to comment, before acknowledging the documentation with their signature. This was required before a supervisor could use the information to justify an employee's non-recommendation, or place the negative documentation in the employee's personnel file.

One afternoon, I happened to be at CID Headquarters, which at that time was located at the old SSD Headquarters in Jessup, Howard County. I stopped by the commander's office to say hello. The division commander, Captain Steve Rupard, greeted me, and invited me to come in and have a seat.

Captain Rupard was one of the most energetic, hard-driving, and personable individuals I have ever known in the MSP. Like most of the outstanding leaders I encountered, he too possessed one of the most desirable qualities you can have moving up through the ranks: "Never forgetting whence you came." The captain was also very sincere. When he asked you how things were, he really meant it.

As was his nature, the captain wanted to know how I was getting along. I told him I was ok, and happy that my guys were doing excellent work. Astutely, the captain could see through my facade, sensing I had something on my mind.

I rarely felt the necessity to complain about things I could work out at my level; But as I trusted the captain's sincerity, I relented, telling him my regional lieutenant and I were having some issues. I assured the captain I would deal with the matter correctly. Captain Rupard said he sensed as much. Evidently, the lieutenant decided he was only recommending four out of the five detective sergeants in our region for promotion. I was the only one he was not recommending.

Before I could say anything, the captain said he noticed there was no supporting documentation on the lieutenant's corresponding Form 17, justifying my non-recommendation. When he brought this to the lieutenant's attention, the lieutenant attempted to qualify his actions by citing incidents that amounted to personality conflicts, not job performance as his reasons, the captain said.

At one time, Captain Rupard was the detective sergeant at Waldorf. He knew if there were any issue with my performance, he would've heard about it from the people there. The captain said he told the lieutenant I was to be recommended, and to resubmit an updated Form 17. Captain Rupard told me not to worry about it, but try to iron out the differences between myself and the lieutenant. I was very appreciative of the captain's fairness, and his willingness to hold the lieutenant accountable for disregarding policy.

The next morning in my office, I received a telephone call from the lieutenant. He was calling me to discuss whether or not he was going to recommend me for promotion. I didn't say anything; I just let him talk. The lieutenant began by saying he wasn't thoroughly pleased with my performance. But last night before he went to bed, he prayed on it, and decided to recommend me. I had no intentions of revealing the conversation I had with Captain Rupard. I just thanked the lieutenant, and asked him to excuse me, as I had to attend a meeting. That was just a pretext to get him off the telephone, before I said something I would regret.

What a colossal gall the man possessed. Not only did the lieutenant violate my rights as an employee, but then he tried taking credit for his lack of integrity, by shamefully evoking a religious element to his hypocrisy. But as I say throughout, the MSP is a place full of fateful irony; and the lieutenant needed to ask his Magic 8 Ball about his future.

Towards the end of June, I received a telephone call from Lieutenant John Davis. You may recall he was the administrative sergeant in the Fugitive Unit's Warrant Section, who helped me prepare for my sergeant's exam. Lieutenant Davis was now in command of CID's Attorney General's (AG's) Section, located in Baltimore City.

Lieutenant Davis asked me to be his detective sergeant, overseeing the investigators assigned to AG's Criminal Investigation Division. As his assistant commander, I would be responsible for the White Collar Crime Unit, and the Environmental Crimes Unit. Lieutenant Davis would oversee the Insurance Fraud Unit, along with his other divisional command responsibilities. This was both a challenge, and a great opportunity.

I was honored to be asked. Before I could answer, Lieutenant Davis told me it didn't matter, because he was not taking no for an answer. We both laughed. I didn't have to think twice about working for someone I greatly respected like John Davis.

Chapter 44
Trooper Please Help My Son

The evening before my last day at Waldorf, I was working late making sure things were in order for the new detective sergeant, Tom Parker. On my way home, before reaching the county line, I heard a call for service radioed by the barrack. The PCO directed the trooper to proceed to a call involving a possible suicide attempt. The victim had reportedly suffered a self-inflicted gunshot wound. I advised the PCO that I would respond as well.

I arrived first, and parked my vehicle a house down from where the incident reportedly took place. As I approached the residence, the victim's elderly mother hurried towards me crying, and pleading with me to help her son. I put my arm around her, and attempted to comfort her as we walked back towards the house. Keeping my eyes forward, I scanned the house as we hastily moved forward.

Even though I was unaware of what I could do, I advised the mother that the ambulance was coming. Although time was of the essence, I had to ensure it was safe to approach the scene. I asked the mother what type of weapon was in her son's possession. She told me he had a shotgun, and said he wouldn't hurt anyone else. This was important to know before running into possible exchanges of gunfire, especially if her son had issues with the police, or was mentally unstable.

I asked was there anyone else inside. She advised her husband was in the basement with their son. By this time, the uniformed trooper arrived. I quickly told him what I knew as we entered through the front of the house. After asking for her son's first name, I requested the mother remain upstairs. Slowly making our way down the stairs to the basement with our weapons in hand, I started calling out to let the son know the police were there to help him.

Reaching the basement, we saw the father standing in an open space near the laundry area. When the ambulance arrived, I told the trooper to tell them to wait until we knew it was safe. I asked the father exactly where his son was. He pointed to an enclosed part of the basement that was used as the son's room. The father said he didn't think his son was alive.

I wasn't disregarding his statement, but before entering the room, I needed to be sure it was safe. There was still a weapon inside. If by any remote chance the son was still alive, we had to move quickly, but cautiously. Moving towards the room, I continued trying to get a response from the son. Crouching on an angle close to the door frame, I could see a bed to my left but no sign of the son.

With the trooper now behind me coving my forward movement, I began to widen my angle further left a few small strides at a time. Reaching the left side of the door frame, I was able to see the son's boots and jeans up to his knees, on my right. The son was in a seated position, as though he were propped up against something. After looking up at the drop ceiling, I had my answer. I saw blood, and pieces of brain matter hanging from the ceiling. Sadly, I knew it was safe to enter the room.

Evidently, after propping himself against the entertainment center, the son took a shotgun, put it in his mouth, and blew off the top of his head. After a closer examination, I could see his neck stem showing. The shotgun was laying across his lap.

The EMTs were alerted it was safe to come down stairs. After taking a look, they said they were not transporting the victim to the hospital. As I mentioned before, it is a most difficult duty for the police to notify families of a death, and this was no exception.

Although the father knew, it was heartbreaking having to tell the mother, especially when she thought her son was still alive. Before the EMTs left, I asked them to check both parents. A neighbor or two, came over to help comfort them.

The trooper was new, and I wanted to be sure he was ok. I asked him if he was up to seeing this type of carnage for the first time. The trooper assured me he could cope. At that time, all MSP patrol and investigative vehicles, were equipped with instamatic cameras. The department provided film cartridges, containing 12 exposures each, for taking photos at crime scenes, accidents and other related incidents.

I had the trooper retrieve his camera, and asked him to start taking pictures of the scene. Walking the trooper into the room, I told him where I wanted pictures taken, and to be careful of getting anything on him. In the meantime, I would be checking the scene closer, until my on-call investigator arrived.

As I went about taking notes, I could hear the trooper's camera clicking several times. I thought it had to be more than 12 clicks. I just figured he used more than one roll of film.

When he stopped, I asked him how many pictures had he taken. He said he never counted. Taking the camera from the trooper, I opened the rear compartment, and saw there was no film in the camera. I looked at him and shook my head. I told him one day you'll be a supervisor, and this would be something funny he could tell his troopers about.

Depending on the circumstances, troopers had to do more than investigate an incident, and leave the scene. Sometimes out of compassion for the family, we also tried providing necessary information to help them deal with the aftermath of a crisis. The department also offered our chaplain services, if a family didn't have their own clergy preferences. The hazardous body fluids and matter, scattered throughout their son's room, couldn't be cleaned safely by ordinary methods. I asked one of the neighbors to help them contact a local restoration cleaning business, who could respond after we secured.

As their son's body was not removed from the premises by the EMTs, we had to notify the State's Medical Examiner's Office to respond to the residence. If the medical examiner required an autopsy, then they would remove the body for transport to their office in Baltimore City. If the medical examiner decided that under the circumstances no autopsy was needed, the family would have immediate need of a mortuary service.

My section's supervisor, Sergeant Van Der Heyden, was the on-call investigator that evening. When Willem arrived, I turned my notes over to him. After briefing him, I started for home again. That was some way to end my last official working day at Waldorf.

As predicted, that new trooper was eventually promoted to sergeant. When we see each other at different MSP functions, we still laugh about his photography skills. "Just one of those things that happens," I tell him. We've all been there in one way or another.

Waldorf was a great assignment with great people, but I did look forward to the challenges of the AG's Office. It came as no surprise that all three of our investigators, would go on to make the rank of sergeant before they retired. I knew they had it in them. Happily, I've maintained my contact, and friendship with them, and several others from my days at Waldorf, throughout these past years.

Chapter 45
The Attorney General's White Collar Crime Unit:
We Are More Than Chauffeurs with Badges Folks

I reported to my next assignment in July 1994. This transfer not only meant a reunion with Lieutenant John Davis, but also with my academy classmate Sergeant Rick Norman. The Maryland Attorney General's (AG) Section, is considered a high-profile, politically sensitive assignment. The AG's Criminal Investigation Division investigated and prosecuted criminal activity considered "white collar" in nature, committed against and within state government.

Those cases involved theft, fraudulent misappropriation by a fiduciary, misconduct in office, bribery, perjury, and falsifications of public records. The division also investigated health care fraud, gun trafficking, insurance fraud, multi-jurisdictional crimes, and criminal violations of Maryland's tax laws. The White Collar Crime Unit was supervised by Sergeant Norman.

The other component to the AG's office I'd be responsible for was the Environmental Crimes Unit (ECU). The ECU enforced the state's environmental articles governing air and water pollution, hazardous waste, and commercial littering. The ECU was supervised by Sergeant Shelly Clemens.

Our investigators were there to conduct criminal investigations which were initiated by the attorneys, who were also responsible for case management, and the prosecution of those cases. Arrest or search and seizure warrants, had to be obtained and served by law enforcement officers. Attorneys are officers of the court, and have no powers of arrest. As an added benefit, we provided protection for the attorneys, and accountants, while they conducted their duties in the field.

Shortly after my arrival, we received a new investigator. I met her at our CID Headquarters which was now in Columbia, Howard County. After I was introduced to Corporal Terri Wilkin, I had her follow me to our designated parking garage. The garage was a few blocks from the AG's office building.

Corporal Wilkin began unloading some of her things in boxes. The boxes looked a bit heavy. As I would have done if she were a male, I offered to help carry something. Corporal Wilkin said, "No thanks, I work-out."

After walking a few blocks, I noticed the corporal looked a little flushed. Those boxes were starting to weigh her down. As I walked along side of her, I saw people passing us looking at me with disdain. They were probably wondering what kind of gentleman I was.

Making light of the awkward situation, I said to the corporal I knew she worked out, but was she sure I couldn't help carry something. This time she accepted my help. We both laughed. Whenever we would see each other years later, she'd flex her bicep, and say she was still working out.

Once I settled in, I inquired about any concerns on the part of the investigators. I got the impression that the investigators were sort of walking around on eggshells. After becoming acquainted with the AG's protocol, I availed myself to the assistant AG (AAG), supervising the division.

Our initial meeting was pretty standard. He made his expectations of our role there clear. The AAG told me there were two required staff meetings held monthly. During my first meeting, I just sat and listened. It didn't take long to realize intentionally, or otherwise, the troopers' contributions to the AG's successes, were being generally minimized by some of the attorneys.

During a subsequent staff meeting, the supervising AAG voiced his displeasure about our lack of effort, when it came to serving the division's outstanding arrest warrants on file. This was my first time hearing about that. I told the supervising AAG I would look into the matter, and address it accordingly. I requested that any such future concerns be brought to my attention, before they caused any unnecessary public aggravation.

After being directed to the file cabinet housing the warrants, I reviewed them with Sergeant Norman. There were fourteen open warrants on file. The warrants were divided amongst the five investigators. Taking one myself, I went out that afternoon to locate the defendant.

My defendant had a business close to the AG's office in downtown Baltimore. Not wanting to alert the defendant he was being sought, I telephoned him pretending I wanted to use his business' services. Unwittingly, the defendant invited me over, unaware he was about to be arrested.

Utilizing Corporal Wilkin as though we were business partners, the defendant was at ease in our presence. Once the defendant was positively identified, he was arrested without incident. Within the next few weeks, eight of the warrants were closed by arrest, or other means. The supervising AAG seemed reasonably appeased with our stepped up effort… at least for the time being.

One of the more complicated efforts to locate a defendant came, when Corporal Jackie Whitaker used a pen register to help pinpoint the whereabouts of her elusive defendant. A pen register is an electronic device, used to record the telephone numbers called between one telephone-line to another. Use of a pen register required a court order, and the cooperation of the local telephone company.

In addition to her interviews with several of the defendant's known associates, Corporal Whitaker was able to locate the defendant after a series of telephone numbers listed to the defendant's known associates, were linked by the pen register to a number in Pennsylvania. As part of the court order, the telephone company identified that Pennsylvania number as the defendant's. With the help of the local Pennsylvania authorities, the defendant was arrested, and processed for extradition.

After I became aware that a particular high-profile case was released to news affiliates without mention of our involvement, I called the AG's public information office to inquire why. The public information officer candidly said he was unaware of any state police involvement. I politely informed him our investigators were more than just chauffeurs with badges. He assured me that he would be certain to include our contributions where appropriate in the future. The gentleman kept his word; we were given our accorded due credit in all future press releases.

Before the bi-monthly staff meetings ended, everyone would have an opportunity to bring out something of interest, or concern for the good of the order. After the next meeting, I listened as the attorneys touted their activities. When it was my turn, I congratulated my investigators on their latest effort to reduce the backlog of warrants. The supervising AAG casually responded, "Oh yes… good job."

Generally, the environment became a bit more congenial, with only an occasional display of tension. On two separate occasions, I had to intervene as the same investigator was chastised on the basis of inaccurate information. After looking into both instances, I found that rather than hear the investigator's side of things, the two involved AAGs, just reacted to the first version reported to them.

I had to remind them both, that the troopers were my responsibility. Since we were just down the hallway from each other, there was no reason to jump to conclusions without informing me first. I said that would keep them from making an unnecessary spectacle of themselves, by overacting to misleading or false information. (Sort of like the old saying: "People are innocent until proven guilty.")

We were all aware there was immense pressure on the various units to provide positive outcomes on investigations, especially during an election year. As it was my expectation that we perform at a high level regardless of whether it was an election year or not, there was no need for people to start bleeding all over the place before they were cut. After the incumbent AG was re-elected, eventually things settled down, and there was less noticeable acrimony.

The AG's office received information that the superintendent for buildings and grounds under the Department of General Services (DGS) in Baltimore City, was suspected of stealing money, and state owned equipment for a period of two years. AAG Norman Smith and I, began an extensive document search through DGS invoices, looking for illegal authorized payments for services, allegedly being used for the suspect's personal benefit. Additionally, we began an inventory, looking for equipment allegedly taken off the premises by the suspect.

At the initiation of the investigation, the suspect was placed on suspension. On our very next visit to the Baltimore DGS complex, missing tools, and other equipment had suddenly reappeared. It didn't matter though. We had already noted their absence at the time of our inventory. After I obtained an arrest warrant charging the suspect with theft, he surrendered himself to me through his attorney, at the Glen Burnie Barrack.

During a pretrial meeting at the AG's office with the defendant and his attorney, AAG Smith offered them the opportunity to accept a plea agreement. As the investigating officer, I was also present. The defendant was vehemently opposed to my presence in the room. AAG Smith ask that I wait nearby, outside the conference room.

At the conclusion of the meeting, the defendant's attorney came over to me and apologized. I asked him what for. He told me for his client's use of racial remarks directed at me after I left the room. He said he hoped that wouldn't influence my zeal to prosecute his client. I just laughed, and told the attorney I had been called worse by better people than his client.

Through a letter from his attorney, the defendant refused to accept any plea agreement offered by AAG Smith. Instead, the defendant arrogantly opted to stand trial. The defendant received guilty verdicts on two counts of felony theft. Prior to sentencing, the presiding judge admonished the convicted defendant telling him: "A thief is a thief is a thief."

In January 1995, there was a new governor elected. He appointed Prince George's County police chief, David Mitchell as the new superintendent. In November, the section was working on a major corruption case. We were serving search and seizure warrants in Maryland and Pennsylvania. That particular day, the operation went well into the evening hours. When we returned to the office, I was notified I had been promoted to lieutenant.

Although the transfer assignments were unknown at that time, it didn't matter to me. Getting promoted was the hard part. Driving to your new assignment was the easy part. We have a saying in the department that goes: "It's never too far in an MSP car."

During my time at the AG's office, I developed a relationship of mutual appreciation and respect with AAG Scott Lewis. AAG Lewis was an excellent prosecutor, and I always appreciated his demeanor, and respect for the investigators. After Scott left the AG's office, he went on to have successful tenures as an assistant prosecutor with the Harford County, and the Cecil County State's Attorney's Offices respectively. Years later we still exchange Christmas cards.

The investigators in the unit were outstanding to work with. Each one distinguished themselves as knowledgeable in the complexity of their assigned investigations. In the years that followed, several would go on to supervise, or command their own assignments.

In the White Collar Crimes Unit, Sergeant Rick Norman, Corporal Eric Danz, and Corporal Terri Wilkin, would all be promoted captains before they retired. Corporal Jackie Whitaker retired as lieutenant. Corporal Joe Price retired as a Detective Sergeant. Corporal Harvey (Tyrone) Waters was promoted to sergeant and TFC Pat Jamison to corporal. In the Environmental Crimes Section, Sergeant Shelly Clemens would later go onto supervise the criminal section at Rockville Barrack. TFC Tim Frye made lieutenant, and TFC Dave Riggs made sergeant.

In tribute to my mentor, and friend Lieutenant John Davis, I owe him a special thank you. He was my kind of leader. Like the others I hold in high regard, he too cared about his troops, and loved the MSP.

After he retired in 1996, we stayed in contact with an occasional telephone call. I'm glad I took every opportunity to let John know how important he was to me personally. Sadly, John passed in 2011. Retired Lieutenant Rob Garber, retired TFC Lee Ordway, and I gathered to visit with John in the hospital before he passed.

Like so many others I have mentioned, John help make the MSP what it will be for years to come. As I said before, they don't make them like that anymore. John and his widow, retired MSP Lieutenant Nina Hook, have a son named Colton. Following in his parents' footsteps, Colton is now a trooper too.

Chapter 46
Bureau of Drug and Criminal Enforcement:
Lower Eastern Shore

On November 20, 1995, a MILES message came out announcing assignments in the newly formed Bureau of Drug and Criminal Enforcement (BDCE). The department consolidated the criminal, and drug operations into one bureau. I was one of the seven lieutenants assigned to the bureau as an area commander. My new command structure included the criminal sections, and drug enforcement operations at Salisbury Barrack "S" (Wicomico County), Berlin Barrack "V" (Worcester County), and Princess Anne Barrack "X" (Somerset County).

A month before my arrival, on October 17, 1995, Ivan Lovell accompanied by his passenger William Lynch, were traveling southbound on U.S. Route 13, south of Princess Anne, in Somerset County. They were transporting a large quantity of crack, and powdered cocaine worth a street value estimated at $63,480.00. Lovell was armed with a .45 caliber semi-automatic handgun. Lovell was on parole in North Carolina, after serving less than one year of a 12-year sentence for a drug conviction.

Shortly before 1:00 a.m., TFC Edward Plank, Jr., and Trooper Dennis Lord, were on road patrol working out of the Princess Anne Barrack. Operating radar, TFC Plank observed Lovell's vehicle being driven over the posted speed limit, and gave pursuit. Immediately after, Trooper Lord pursued a different vehicle for another observed violation.

Trooper Lord effected his traffic stop in the opposite direction, north of where TFC Plank had stopped Lovell. After his initial contact with Lovell, TFC Plank became suspicious of Lovell's true identity, and radioed for backup from Trooper Lord. Trooper Lord then drove south on Route 13, and parked behind TFC Plank's vehicle. TFC Plank shared his concerns with Trooper Lord. Trooper Lord walked back to his vehicle, and retrieved his handheld radio.

TFC Plank again approached the driver's side of Lovell's vehicle. Now in possession of his radio, Trooper Lord began walking back towards Lovell's vehicle as well. Suddenly, Trooper Lord heard a gunshot. He saw TFC Plank fall to the ground. Trooper Lord immediately fired two shots at the driver's side of Lovell's vehicle. Lovell then returned fire at Trooper Lord.

Trooper Lord's rounds broke the rear window. One of Trooper Lord's rounds passed through Lovell's right forearm, and another grazed his scalp. Lovell then sped away from the scene. Trooper Lord radioed the barrack for assistance, but in the end, TFC Plank's wounds proved fatal.

After fleeing the scene, Lovell came upon a nearby pond, and submerged his vehicle. After he and Lynch separated, Lovell then broke into a nearby residence. Lovell accosted the two startled homeowners, who bravely fought off Lovell. Despite being shot at and terrorized, by Lovell, the homeowners eventually overcame him. Several hours into the search for Lynch, he was found hiding in a nearby wooded area, and surrendered.

Lovell would go on to confess, and received the death penalty. The sentence was eventually overturned to life without parole. Lynch on the other hand, was charged with drug related violations. It was determined that in order for Lynch to receive a fair trial, a change of venue was necessary. The case was scheduled to be tried in Cecil County. The lead investigator in the case was TFC Joe Gamble, BDCE Salisbury Barrack. TFC Gamble told me that a lot of troopers were outraged, over the state's attorney's decision not to prosecute Lynch in anyway with TFC Plank's murder.

Although emotional reactions can't always determine what charges can be legally preferred against an accused suspect, I certainly understood the frustration felt by those closely affected by TFC Plank's death. As I had no clue what could be done at that time, I sought advice above my level for guidance. The response was to leave the matter to the state's attorney's office, and not get involved.

Based on the circumstances, I at least expected to be asked for any suggestions. Even with nothing to offer at that time other than the problem, I felt some collective consideration might have resulted in a viable solution. If there had been none reached, at least there would have been an effort. Those who expressed concern would now understand the limitations of the situation, and hopefully learn from it.

As I was just promoted, I didn't want to start off on the wrong foot in my new bureau. However, I was taken aback with the reluctance to even consider the matter. I know you want to tread lightly in someone else's territory, but that response was disappointing. The message was relayed to TFC Gamble. I apologized for my lack of success with the first thing that was asked of me.

Later that night, I was home watching television. While I was channel surfing, I came across a program highlighting the in-car camera video footage, of Texas Constable Darrell Lunsford. On January 23, 1991, in Garrison, Texas, Constable Lunsford stopped a vehicle occupied by three Hispanic males. Constable Lunsford discovered they were transporting marijuana in the trunk of their vehicle.

Within seconds, Constable Lunsford was attacked, and taken to the ground. A passenger exited the vehicle and joined in the attack. Constable Lunsford was stabbed, kicked, and fatally shot with his own sidearm. What his attackers didn't realize, was that on the dashboard of the constable's vehicle, was a video camera recording the incident.

The recording proved to be invaluable in the suspects' subsequent capture and prosecution. The narrator commented that all of the suspects were charged and serving time federally, in connection with Constable Lunsford's murder. The next day, I told TFC Gamble about Constable Lunsford's case. I felt there was some similarity between TFC Plank's case, and Constable Lunsford's. I told him it wasn't my intent to disobey an order, but I was going to reach out to a friend in the United States' Attorney's Office for his opinion.

Andrew Norman, a former Washington County Assistant State's Attorney and friend, was now an Assistant United States' Attorney (AUSA), in Baltimore. I felt there was a legitimate reason to explore any possible means to seek an alternative prosecution avenue against Lynch; One that exceeded any concerns over political expediency, or any other reason for that matter. Certainly no one would publicly say they didn't want the full extent of the law applied in this case.

In the department you were encouraged to use all available resources when necessary. So using mine, I telephoned AUSA

Norman at the Edward A. Garmatz U.S. District Courthouse in downtown Baltimore. Andrew was more than happy to hear what I had in mind. After briefing him with all my details, Andrew said he would love to take on this case, however he had just been transferred out of the drug unit. He advised me that any federal jurisdiction in this matter, would require a nexus to an existing drug operation on the part of Lynch and Lovell.

Andrew said he would personally see that my information was given to the right section for their attention. Although he couldn't promise anything, I was encouraged there was an outside chance to seek a case against Lynch within federal jurisdiction.

When I next spoke to Andrew, there was good news, and some that could have been problematic. The United States' Attorney General (USAG), for Maryland, the Honorable Lynne Battaglia, was willing to assume the case, but only after an official request from the county's state's attorney. Now it was up to TFC Gamble and me, to convince the Somerset County State's Attorney, Logan Widdowson, to embrace the idea of inviting the USAG into the case.

After a meeting with much discussion, Mr. Widdowson agreed to at least meet with the USAG. He and TFC Gamble traveled to Baltimore, and met with AUSAs Norman and Andy White. Paperwork was completed to formally request an open case file that would be assigned to the drug unit, if Mr. Widdowson agreed. At the conclusion of the meeting, Mr. Widdowson finally agreed to formally request the USAG seek prosecution against Lynch.

In the days that followed, AUSA Kathryn Armentrout and TFC Gamble, would devote dozens of hours driving back and forth from Maryland to North Carolina. Thanks to the Asheville North Carolina Police, Joe located witnesses and acquaintances, who were willing to speak freely and factually, about Lovell's, and Lynch's alliance in the local drug culture. Having secured the information required by federal guidelines to prove Lovell's, and Lynch's use of violence in their prior illicit drug activities, the case against Lynch could proceed. Combining this information with the previous evidence in the original MSP case, AUSA Armentrout, and AG Battaglia, successfully prosecuted the case against Lynch in federal court.

Lynch received a sentence of 20 years without parole for his role in TFC Plank's murder. Thanks to the total dedication of our investigators, and the full cooperation of the USAG's Office, the Asheville Police, and Mr. Widdowson, the federal case against Lynch was made possible. But I wouldn't have gotten the idea, had it not been for the tragic death of Texas' fallen hero, Constable Darrell Lunsford. Mr. Widdowson who retired in 2005, after serving as the Somerset County's State's Attorney since 1976, passed in 2009.

Another irony to this story, is that AG Battaglia, was also a law professor. One of her law students at that time was the new superintendent. During a preliminary meeting with TFC Gamble, AG Battaglia telephoned Colonel Mitchell, to give him an updated status of the case as a courtesy. After she put TFC Gamble on the line, the colonel asked him what he thought. Joe stated we should proceed. And as the saying goes: "The rest is history."

Towards the unexpected end of my tenure on the lower shore, I was at the Golden Ring Barrack (my regional headquarters) dropping off my region's MSP Form 31s (Employee Work and Leave Report). My immediate supervisor (a captain) said the major wanted to have a word with me before I left. We were joined by the captain, as I sat in front of the major's desk.

The major asked if everything was ok with me. I told him as far as I knew, it was. When I asked if there was a problem, the major said he had information I was not regularly reporting for duty at my Salisbury Barrack office. Furthermore, he said, there were days when I arrived past the standard reporting hours, and leaving early before the end of my shift on those days. I thought, "Here we go again."

After hearing this, I asked the major where he got his information. Of course he wouldn't reveal his source. I told the major it didn't matter. As far as I was concerned, if this was more than a general characterization, then who ever said it, and I didn't care who, was a liar.

When occasionally some legitimate business kept me in the Baltimore area past one o'clock in the afternoon, I admit that I didn't take that three hour drive to my office afterwards. I thought that was reasonable. If I wasn't going to be on the shore, our supervisors at my three locations were informed, and knew how to reach me if needed. In those instances, there were no reported incidents that required my presence. I explained as needs varied, so did my arrival time.

As for the suggestion that I regularly left early, I told the major the last thing I wanted was to leave early, and have to go back in the event of an emergency. Then I would have to explain why I wasn't there when the emergency occurred. I also gave the major examples of being asked by the barrack commander to mind things while he was out, in the event of a need for a command presence at the scene of an emergency.

I recounted times the Field Operations Bureau chief, Lieutenant Colonel Ernest Leatherbury, requested to meet with me. Even if he arrived past my duty hours, I was still there waiting for him. Having had enough of this absurdity, I asked the major for an MSP Form 181 (Notification of Charges).

When he asked why, I told the major I was tired of defending myself against the stupidity of others. I said I would sign a blank charge sheet, and invited him to call the barrack commander, the first sergeant, or any of my investigators in reference. If any one of them claimed I was inappropriately avoiding my time requirements, he could fill in the blanks, and I would see them at the hearing board.

The captain attempted to add his perspective, telling me, "Perception is nine-tenths of the law." I reminded the captain that facts are 100% of the law. I told them both my explanations could easily be verified. When facts are on the table, perception in this case is a false accusation, I said.

The major declined to telephone those who could verify my side. As this was getting me nowhere, I asked the major for the bottom line. The major replied, I would have to be at my office at 8 a.m. from here out. I said that was fine, and ended any further discussion on the subject.

A few weeks later, I received a telephone call from the deputy superintendent, who was also BDCE's bureau chief, Lieutenant Colonel Larry Harmel. Lieutenant Colonel Harmel told me it was time for me to come back north, as commander of the southern region. I would be replacing the lieutenant who was being transferred to command of the JFK Highway Barrack.

When the transfer list came out, I was replaced by a lieutenant who left the governor's executive protection detail. It was common knowledge in the field, that personnel leaving executive protection, were generally given favorable choices of reassignments. That lieutenant lived in the area, and requested the lower shore command.

Although the eventual end my tenure in the region was precipitated by unnecessary drama, I was proud that we were instrumental in the outcome that saw complete justice for TFC Plank and his family. TFC Gamble would eventually achieve the rank of lieutenant, and become commander of CID's homicide unit. He is now the elected sheriff of Talbot County.

Although I was falsely accused of neglecting my required hours, that didn't stop me from finding enough time to establish a great working relationship with Salisbury's three administrative aides, Deborah Pheasant, Karen Timmons, and the late Sandy Carroll. "The Weekend Bail-Money Trio," as I called them, were some of the nicest, funniest, and dedicated people I had the pleasure of working with. They certainly personified what was best about our civilians in the MSP.

Chapter 47
Bureau of Drug and Criminal Enforcement:
Southern Maryland

I began my new command in July 1996. The command included the criminal section and drug enforcement operations at Glen Burnie Barrack "P" and Annapolis Barrack "J" (Anne Arundel County), Prince Fredrick Barrack "U" (Calvert County), Leonardtown Barrack "T" (St. Mary's County), and Waldorf Barrack "H" (Charles County). I was back in Charles County where I was the detective sergeant. Unlike before, the drug investigators were now part of the command.

Speaking of irony, the lieutenant I replaced was that same lieutenant I had at the Waldorf Barrack, who didn't want to recommend me for promotion. That slight was behind me now. After he briefed me on several outstanding issues that were now mine, we shook hands, and wished each other luck in our new assignments.

My headquarters would be at the Glen Burnie Barrack. In that criminal section was Jackie Whitaker, from the AG's section in Baltimore. She had been promoted to sergeant. The barrack commander was Lieutenant Ray Grissett (who had a personal hand in helping me get off probation, when I was a new trooper at the JFK Highway Barrack).

Other than the usual required criminal and administrative investigations, our most unique responsibility involved conducting investigations into all homicides, occurring at the Department of Correctional facilities (DOC), in Jessup, Anne Arundel County and in Baltimore City. These DOC facilities included intake, pre-release and maximum security centers, and those housing juvenile offenders. On occasions, we jointly worked with DOC's Internal Investigation Unit upon request.

As you can imagine, being assigned to the ID section at Glen Burnie Barrack was not the most coveted assignment within the department. Not many people, or even police officers like going into the prisons. If having to investigate inmates for murder wasn't bad enough, there was always the possibility that an investigation could reveal some breach of policy by a correctional officer. There were so many challenges to face by the time we arrived, especially if the incident occurred after regular business hours.

We had to rely on DOC personnel at the correctional facility to maintain the scene, secure evidence, keep witnesses available and importantly, not tamper with or destroy evidence. This is by no means meant to reflect as negative commentary on the correctional officers we encountered, however, there were times when the crime scenes were clearly compromised prior to our arrival. We weren't happy about those instances, but with no proof of who was responsible, we had to move on with what we could.

Sergeant Whitaker perfectly described the scenario faced by our investigators: She said, "Imagine arriving on crime scene, only to discover that it had been mopped clean with bleach, perhaps by one of the very inmates involved in the crime. Correctional officers have an unenviable job that many people wouldn't or couldn't do, and that includes many police officers. When you are in a facility you are the guest, and subject to the facility's rules."

Sergeant Whitaker continued to make her point saying, "Rule number one: Your firearm is taken, and locked in a gun locker. As a police officer inside a correctional facility, you are left with no weapons to defend yourself. Rule number two: Contrary to what many believe, inmates are not locked in their cells all day. In many facilities, inmates freely move about for meals, to exercise, to the library, or to one of the many jobs they perform inside the prison. They are within feet or sometimes inches of you, and you never know which of the inmates could have a shank, or other weapon secreted."

"Rule number three: Your ability to navigate through the facility is totally dependent upon the correctional staff. You can't even open a door without a correctional officer unlocking it for you. You find yourself surrounded by inmates in a world over which you have no control, and your focus must be the crime which brought you there. Understanding the culture, you are not surprised when none of the inmates tell you what they saw. If they do, you have to first determine the validity of the information. If true, you have to coordinate the best means for that inmate's protection as a future witness in your case." All of that was quite an earful, but Jackie drove home the situation they faced completely.

The section's supervisor Sergeant George Jacobs, had to deal with that exact scenario, when an inmate agreed to cooperate with the police, after witnessing the death of another inmate. In a murder stemming from an argument between two inmates, Sergeant Jacobs' case was aided by the deceased inmate's cellmate who witnessed the murder. When he became a state's witness to the murder, the cellmate had to be protected. Through an interstate compact agreement, he was moved to an undisclosed state, for the remainder of his sentence.

In a totally different homicide investigation, our Forensic Science Division again played a critical role in helping us solve the case. The success of Sergeant Jacobs' investigation into the death of a young adult male, was facilitated through a unique method of technology, and knowhow. The victim's body was discovered by a state highway employee cutting acreage alongside the on-ramp to Davidsonville, from eastbound Route 50, in Anne Arundel County. Although the victim's body had only been there for only two days, it began to quickly decompose, rendering normal means of immediate identification impossible.

Removing one of the victim's hands, our forensic technician injected a gel substance into the finger joints, causing the epidermis (outer layer) of the skin to inflate and slip off. This epidermis-like glove was then placed over a latex glove worn by a lab technician. The epidermis glove could now be rolled with ink, and fingerprinted as if it were the victim's own hand. You have to take your hat off to our folks in the lab.

After a series of interviews, a suspect was identified. Further inquiries made by Sergeant Jacobs led to the discovery of a wrecked vehicle driven by the suspect. In the trunk of the vehicle which was later found in the possession of a tow company, were traces of blood which was believed to be that of the victim's. Using a phlebotomist, Sergeant Jacobs obtained blood samples from a family member of the victim's for DNA verification.

Sergeant Jacobs reported that the suspect's motive in this case was triggered, when he was allegedly "disrespected" by the victim. The victim was shot by the suspect with a stolen handgun. The shooting took place inside a wooded area in Prince George's County. The victim was taken to Anne Arundel County, which borders Prince George's County, on Route 50, and left in the acreage adjacent the on-ramp. In the end, although there was enough creditable evidence to convict the suspect, the case was dismissed after a jury trial.

Unfortunately for justice's sake, Sergeant Jacobs said he overheard a Black female juror, tell a fellow Black juror, she was not about to send another Black male to prison. That's very charitable when it's not your child lying decomposed in the grass next to an on-ramp. It is a sad commentary that she apparently cared more about a living Black murderer, rather than an innocent dead young Black man: One whose only crime was he allegedly said something that disrespected the murderer's so-called manhood.

Being a veteran investigator, George understood his job ended when he provided the state with the best evidence, and subsequent testimony he could. No matter how disturbing that juror's sentiment was, he knew all too well that no judge, or jury will be the same in their views, but he never saw that one coming.

When I first arrived, I had to immediately deal with a unique personnel matter involving severe allegations against an investigator assigned to the Waldorf Barrack. The unusual thing about this matter, was that under normal circumstances, the investigator would have had his police powers suspended based on the nature of the allegations. But as the matter was still being investigated by another agency, only his access to computer based state, and federal public safety records were restricted. The investigator was not told the reason for the restriction of his computer access.

I was briefed about the allegations by the outgoing lieutenant. The investigator Sergeant Mike White, inquired if I could advise him on the exact cause of his status. Sergeant White said that the previous lieutenant told him, he (the lieutenant) had no idea. Unlike my predecessor, I didn't pretend I was unaware of the allegations. Instead I was honest with Sergeant White. I said although I was made aware of the allegations, I was prohibited from sharing them with him. As he was still investigating administrative background cases, I decided to treat him as I normally would, until I was told to do otherwise. That's exactly what happened the following case.

In August 1993, the Maryland Department of Natural Resources Police (MDNRP), investigated the mysterious death of Nancy Manni. Ms. Manni's body was discovered floating in the Chesapeake Bay, off of Cove Point, in Calvert County. At the time, it couldn't be determined if her death was the result of murder, suicide, or an accident. Still unsolved by 1996, a local politician voiced his criticism of the MDNRP, publicly claiming they were derelict, by failing to find evidence against the two initial suspects, both who dated the victim at one time prior to her death.

It was under this public scrutiny, that the MDNRP requested the MSP conduct a follow-up investigation into Ms. Manni death. I assigned the investigation to Sergeant White's supervisor, Detective Sergeant Mike Spaulding. Detective Sergeant Spaulding was about to depart on an already planned vacation. He would immediately begin the follow-up upon his return.

On February 2, 1996, Ms. Manni's case aired on the syndicated television program "Unsolved Mysterious," staring actor Robert Stack. It was unknown at the time, but the actual suspect responsible for Ms. Manni's death, was incarcerated at a detention center in Polk County, Florida.

An inmate named John O'Meara, was serving time there on local charges. Miraculous, that particular episode was aired when O'Meara was watching television with other inmates. O'Meara subsequently told a fellow inmate that he was responsible for Ms. Manni death. That inmate later became an informant relative to this case. O'Meara was not one of the original suspects, and had no known prior connections to Ms. Manni.

According to the informant's information, O'Meara said he met Ms. Manni socially in a bar before inviting her back to his boat. Possibly, after Ms. Manni rejected O'Meara's alleged sexual advances, he either pushed her overboard, or she fell over during a struggle. O'Meara is reported to have said he may have struck Ms. Manni with his boat while she was in the bay.

The informant's story was relayed by Florida authorities to the MDNRP, who notified Sergeant White. Sergeant White informed me of this unbelievable turn of events. Detective Sergeant Spaulding was not due to return from his vacation for a few more days. As Sergeant White was familiar with the case, I asked if he felt comfortable assuming the investigation. Sergeant White said he was, but expressed concerns over his status, wondering if I would get into trouble as a result.

I appreciated his concerns, but I was more concerned about getting O'Meara to formally confess. I said there'd be more trouble if I waited for his detective sergeant to return from vacation, and the suspect decided to clam-up, or change his story.

When Sergeant White called me back saying O'Meara was due to be released in a few days, I authorized Mike to fly down to Florida to interview O'Meara. He was accompanied by MDNRP Corporal Dennis Leland. Corporal Leland was the original case investigator. I notified my major of my decision. Of course there was no joy to be had.

That afternoon, I was summonsed to BDCE Headquarters at Camp Fretterd in Reisterstown, Baltimore County. The major didn't say too much, but he delivered a message from the BDCE bureau chief, asking me who (the blank) did I think I was, making such a decision based on Sergeant White's status. I asked the major if I should've waited for Detective Sergeant Spaulding's return from vacation, or lose the opportunity to solve a three-year-old murder investigation. Nevertheless, I was told I had not heard the end of this, and I was dismissed.

When Sergeant White and Corporal Leland arrived at the correctional facility, O'Meara agreed to speak with Sergeant White without counsel, and consented to a tape-recorded interview. As I feared, O'Meara denied he had any knowledge of Ms. Manni, or even being in the area at the time of her death.

Using deception, Sergeant White cleverly led O'Meara to believe the police discovered a copy of a written warning issued by the MDNRP. O'Meara was told the warning was written on the evening Ms. Manni was last seen. Sergeant White convinced O'Meara that the warning was placed on his boat by the police, after O'Meara had improperly moored it at a pier, near the bar where Ms. Manni was last seen.

Faced with this sudden revelation, O'Meara began to change his story about being in the area. Next, Sergeant White persuaded O'Meara to think about the spiritual implications of his lack of forthcoming. In recounting those moments with O'Meara, Sergeant White told me he and Corporal Leland even got on their knees with O'Meara to pray for guidance.

O'Meara eventually relented and confessed his involvement. He claimed that Ms. Manni fell over the side after smoking marijuana.

He said he tried to look for her, but thinks he struck her with his boat after she fell overboard. As O'Meara was due to be released in the coming days, Sergeant White telephoned the Waldorf Barrack, and requested TFC Chip Ewing prepare a district court statement of charges, in order to have an arrest warrant issued for O'Meara.

TFC Ewing then had the PCO enter the warrant into NCIC, allowing the Florida authorities to place a detainer on O'Meara. The detainer prevented O'Meara's release, until we could seek extradition proceedings. When news of Mike's efforts made the news, plenty of bows were being taken up on the "Third Floor." Predictably, no one bothered to apologize, or even acknowledge they "bled before they were cut."

Because of Sergeant White's unusual circumstances, we took into account there could be concerns over his status being called into question by the defense, during a subsequent court trial. Regardless of his status, any confession obtained in a one-on-one interrogation, could have been disputed by O'Meara. O'Meara could have easily changed his mind, and claimed he was coerced, or that his rights were violated. Corporal Leland not only acted as a witness, but as the initial investigator, he had firsthand knowledge of the case that Sergeant White didn't. They were perfectly paired as the results bear out.

On February 12, 1997, O'Meara was returned to Maryland, where he was charged with murder. O'Meara pled guilty to second-degree murder in the death of Ms. Manni, and was sentenced to 15 years in prison, thanks to "Unsolved Mysterious," the informant, and Sergeant White. That case was certainly one for the books.

Incidentally, Sergeant White was subsequently exonerated, and reinstated to full duty. In 2003, the newly elected governor publicly apologized to Sergeant White, for the manner in which he was treated by the department's previous administration during his suspension. Now retired, Mike is enjoying life after MSP.

Chapter 48
The Old "Oreo Cookie and Institutionalize Racism" Ploys

One of the very things I prided myself in was being someone with a reputation of fairness. However, there were some who still tried taking advantage of my nature. One such instance came when my newly promoted detective sergeant at Glen Burnie, created a nuisances of himself with Lieutenant Grissett. As we were guest in the barrack, we had to be mindful of just that.

Lieutenant Grissett said the detective sergeant was becoming an unwanted nuisance by involving himself in barrack affairs that didn't concern him. Ray asked if we could have a sit-down meeting with the detective sergeant. He and I met with the detective sergeant in my office.

The detective sergeant was literally seated between me and Lieutenant Grissett. Ray opened the discussions while I listened. When he was done, I asked the detective sergeant if he understood the lieutenant's position.

Trying to ease the slight tension, I assured the detective sergeant that the matter would go no further. I merely considered it as a discussion between the three of us to clear the air. Making light of the situation, I said I didn't want him to think he was sandwiched between two lieutenants like he was an "Oreo Cookie."

Let me be clear here: What I said had no inference to the detective sergeant's ethnicity. It was simply to suggest he was being squeezed in the middle between Ray and I over this matter. The fact that Ray and I are both Black, and the detective sergeant wasn't, had nothing to do with my comment. To be honest, I thought I noticed a slight reaction from Ray after the comment. But as we all ended up laughing afterwards, I thought they got the gist of my seemingly innocent comment.

The detective sergeant and I briefly spoke afterwards, and he requested permission to leave early. I felt he needed to take a breather, and as it was a Friday, I granted his request, and told him to have nice weekend. At no time did he tell me, or Lieutenant Grissett, that he was offended by my "Oreo Cookie" reference to him.

The following Monday, I was visited by the department's Fair Practice officer, Captain Edward Brown. Captain Brown advised that the detective sergeant had filed a complaint of racism against me. The detective sergeant said I referred to him as an "Oreo Cookie." "So that's why he wanted to leave early," I thought.

I recounted the situation with Captain Brown, telling him had I known I offended the detective sergeant, albeit unintended, I would have most sincerely apologized, and reported the incident to my next level of command. I understood my intent didn't matter, it was how the victim perceived what was said that counted. I had a scheduled meeting, and left the barrack for the day.

The detective sergeant and I had known each other previous to his assignment to Glen Burnie. While I was at the Valley Barrack, he was the corporal who got assaulted by a drunken football player while DJ'ing at a campus party. I also interviewed him twice as a witness, when I was in IAU.

This was the first time in my life, much less my career, that I had been accused of racism. I was certain he knew better. Regardless, this didn't excuse my comment if he took exception to it. Over the years, I came to know this detective sergeant as a conniving individual, with his own form convenient bias. Even so, I tried to embrace his presence as I did with all of my staff.

Due to the lack of office space at the barrack for BDCE personnel, I allowed the detective sergeant to temporarily share my office space. When he unlocked the door, he was startled when he realized I was sitting at my desk. You would've thought I was his best friend at that moment.

Apparently, the detective sergeant was unaware I had been notified of his complaint. He wanted to know how I was doing. I responded not bad for a racist. He got flustered, and said he could explain. I told him if he wasn't up to his old tricks, he should've explained before going to fair practice. I advised the detective sergeant to save his explanations, because I couldn't discuss the matter while it was still under investigation.

Subsequently, I was called to the "Third Floor" to explain what I meant by "Oreo Cookie." I welcomed the chance to expose the detective sergeant's feeble attempt at turning the tables on me.

I explained that the phrase was known as a derogatory term used amongst Black people, when mocking another Black person. The term implies the person being mocked, prefers White attitudes and values to their own Black heritage. The awkward facial expressions of those in the room, told me they were unfamiliar with the meaning of the phrase.

I said that using "Oreo Cookie" in my description of the situation had nothing to do with the detective sergeant's ethnicity. I ended telling them, if I wanted use a derogatory, or racist term against the detective sergeant, it wouldn't have been that.

In the end, Fair Practice found no racist intent on my part. In hindsight, I did admit I should have used a less controversial phrase describing the detective sergeant's predicament. I was given a verbal reprimand, which I certainly appreciated. Apparently, the detective sergeant was unhappy that his little reverse racism maneuver didn't work. Predictably, his head got too big, and soon he was to tell one lie too many.

One morning, the detective sergeant telephoned me complaining that our new major had cursed at him, apparently disturbed over some issue. The detective sergeant who sounded upset, said he just got off the telephone with the major. I telephoned the major to find out why he spoke to my subordinate that way. When I told the major what the detective sergeant accused him of, the major was beside himself, and vehemently denied using profanity towards the detective sergeant.

Seeing is believing. The detective sergeant's attempt to turn the tables on the major, convinced him who was the problem. The new bureau chief and major, had the "Town Liar" transferred to another division. Even after being hoisted on his own petard, the detective sergeant just couldn't leave without performing one last act of stupidity. He was replaced by my academy classmate and friend, Detective Sergeant Nick Plazio.

The ousted detective sergeant tried in vain to convince Detective Sergeant Plazio that he should watch his back with me, etc., etc. Not letting on he and I were friends, Detective Sergeant Plazio just listened. Detective Sergeant Plazio telephoned me, and jokingly told me about the excellent character reference I just received from his predecessor.

When I arrived at the barrack that morning to greet my new detective sergeant, he and the investigators were gathered in their office space. Obviously happy to see one other, Nick and I happily embraced. While looking directly at the surprised detective sergeant, we loudly quoted our favorite saying from the past: "We don't care!" You could just hear that narrator asking the mortified detective sergeant: "Wanna Get Away?" The detective sergeant must have really enjoyed the taste of his foot. He had just barely got it out, before sticking it in his mouth again.

Somehow the "Oreo Cookie" story got around the region. My longtime friend, the late Lieutenant Rob Garber, was never one to let an opportunity to callout someone's stupidity go unchallenged. In response to the detective sergeant's alternate reality, Rob filled a child's "Dick Tracy" character lunchbox with Oreo Cookies, and sent them to me through the barrack mail. I still have the lunch box today.

Apparently, it was the season to play the reverse-race card game. A sergeant who supervised the region's drug unit, was personally recruited, and transferred to the Executive Protection Unit. When the governor's itinerary had him traveling abroad, executive protection got the idea they should quickly recruit someone of the sergeant's ethnicity to be part of the detail's entourage.

After the assignment abroad was over, the sergeant was placed on the unit's normal shift rotations, back at the governor's mansion. Shift work apparently interfered with the sergeant's desire to further his off duty educational pursuits. The sergeant decided he wanted out of executive protection. As I mentioned earlier, if a trooper wishes to leave executive protection, the department will generally reassigned the outgoing trooper to an assignment of the trooper's choice. The sergeant requested a return to his former supervisory position in the drug unit.

When I was contacted by the executive protection commander, I advised him that the position was no longer available. As the current supervisor was doing an excellent job running the unit, I was not about to uproot him simply because the sergeant's green grass dried up. I made it clear the sergeant was welcome to return to the region, but the only opening available was in the Leonardtown Barrack's ID section. The section was under the command of the "Fabulous Redhead," Detective Sergeant Don Holloway.

In response, the sergeant authored a scathing detailed report questioning my motives. So once again, I had to report to the "Third Floor" to meet with the lieutenant colonel, and the major as well. The lieutenant colonel handed me a copy of the sergeant's report. After reading the report, I came across the part where the sergeant alleged that due to my actions, he was the victim of "institutionalized racism."

I chuckled at the notion, and they wanted to know what was funny about it. I said he's trying this race business on the wrong person. I asked them to consider why executive protection went out of their way to recruit the sergeant in the first place. I opined because the governor wanted to have a trooper of his ethnicity in his entourage, based on where they were visiting abroad.

Although my assessment made the room a little uncomfortable, I was not about to mince words. This was a serious allegation, and one I felt was based on a personal agenda, conveniently playing the "race card." I didn't accept unsubstantiated claims from Black personnel, and I wasn't about to accept it in this case either.

The sergeant never shared with me that he had a transfer request in for executive protection. When I learned he was being transferred, I was happy for him. But now that rotating shifts were cramping his off-duty pursuits, he expected me to uproot a corporal who was doing an excellent job supervising the unit, just for him. I asked why that constituted any form of racism. To further my point, I said the sergeant didn't seem to mind letting executive protection use his ethnicity when it suited him. But now I'm a racist, because I have infringed upon his "I'm-special rights," to demand his choice of assignment at someone else's expense.

In an attempt to justify his position, the sergeant said he had never worked as a "criminal investigator" before. He said his only investigative experience was as a drug investigator. I told the lieutenant colonel, as the sergeant was a former drug investigator, he should have an easier transition than others coming in with no prior investigative background. I reminded them the sergeant never worked in executive protection before, but that didn't seem to trouble him too much. I said, "I guess throwing yourself in front of a deadly threat to protect the governor, is something that came natural to the sergeant."

I assured them as long as the sergeant was willing, Detective Sergeant Holloway would teach the sergeant all he needed to know about being in CID. After that exchange, the lieutenant colonel and major finally relented. I appreciated the lieutenant colonel hearing me out, and doing what was right; not just what was politically expedient for the moment.

With few choices at his disposal, the sergeant accepted my offer, and reported to Leonardtown. I was told the sergeant settled in, and did his job accordingly. Thanks to the "Fabulous Redhead," the sergeant evidently acquired a new skill set. He could now include "criminal investigator" on his resume.

As expected, Detective Sergeant Holloway was flexible about the sergeant's off duty educational pursuits. In the end, there was no "institutionalized racism" just the sergeant's cry of foul where none existed. Happily for the sergeant, he would go on to advance in his career, and was eventually promoted to lieutenant before he retired.

A new system of operational accountability called the Geographical Management Accountability System (GMAS), had been initiated within the department. Appearing before the superintendent and the three bureau chiefs, barrack and ID commanders were questioned about enforcement activities, and other related public safety issues in their respective jurisdictions. GMAS was sometimes amusingly referred to as "Give Mitchell A Story." It was a tongue-in-cheek reference to Colonel Mitchell, who presided over the process.

With the existence of BDCE in place, the barrack commanders felt they lacked control to focus criminal investigative resources to address the issues they were being questioned about. Subsequently, an executive decision was made to return the control of the BDCE investigators assigned to the barracks, back over to the barrack commanders.

Criminal enforcement and drug operations, were separated once more. Some of BDCE's lieutenants remained in drug enforcement operations. The remaining lieutenants were transferred to other assignments. I was reassigned to FOB, and became commander of the Rockville Barrack.

Sergeant Jacobs would soon be promoted to detective sergeant. George commanded our Washington Area Vehicle Enforcement Unit (WAVE), before he retired. George moved out of state, and began a career in the private sector, marketing registration plate recognition systems ("Tag Readers").

Sergeant Whitaker (who started out her career in the MSP as a PCO, before deciding to apply to the academy) was eventually promoted to detective sergeant, and assumed commanded of the ID section at the Glen Burnie Barrack. Jackie was promoted to lieutenant before she retired. We worked together again for a third time, when I requested her transfer to the Inspection Support Services Unit. She would always joke that she couldn't get rid of me.

Detective Sergeant Plazio was later transferred to the Westminster Barrack, where he commanded the ID section. Nick was later promoted to lieutenant, and commanded the College Park Barrack before he retired. We have all remained great friends throughout these many years.

Chapter 49
Commander, Rockville Barrack "N"

In 1998, I was reassigned to the Field Operations Bureau (FOB), as commander of the Rockville Barrack in Montgomery County. Montgomery County is considered a suburb of the District of Columbia, bordering the District and Virginia. The barrack shared joint jurisdiction with the Montgomery County Police Department (MCPD). This marked my first return to uniformed duty since 1983. Being a barrack commander is an awesome responsibility. It is analogous to running your own police department within that county.

The newly promoted assistant commander was my academy classmate and friend, First Sergeant Rick Norman. In 1994, Rick worked with me at the AG's office in Baltimore. Like me, it had been years since Rick worked at a barrack. Prior to the AG's assignment, we both worked undercover. He in drugs, and I in criminal enforcement. We knew we had our work cut out for us.

There were two other of my former co-workers at Rockville as well. Corporal Scott McCauley and I were patrol partners in the lower end of the county at the Westminster Barrack. Scott was one of the patrol supervisors. Sergeant Shelly Clemens who supervised the Environmental Crimes Unit at the AG's office, was the barrack's criminal section supervisor.

Being of the same mind regarding our limitations, Rick and I agreed that the last thing to do was come in, and unnecessarily start changing things. Instead, we opened our doors to discuss concerns and best practices, with both our sworn, and civilian personnel.

Like the JFK Highway, Golden Ring, College Park, and Forestville Barracks, Rockville was referred to as a "traffic" barrack in the field. The barrack's patrol areas consisted of Interstates 495, and 270. On my very first day, the barrack investigated an accident that was nearly a catastrophe. One of our troopers was standing by his vehicle on the left shoulder, northbound on I-270. A motorist watching the trooper, suddenly slowed his vehicle in front of a car-carrier tractor-trailer.

Not wanting to rear-end the vehicle in front of him, the operator of the tractor veered onto the left shoulder, and wound up rear-ending our patrol vehicle. The impact pushed the rear of the patrol vehicle nearly up to the front seat. Thankfully the trooper saw the tractor approaching, and jumped over the medium-height barrier, onto the shoulder of southbound I-270. After I reached out to TFC Howard Hersch, making sure he was absolutely ok, TFC Hersch said, "Welcome to Rockville sir."

As you will continue to read throughout the book, the MSP is large in one sense, and a small world in another. The minute I learned I was being assigned to Rockville, I knew I may have to quickly address a personnel matter, once I got there. The corporal I investigated for his use of the "N-word" when I was assigned to IAU, was a patrol supervisor at the barrack.

It was obvious the corporal wasn't happy to see me coming, especially since I sustained the charges against him. I wanted to establish from the beginning what my expectations of him were. Meeting with his sergeant, I asked the sergeant if he was aware of his corporal's prior history with me. He said he was. I told the sergeant that was in the past, and I had no agenda against the corporal.

All I expected was that the corporal conduct himself professionally and take care of his group, I said. That was the same expectation I had of all the staff and myself. I told the sergeant that I needed his corporal to concentrate on his business, not wondering if I harbored ill feelings towards him. I ended the conversation by assuring the sergeant I wouldn't hesitate to act accordingly in addressing any negative personnel matter involving the corporal, if it became necessary.

Shortly thereafter, a speeding complaint on the corporal came across my desk. The sergeant came to me, and requested he be allowed to address the matter. Apparently the sergeant was still unsure of my intentions when it came to his corporal. I told the sergeant it was his job to address his corporal's conduct issues at that point, not mine. However, I reminded the sergeant that the corporal wanted to be a supervisor, so he was expected to act like one.

We wanted our supervisors to be positive example for the troopers. No less was accepted. It was good to witness the corporal adjust his attitude, and accept his responsibilities in short order. When you treat your people fairly, more times than not, everybody wins. The relationship between the corporal and I became genuinely congenial afterwards, and still is today in our retirement.

Rick and I quickly established that we wanted the troopers and supervisors, to take ownership of their respective responsibilities. We gave troopers the autonomy to come up with ideas to enhance public safety. The feedback we received was very positive.

One of the earlier examples of this came, when we addressed complaints about reckless drivers. During morning rush-hour traffic, the barrack would be inundated with calls from motorists complaining about reckless drivers. Studying the problem, TFC Rob Maroney, Rick and I came up with a plan that TFC Maroney dubbed, "Operation Stealth."

Using an unmarked vehicle other than the standard patrol fleet's Ford Crown Vics, the trooper assigned as the "spotter," would travel along the predesignated area of the interstate, watching for motorist who were operating recklessly. When a violation was detected, the "spotter" would radio the violator's vehicle information to a member of the "stop-team" already operating in the immediate area.

The "spotter" would continue to follow, and observe the violator's vehicle. When the violator was pulled over by a member of the "stop-team," the "spotter" would then verify that the correct vehicle had been stopped. The "stop-team's" member (a uniformed trooper), would identify the operator, and issue the appropriate citation(s), based on the "spotters" observations. Both troopers would then testify to their respective roles in the operation, at any subsequent court trial if necessary.

In preparing for the operation's kickoff, TFC Maroney, who also served as the barrack's public information contact, notified the local news affiliates, who were more than happy to witness this innovative traffic enforcement operation. The big day arrived, and there were radio and television crews in attendance. It was positively received, and went well until it started raining heavily. The operation was called off as a result.

Unfortunately, one of our newer troopers apparently didn't get the message. In his zeal to pursue a reckless driver, the trooper wound up in a departmental accident, totaling his vehicle. We were extremely fortunate that only our property was damaged, and the trooper's injuries were minor. Of course when I reported the departmental accident to the region commander, he questioned my judgement on allowing this to happen. I told the major that the mission was called off, and I had no idea someone didn't get the message.

Accepting the good and the bad is a part of a barrack commander's life. I accepted my verbal undressing from the major. Through his supervisor Corporal McCauley, the trooper was dealt with accordingly. In the future, all units would have to acknowledge the end of the operation over the radio. We all learned a lesson, and life went on.

Although our big day was somewhat tarnished, it gave the troopers a sense of pride and accomplishment. Despite the inauspicious start, the operation was eventually recognized by the superintendent, and we were awarded a "Superintendent's Salute," in recognition of the unique plan to enforce public safety on the highways of Montgomery County.

We were in the times of a new management concept. To ensure that state employees were focused on their jobs, the new gubernatorial administration employed a principle called "Managing for Results." This was a structured system of determining the measurable results of an employee's performance, while ensuring accountability for reaching established measurable goals. In my opinion, that only seemed to apply to state employees, not those politicians who were living the "Life of Riley," in Annapolis. They certainly enjoyed naming renovated buildings, and palatial meeting rooms after one another.

Instead of needed resources, and competitive pay scales on par with other police agencies (especially for our civilians), all we got were their catchy clichés. The one thing I always said about the MSP, was regardless of what hand we were dealt, we wouldn't fail to meet our mandated challenges. It's the MSP way. I attribute it to the character of our troopers, and civilians. Our friends in the state capitol knew it, and counted on it.

Things were moving along well, and I began to venture outside the barrack to meet with other law enforcement officials in the county. There was a genuine feeling of partnership, and I assured them I wanted nothing more than to continue in that vain. Although compared to county's police resources, we were minuscule, but I assured those I met that our resources were at their disposal if needed.

In the event our troopers would have to assist another officer, or need to pursue a violator off the interstate, I wanted them to get a feel for the county in close proximity to the interstates. I invited the different county district commanders to contact the barrack, so we could join them in some of their enforcement, and community activities.

One of the allied executives I met was Chief Pablo Mitchell, head of security at the Carderock U.S. Naval facility in Bethesda. Chief Mitchell came to the barrack and introduced himself. He graciously made the base's conference room available, if I needed to host an event too large for the barrack. Pablo and I developed and continued a longstanding friendship, well after he left Carderock for another law enforcement opportunity in Prince George's County.

A major concern for any barrack commander is the number of fatal accidents that occur in the barrack's jurisdiction. At that time, Rockville had a low number, due in part to the heavy volume of traffic during rush hour. We referred to our roadways as rolling parking lots. During these times, no one could go past 30 to 40 miles per hour. While it made for long hours of drive time, at least people weren't dying in accidents.

We did experience three fatalities while I was there. Two of these accidents occurred during the dark early morning hours of night patrol. One happened near the end of a ramp, when an oncoming vehicle ran into the rear of a disabled vehicle. The victim was standing outside of his vehicle looking in the trunk, when he was struck by an approaching vehicle driven by an inebriated motorist.

The second involved an individual who had just been released from the county's detention center. After walking out into the middle of I-270, he inexplicably laid down on his back, and was run over by oncoming traffic. The third involved a school-aged young man who was struck by one of our vehicles. I will elaborate on that incident at the end of Chapter 51.

Generally, as the barrack commander, you didn't initially get involved with the internal investigations on your personnel. As the final reviewer of the investigative reports, you were also responsible for disposition of the recommended penalties, or concurrences of innocence on the part of your personnel. However, there were times when complaints of a sensitive nature came to my immediate attention, when the complainant requested to speak with "Whoever is in charge." In one such case, I found myself engaged with a complainant, who accused a newly reassigned corporal of a serious act of misconduct.

One late afternoon, a motorist telephoned the barrack to complain about receiving a citation. The caller identified Corporal Mike Brady as the trooper who stopped her. I hadn't had the opportunity to greet the corporal up to that point. The caller demanded to speak to the person in charge, so she was transferred to me by the duty officer. From the start, the caller was agitated. She angrily began telling me about her objections to being issued a citation for driving in the high-occupancy lane (HOV).

I asked the complainant how many people were in the vehicle with her when she was stopped. The complainant stated she was alone. I advised her that during the hours the HOV lanes were in effect, there had be at least two people inside a vehicle in order to use the lanes. I further explained that requirement appeared on the posted signs alongside of the HOV lanes. I told the complainant that the corporal was correct in issuing her a citation. I said I was sorry, but she had no complaint about receiving a citation.

The complainant was informed that her only recourse at that point, was to request an appearance in the district court, and contest the citation before a judge if she wished. When I asked the complainant if the corporal was discourteous, she then accused Corporal Brady who is White, of calling her the "N-word" during the traffic stop. The complainant revved up her distain, and threatened to report me to the local chapter of the NAACP.

I had gathered the complainant was still driving. I told her I didn't want her to get a ticket for talking on her cell phone. I invited the complainant to come to the barrack, so a formal statement could be taken from her. I advised the complainant that this was upsetting to me, but I had to get both sides of the story first, beginning with her version of the events.

The complainant's tone changed, and she seemed very pleased with herself. I assured her that the department didn't stand for such conduct, and I would personally see to it that the appropriate measures were taken, if there was evidence to support her allegations. I told the complainant that while I was waiting for her, I'd be reviewing the corporal's in-car-camera video. She didn't comment. I told the complainant if I didn't hear the "N-word" as she alleged, I would personally see that she was charged criminally, with knowingly making a false report on the corporal.

I told the complainant to take her time, as I would be waiting. I waited for more than an hour, but she never arrived, or called to say she had been detained. I had Corporal Brady report to my office. I informed Corporal Brady of the complaint against him. The corporal immediately assured me that he absolutely did not use that word. I reassured Corporal Brady I believed him. I told him not to worry, because after my conversation with the complainant, she had no intentions of coming to this or any other barrack for that matter.

I explained to the corporal, that common sense dictated that most people wouldn't call, and complain about receiving a $25.00 citation for five minutes, and then only after giving them an opening about his conduct, suddenly remember he called them the "N-word." I told him I felt she tried bluffing me, when her complaint about the citation got her nowhere. I shared with Corporal Brady how I made believe there was an in-car video camera in his vehicle. The complainant had to think that meant the whole encounter was visually, and audibly recorded.

Corporal Brady asked what if she had called my bluff and showed up. I said, I'd have no choice but to follow procedures. I told him I knew I was taking a calculated risk, but I had faith in human nature. If she were telling the truth, she would have been here by now outraged over the use of that word, not a $25.00 citation. At that time, JFK Highway was the only barrack in the state with video cameras in their patrol vehicles.

In the end, the complainant paid the citation rather than contest it in court. I presumed my faith in what Judge Learned Hand called "The eventual supremacy of reason," convinced the complainant that filing a false report wasn't in her best interest. Corporal Brady would eventually get promoted to the rank of captain, and command the Internal Affairs Unit before he retired. How's that for irony?

Another case involved a trooper using our laser speed-detecting equipment. During the early morning hours of his night patrol, the trooper detected a vehicle traveling over the posted speed limit while working from a stationary position on I-270. The trooper effected the stop, and issued the operator a citation. Days later, the operator's sister wanted to report a case of racial profiling against the trooper.

Reportedly, her brother had been injured in a non-related matter, and was incapacitated. Acting on his behalf, she wanted to file the complaint. Her call was transferred to me by the duty officer. I asked her why she was making the complaint instead of her brother. That's when I learned of her brother's misfortune. Under those circumstances, she could certainly initiate the complaint. But unless her brother was physically unable to provide his account, we still needed to hear from him at some point. I asked was she present at the time of her brother's contact with the trooper. She said she wasn't.

To get the inquiry started, I asked her for the basis of the allegations against the trooper. She replied that her brother was singled out because he was a Black man driving a luxury vehicle, and the trooper being White was biased. That was the extent of her account. I told the complainant that I would get back to her on the matter. I obtained copies of the trooper's citations for that shift. The citations were checked for time and location of the stops, and the method used to detect the violations.

When I called the sister back, I asked her to repeat the nature of her complaint. She was given the time to state her version, as well as express her outrage over our "practiced racism." When she concluded, I asked her how at 1:00 a.m. on a low-lit roadway, about 100 feet or more away, could the trooper see who was behind the wheel of any vehicle, luxury or otherwise. I told her all the trooper saw was a vehicle coming towards him traveling over the posted speed limit. I asked her to please explain how the operator's race could be determined under those circumstances.

As there was no use of infrared night-vision equipment, the only thing the trooper saw I told her, was a vehicle entering the beam of influence on his speed-detecting equipment. That provided the trooper with probable cause to stop her brother's vehicle, and charge him accordingly. The trooper wrote several citations from that location, and they were issued to more than just Black people, I said. In the end, she nor her brother had a valid complaint. I told her the only thing my troopers profiled were violators, and they came in all races, not just those who looked like her brother.

It was our practice to ensure that those under our command understood we wanted them to be aggressive, but safe. We made it clear their enforcement activities had to be within the rules. We engaged our troopers and supervisors, to pay attention to what trends were in the public's concern, and act accordingly.

Early on, an accountability was developed between the troopers, supervisors and the command staff. As the commander, troopers and their supervisors usually follow your leadership, and established traits. They were all accountable to me and the first sergeant, but just as important, Rick and I let them know we were accountable to them as well. Unquestionably, there was a genuine good nature and respect between the command staff and the barrack personnel, especially when one of our PCOs Brian (Cousin Skiddy) Skidmore, and Sergeant Bryan Davy, were working together on late patrol.

Sometimes at the end of my shift when I called 10-8, one or the other would respond, "10-4, N-1, we'll be making that call to Waterloo in reference." That was to jokingly signify they'd be alerting the major or captain I was leaving early. They knew how tentative things were between me and my immediate upper command. It was their way of making light of the silly reality I sometimes faced. They always made me laugh when they did that; and I always appreciated them for it.

Chapter 50
Incidents on the American Legion Bridge

One morning while checking the area before going to the barrack, I responded to a call for an abandoned vehicle on the northbound side of the American Legion Bridge. The operator was seen getting out of his vehicle by a Maryland State Highway Administration (SHA) employee. Traveling southbound, the SHA employee crossed into Virginia, and returned to the bridge, only to find no sign of the operator. After contacting the barrack, the SHA employee parked his truck with its emergency amber lights activated behind the abandoned vehicle, until a trooper arrived.

When I arrived, the SHA employee explained what he saw. Initially, we thought the operator may have received a ride from a passing motorist, and driven to seek a tow truck. Due to the immediate hazard, we had to have a tow truck respond, and remove the vehicle. It was anticipated we would hear from the operator after he returned and found his vehicle missing.

After not hearing anything from the operator, we later received a telephone call from the operator's wife. The operator who resided in Virginia, was en route to his job in Baltimore County. When he failed to show, the employer contacted his home. The wife checked, and discovered that her husband hadn't taken his wallet, and other personal items that he normally would. This led us to believe that he may have jumped off the bridge. The wife couldn't offer any reason why her husband would want to end his life.

An immediate request went out to the county's emergency search and rescue service. A search of the area at the bottom of the bridge, and in the Potomac River was initiated to no avail. One of the marine searchers advised if the operator was in the river, with the current heat conditions, he'd probably surface in a few days. He had seen it before, he said. Two days later, a man's body washed up along a shore line further down river. The body was discovered by some people fishing. That part of the river geographically bordered

Maryland, Virginia and Washington D.C. As I gathered amongst the represented officials, I was the only one not trying to claim jurisdiction over the victim's body. I just stood by and listened.

The victim was bloated, and lying face down. When emergency responders pulled the victim's body towards land, his body which had become translucent, burst when exposed to the air and heat. In all of my experiences, I had never seen anything like that. In the end, it turned out to be the D.C. authorities who had jurisdiction. They were provided with our initial report. You really had to feel for the family, but now their dreadful wait was over.

Later one afternoon towards the end of my shift, I was notified by the duty officer there was a male subject standing on the bridge threatening to jump off. To complicate matters, it was minutes before we could expect the beginning of evening rush-hour traffic. First Sergeant Norman headed to the scene, while I notified regional headquarters. The scene was on the northbound side of the bridge south of the Virginia line. When I arrived, I was briefed by the first sergeant.

First Sergeant Norman was a member of the department's Hostage Recovery Team (HRT). When Rick arrived, he found a husband and wife who were U.S. Park police officers (USPP), and also HRT trained, on the scene. They were on their way home, and stopped to help what they thought was a disabled vehicle/motorist. After they determined the subject was a potential jumper, they notified 911, and began a dialogue with him. Rightly, Rick allowed the park officers to continue rather than interrupt them, and start over.

There were many other related issues that came about quickly, and had to be addressed dealing with this would-be jumper. First there was a concern on whether or not the subject possessed a weapon. If it was a firearm, that would have caused a retreat to a safer distance, and prohibit traffic from crossing either side of the bridge. This scenario would most certainly require the presence of our Special Tactical Assault Team Element (STATE) or the county's equivalent SWAT unit.

If none of the above applied, then there would be the pressure of maintaining the free flow of evening rush-hour traffic. The SHA representatives were anxious, because their superiors were breathing down their necks about the traffic conditions. If this went on longer than someone's idea of reasonable, regardless of what we had to consider, I would have to answer for it.

Secondly, there was the media coverage that insisted on having access to the scene. Then there was that who has jurisdiction thing as we shared concurrent jurisdiction with the county police. Lastly, there were demands for updates coming from my captain, who insisted I call out our STATE team, and not use the county's SWAT. Our Public Information Office (PIO), was looking for updates for news inquiries, and to update the superintendent. This was no time to be pulled in 10 different directions.

The first order of business was to ensure contact with the would-be jumper was still safe. I had First Sergeant Norman engage with the two USPP officers, while troopers stood nearby to ensure their safety. Next we had to get the necessary fire department medical, and marine units on the scene, should the subject suddenly attempt to jump.

I informed the county police this was an MSP operation, and their assistance was greatly appreciated. I requested that they contact the necessary county emergency units, and have their officers, deal with traffic on the southern side of the bridge. When the Virginia State Police arrived, I requested they do the same for the northern side leaving Virginia. Chief Pablo Mitchell came by, and kindly offered Carderock's base if I needed it for a helicopter landing. He then asked how he could help. I asked if he would assist by keeping the media at a safe distance.

The barrack radioed telling me the captain wanted me to telephone him. The captain wanted to know if I requested STATE yet. I told him not at this time. It didn't make sense knowing that it would take them time to assemble and get there, especially during the rush hour. Furthermore, I had use of the county's closer SWAT on standby, and at my disposal if necessary. As there was an ongoing dialogue, and no sign of a firearm at that time, I saw no need to delay the possibility of ending the matter with the resources on hand.

By now the two USPP officers needed to be relieved, but they had made a breakthrough with the subject. They were greatly thanked, and left the scene. First Sergeant Norman re-established a dialogue with the subject. The subject said he was thirsty. One of our troopers had a cooler with water in his vehicle. I told the trooper to wait until

I spoke to the first sergeant before making the water available to the subject.

The subject's vehicle was in the far right lane next to the solid concrete barrier overlooking the river. The front passenger door was open. The subject had been standing between the outside of the door and the bridge's barrier. By now the subject was seated sideways in the front passenger seat, apparently weary of the ordeal. After briefly conferring with First Sergeant Norman, we agreed it was time to end this. When the subject was first asked if he had any weapons, he willingly displayed a small-bladed pocket knife to the USPP officers. We were fairly sure that's all he had.

The plan was to have First Sergeant Norman carefully approach the subject with the water. When the subject reached for the water, Rick would grab his arm, and the four troopers surrounding the vehicle would quickly rush the subject, using the door to block him from possibly jumping over the barrier. The trooper with the water approached the other three troopers with the plan.

Back then the cellphones had pull up antennas. From my vantage point, once I saw the first sergeant got close to the subject, I would pull up the antenna on my cellphone. That would be the signal to rush the subject. The timing of the plan worked. The subject was overpowered, and in custody without injury to any of the troopers or himself.

What seemed like hours, only took about 50 minutes to complete, and reopen the traffic on both sides of the bridge, once we took over from the USPP officers. For all of us, especially those newer troopers, this was a real-life training experience they wouldn't soon forget. It was an example on how to best apply the use of your own resources, while engaging allied public safety resources to assist.

I knew that public acknowledgement of our actions was valued by those above me. Equally important however, is acknowledging those who assisted you. The worst mistake you can make, and will surly sever relations, is failing to acknowledge those who assisted you, no matter how little. In other words, there was plenty of credit to go around. So there was no need to exclude anyone, or take all the credit. Finally we could take a deep breath. Now came the cleanup, and the critique of dealing with this type of an incident. Not to be overlooked, was that traffic was soon back to normal, and everyone could safely go on their way.

Back at the barrack the gentleman admitted to embezzling money from the bank where he was employed. He had hoped to replace the money at some point, but an unexpected audit ensured his theft would be discovered. It seemed he was more so crying out for attention and help, rather than wanting to jump off the bridge. Sergeant Clemens obtained an emergency petition to have the gentleman evaluated at a local hospital's psychiatric ward. After his release, she assisted the Virginia authorities with their follow-up, and his extradition back to Virginia.

Hoping to receive recognition for my folks involved in the successful handling of this incident, I submitted a detailed report through my chain of command, to the Awards Review Committee (ARC). Almost a year later after I was no longer at Rockville, I inquired about my report to the ARC committee's chair. The captain told me she never saw my report. I smelled a rat at the regional level, but I couldn't prove what I suspected happened to my report.

The department authorized commanders to issue "Commander's Ribbons," that can be awarded to deserving personnel at a commander's discretion, without going through the ARC for consideration. Attempting to make up for this after the fact, I immediately requisitioned the ribbons from the Quartermaster's Division. With my personal letters of appreciation, I mailed each member involved a commander's ribbon, in recognition of their outstanding performance that day on the American Legion Bridge.

Chapter 51
Why Did Your Troopers Write So Many Citations?

In preparation for an upcoming Geographical Management Accountability System (GMAS) session, all of our regional barrack commanders met at region's headquarters at the Waterloo Barrack. This particular session followed a Labor Day holiday weekend. The superintendent was interviewed by the news media, on the department's anticipated enforcement activities taking place that holiday weekend.

Colonel Mitchell appealed for motorists to adhere to standard safety sensibilities, alerting the public that troopers would be out in full force, ensuring that public safety measures were enforced if necessary. During that weekend, Rockville troopers again employed an innovative approach to detect traffic violations. Led by TFC Rob Maroney, speeding motorist were identified, by using laser equipment from inside the bed of a borrowed SHA dump truck.

Once more, our troopers distinguished themselves when they issued a significant number of citations for traffic violations that weekend. The captain asked me what did I attribute this effort to, by my troopers. I thought the answer was very obvious. I responded by saying our troopers were there to do their job, which was to detect violations that were traditionally committed at higher levels during the holidays.

Apparently, that was not a sufficient enough explanation. So I added, "True to their commitment to the department's mission, they used their ingenuity, and acted accordingly." The captain was still not feeling my response, so facetiously I replied, "Well since the superintendent was on television warning the public troopers would be out there, they proved him right."

The captain was not amused with my response stating, "We can't say that to the colonel." I asked what was it he expected me to say. As far as I was concerned, our troopers performed exceptionally, and any superlatives should have come from the captain and the major as mine already had. There was no reason for them to be unaware that we established an environment where our troopers could excel.

It was obvious our troopers had a voice in how things were done, and morale was excellent. TFC Tom Lubinski, was recognized by the Maryland Trooper's Alumni Association as their "Trooper of the Year." TFC Howard Hersch, was lauded for saving the life of a newborn in the back of an ambulance, when he removed the umbilical cord from around the infant's neck. None of this was a secret to anyone. From "Operation Stealth," to many other positive things, the troopers were doing excellent work.

Yet there was not one word of praise from either the captain or the major, for all the good things we were doing in the time I had been there. Now they wanted me to play this game of analyzing the psychology behind why the troopers wrote a lot of citations on a holiday weekend: One notorious for its traffic safety concerns.

In November 1998, a few months before our American Legion Bridge incident, a would-be jumper tied up traffic for five hours on the Woodrow Wilson Bridge, in neighboring Prince George's County. The jurisdiction for that section of the bridge occupied by the would-be jumper, belonged to the Washington Metropolitan Police Department (WMPD). The decision to close the bridge for five hours to traffic, was on the part of the WMPD.

Despite requests from Maryland, and Virginia authorities to allow some traffic movement, WMPD authorities declined, and erred on the side of caution instead, choosing to keep the lanes closed on their section of the bridge. Notwithstanding the extenuating circumstances faced by the Forestville Barrack commander, our incident was textbook.

Yet, I heard nothing from the region's command staff regarding our success on the American Legion Bridge. Knowing the major's forte, I'm sure I would've been walking the "Green Mile" had it gone in the opposite direction; especially with the emphasis on maintaining the free flow of traffic during rush hour.

After the meeting was over, the captain requested I remain behind. In his office, the captain began the conversation by asking me if I was all right. I responded, "Of course I am." He wanted to know what were my issues regarding his question. I told him candidly, I thought the colonel was smart enough to figure out the nature of the barrack's performance. I said I was sure he'd be happy we met his expectations, rather than try and figure out the psychology behind the troopers' efforts. The captain ended the meeting.

A few days after that, I received a telephone call from Major Gary Cox, Commander of the Southern Region. Major Cox said he'd like me to command the Glen Burnie Barrack, and wanted to know if I was interested. I had a great deal of respect for the major based on my prior interactions with him. I told Major Cox I was honored he asked me, and I would be glad to command in his region. I submitted my transfer request to the Glen Burnie Barrack.

One subsequent evening while I was working a late shift, the duty officer transferred an incoming call to my office. It was my major on the line. The major began the conversation by asking me what I was doing at the barrack that time of night. I reminded the major, he wanted the region's barrack commanders to work at least one evening a week, and this was my night. The major quickly changed the subject. He then congratulated me on my transfer. A promotion/transfer list had come out that evening.

I thought to myself, "If he didn't think I was working, why did he call the barrack instead of my home." Obviously he didn't plan on telling me personally, but instead, leave it up to the duty officer to call me. The major then asked if I lived near Pikesville. I said, "Yes sir." I then asked what did that have to do with Glen Burnie. He said, I wasn't going to Glen Burnie, I was being transferred to the Superintendent's Office of Planning and Strategic Management (SOPSM), at headquarters.

The major told me that my classmate Heber Watts, had been promoted to captain. I would succeed him as the commander of staff inspection, which was under SOPSM's command. I was not going to prolong my time on the telephone with him by asking about my transfer to Glen Burnie; I recognized the familiar foul odor in the air.

When I announced to my staff that I was being transferred, a few days later, the barrack members humbled me with a luncheon in the conference/kitchen area. On and off-duty personnel attended, as did our Volunteers in Police Services (VIPS), Mr. and Mrs. Nat Greene. Chief Pablo Mitchell from Carderock Naval Base, and my high school best friend Ralph Vines also came. Ralph was an investigator with the county's home improvement commission. I couldn't have been more surprised.

But the biggest surprise came when I was told that the luncheon was organized by the corporal I investigated when I was in IAU. His thoughtfulness was a result of just being treated fairly, and given the chance to be better. The next day, I received a telephone call from Major Alan Rodbell, Assistant Chief of the Montgomery County Police. Major Rodbell said he was just told of my transfer. Major Rodbell said he wanted to thank me for my service in the county during my tenure as the barrack commander. The major invited me to lunch, and said he wanted to introduce me to their new chief, Charles Moose.

Formally the chief of Portland Oregon's Police Department, Chief Moose would subsequently gain acclaim for his tenure with the MCPD, during the D.C. sniper case. When we met for lunch, I was surprised that my major had also been invited. Naturally, he was charming, and uttered a most insincere, nose-lengthening praise for my tenure at Rockville. Before we left the restaurant, Major Rodbell presented me with a wrapped gift box. It contained an honorary MCPD officer's badge encased in Lucite. I was surprised and very grateful. It is still one of the most treasured mementos of my career.

The day before my last official day, I began clearing out my office for the arrival of the new commander, my friend and a former supervisor at the Westminster Barrack, Lieutenant Dennis Murphey. That afternoon as I was about to wrap up for the day, the duty officer came in my office to inform me about a pedestrian accident involving a young male student. The young man attended the Islamic Education Center next to the barrack. The young man had been struck by one of our vehicles, after he ran into the street, from behind the front of a transit bus.

The duty officer said the young man's injuries didn't appear to be life threatening. He said the appropriate supervision, and resources were on the scene. I was certainly grateful to hear that the young man's injuries didn't appear critical. I asked which one of our troopers was involved, and how they were doing. The duty officer advised it wasn't a barrack trooper, but the IAU sergeant who had a satellite office in the barrack. He didn't know anymore at that time.

I asked the duty officer had the proper notifications to Pikesville, and regional headquarters been made. He replied it had. About 20 minutes later, First Sergeant Livingston Banks, Commander of the Collision Reconstruction Unit, stopped by my office. First Sergeant

Banks was in his office at the College Park Barrack in Prince George's County, when he was notified of the accident.

Like me, the first sergeant was initially told the accident was not life threatening. Sadly, by the time First Sergeant Banks arrived in the area, he was informed the young man passed while being flown by one of our medic-vac helicopters to Children's Hospital in Washington, D.C. First Sergeant Banks and I responded to the scene.

When we arrived, I was met by the sergeant's commander from IAU, Captain Matt Lawrence. As required, First Sergeant Banks and his team assumed control of the scene, and the investigation. After conferring with Captain Lawrence, he informed me that Colonel Mitchell wanted someone in command to respond to the hospital, and express the department's concern to the family.

Matt said he couldn't go, because he had to remain at the scene with his investigator. By now we were joined by First Sergeant Mark Gibbons, Aviation Division. First Sergeant Gibbons was driving nearby when he heard the radio transmissions, and stopped to offer any assistance. I advised Matt my first sergeant was away in training, and the new commander wasn't officially there yet. I said I'd be willing to go.

As I hadn't been to the Children's Hospital before, First Sergeant Gibbons volunteered to show me how to get there. The whole time we were driving through rush-hour traffic, I was trying to think what I could say to the young man's family that would be enough. I wasn't sure if they even wanted to hear anything I had to say. When we were directed to where the family had gathered, I didn't want to just walk up and invade their privacy. I asked a hospital employee if he would have someone from the family speak to us.

It took a few minutes, but a gentleman who identified himself as the young man's uncle came over. He said the family didn't wish to speak to anyone at that time. I assured him it was completely understood. I explained that all we wanted to do was to sincerely express our sorrow and concern, and tell them that a complete and thorough investigation was underway. At the conclusion, we would provide a transparent explanation of the facts.

The uncle hugged us both. Seeing this, the family waived to us. Not wishing to intrude on them any longer we left. That was completely heart wrenching; but it was one of those things you were glad you did.

The following day was my last official day at the barrack. I went to say my goodbyes to the on-duty staff, and thank them again for all they did to help me while I was there. I posted a typewritten letter of thanks on the bulletin board in the main hallway. Before I headed to Pikesville, I stopped by the Islamic Education Center. I asked to speak to the center's director. I inquired if he thought it may be helpful for me to speak with any of the students about the accident involving their classmate. The gentleman agreed, and allowed me to meet with those who wanted to talk about what happened. Again, I was glad I did.

The barrack had the fortune of having a most dedicated, hard-working administrative aide named Deborah Jeffries. Ms. Jeffries was the sole administrative aide for most of my tenure, and well after I left. Although she lived several counties away, she turned down transfer opportunities that were closer to home, to stay where she was needed. Ms. Jeffries retired in 2019. Like so many of our civilian employees, she represented the very best of the MSP.

Chapter 52
The Unspoken Existence of Black Envy

I was asked to appear with my successor Lieutenant Murphey, at the next GMAS session to field questions he was unfamiliar with. I agreed, and met the regional staff at the Waterloo Barrack for the pre-GMAS preparation. After the meeting, I bumped into my former major in the hallway. This was my first time seeing him since he attended my lunch with Chief Moose and Major Rodbell. I asked him why I wasn't transferred to Glen Burnie, per my documented request. I must have caught him off guard, because he hesitated for a bit.

Gathering himself, he said I was the only lieutenant in the region he kept "F and I" material on. "F and I" material (Facts and Intricacies), is any documented information regarding your observed performance activities. In the old days before job-observation reports (MSP Form 164), were adopted, supervisors recorded written documentation on MSP Form 17s and other methods to compile information, positive, or negative about your job performance. I hadn't heard that phrase used in years. I needed go no further with the major, and said I was just curious. This time that foul odor was emanating right under my nose.

The sad truth of the matter is the major actually violated my rights as an employee. I had every right to see any documented evidence related to any alleged poor performance on my part; especially if he intended to use it against me as he evidently did.

The main purpose of any employee's job-observation report, is to help the employee improve, if there is a legitimate issue that the supervisor, or the department deems as a failure or weakness, on the part of an employee's job performance. It is not just saved for a rainy day to hammer an employee with, because you have a personal issue with them.

If the employee feels there is any bias, or inaccuracy on the part of the supervisor, the employee can factually comment in dispute, or offer extenuating circumstances in their defense. If the information is indisputable, the employee may choose to acknowledge and comment; or the employee may simply sign off without comment.

As I had no idea what the issues were, I had to believe it was my unwillingness to kowtow to his management methodology during my time in the region. Even more so recently, regarding that question about the holiday enforcement posed at the previous pre-GMAS meeting. He obviously didn't intend for me to see this dubious documentation, and just kept it handy until it suited him. The fact that he was able to perpetrate such an act against an employee's rights, is why agencies get sued.

If he was so sure he was correct in his position, then there was no legitimate reason to keep these issues from me. I'm sure he wasn't trying to spare my poor sensitive feelings. I wasn't going to address this with him any further. I knew what I was capable of. It didn't serve to work under the supervision of anyone I had no respect for, and who clearly had none for me. We had known each other since 1977. In the end, none of this came as a surprise. I knew his kind of leopard didn't change their spots.

It was commonly known the major was the heir apparent to the FOB chief's throne. At that point, I had no doubt his greasy fingerprints were all over that bit of maneuvering to oust me from FOB. That was the second time in four years a supervisor who is Black, singled me out amongst the other non-Blacks under their respective commands.

First, there was the lieutenant in CID trying to keep me from getting promoted to his rank with no official provocation. Then a major using his unconfirmed secret dossier to remove me as Rockville's Barrack commander. Opposition to diversity isn't the only form of bias some Black people have to deal with. Sometimes, it's just a simple case of…"That old Black magic."

Chapter 53
The Circle Is Now Complete

Leave it to the hand of fate to give you the chance to put your money where your mouth is. The Staff Inspection Unit was now a branch of the newly formed Superintendent's Office of Planning and Strategic Management (SOPSM), which also included the early version of the Information Technology Section. SOPSM's commanding officer was Major Doug Ward. I had never met the major, but after our initial meeting, I had a high degree of appreciation for his interpersonal skills, and an instant respect for his leadership.

Major Ward said he didn't know much about me either, but he assumed I wasn't very happy with the transfer, since it didn't come with a promotion, or by a request on my part. The major also candidly acknowledged that many considered the assignment akin to being in the "land of forgotten toys." That made me laugh. By this stage in my career, I learned it was best to be with those who wanted you, and leave the others to themselves.

What Major Ward said next is what separates excellent leaders who are motivators, from those who are designated by their ranks as leaders in name only. Major Ward basically told me I could do nothing in protest, or I could look at this as an opportunity to make changes, establishing a system that enhances the process for the good of all, and the department. It was like the major had a crystal ball, and looked back at my own history with staff inspection.

The major said it was up to me. He said I had full autonomy to get things done. He also pointed out that as I was the only lieutenant doing that particular function, I immediately separated myself from many of the other lieutenants, for promotional consideration to captain. The major only asked that I keep him informed of issues, and be mindful that we were on the superintendent's staff. I assured the major I came with no attitude issues, and quickly ventured to follow his sound advice. Once again, it seemed as though fate had a profound sense of irony when it came to shaping my career development.

In that short span between majors, I had just witnessed the difference between how not to lead, and how to lead. The major certainly wasn't a cheerleader, nor was he self-absorbed either. He spoke to me like I was intelligent enough to make the best decision, trusting in my integrity, and dedication. As I've said before, when you have a supervisor like that, you know in your heart, that you never want to let them down.

The first order of business was to acclimate myself with what exactly I was expected to do in the unit. At that time the unit consisted of myself, and my administrative aide, Lori Brewer. Ms. Brewer and I had worked together previously in IAU. Ms. Brewer had been in staff inspection under the last two commanders. Lori was very knowledgeable, and a great help getting me started. We would work together there for the next six years.

Lori and I created a new focus predicated on the unit being more of a support factor first, and when necessary, an enforcement arm of the department second. Before she retired, Lori was assigned to another one of my divisions when I became a bureau chief. Lori was a great asset to me, and the department. I'm happy to still have her as a dear friend after these many years.

When you were promoted from TFC to the rank of corporal, as a first-line supervisor your duties varied, depending on where you were assigned. A new corporal or sergeant transferred to an assignment other than FOB, may not be as involved with administrative responsibilities under the decentralized line inspection (DLI) program. Being a trooper one day, and a supervisor the next, can be daunting when it came to some DLI programs.

As a trooper, you generally didn't engage in the administrative process. So when you took over someone else's DLI program as a new corporal or sergeant, you were at the mercy of your predecessor's efforts. Fair or not, that's the way it was. Aware of this, in my opinion the best way to address this was to be a little more user friendly, so people weren't hiding mistakes, or taking defensive postures when SIU's presence was announced. I also felt whenever feasible, the department should provide the necessary resources to help correct deficiencies as soon as possible.

Some corrective measures involved proper local management oversights, while some were beyond local management's control, and required an executive redress to the problem. I felt that executive management shouldn't just turn a deaf ear to such problems, then when disaster struck, run for cover claiming plausible deniability.

The first thing Ms. Brewer and I did to become proactive, was ask the field installations what were some of their concerns we could reasonably try to address, right out of the gate. One of the issues was health related. As a normal course of business, barracks would come into possession of body fluids during the course of an investigation. In the case of the department's random drug testing program, urine samples were collected from sworn personnel.

Depending on the hour, it was not always feasible to get the evidence, or urine samples to the crime lab, or in the case of the latter, to the medical section. Some of these items were being stored in the barracks' lunchroom refrigerators, along with people's lunches and other food items. I wrote a report requesting the purchase of compact refrigerated units to store these fluids in. The units would be maintained in a secure designated location, and have a sign-in and sign-out policy in place. The refrigerated units would be accessible to supervisory personnel only; Problem solved.

The next thing I wanted to do was change the unit's name to one more user friendly. Staff Inspection became the Inspection Support Services Unit (ISSU). I wanted a name that implied we were there to help, not just find what was wrong. The unit's name would be changed back, and include the word "compliance" after my transfer years later. That was the new commander's prerogative of course.

It was going to be a challenge for just two people to keep up. I was fairly certain I would be there for a while under the current administration. So I knew we had the time to get the job done slowly but surely. Before too long, a promotional/transfer list came out. To our benefit, extra lieutenants were promoted with no immediate available assignments for them. Five were temporarily assigned to the unit. This enabled us to expand our efforts, and start going out in the field to do audits. We were able to effectively review three to four administrative programs during our audits, as a sample size of that barrack's efficiency.

Once the audit was concluded, a report would be generated detailing the installation's compliance, or uncovered deficiencies.

Any noted deficiencies would include our recommendations on how to correct the problem. The installation was provided 30 days to document, and return to ISSU an explanation, and proof of the corrections. Although this was the normal process before I was assigned, the manner in which we interacted with the audited installations was well received by the field.

When Major Ward unexpectedly retired, the newly promoted major replaced him in rank only. SOPSM was renamed the "Office of Professional Responsibility" (OPR). Like SOPSM, OPR would report directly to the superintendent's office. OPR included ISSU, IAU and the Office of Fair Practice (OFP). OFP ensured the department's conformance with state and federal discrimination laws, and administering equal employment practices. No longer under the auspicious of the superintendent's office, information technology became its own division.

On the evening of October 30, 2000, I was home watching the "Monday Night Football" game, when I received a telephone call from Lieutenant Ray Grissett. The call was the kind that gives you a sick feeling in your stomach. One of our covert drug investigators, TFC Ed Toatley had been shot while making what he believed to be a drug buy in Washington, D.C. The supposed buy actually turned out to be a rip-off by the suspect. Lieutenant Grissett was now the commander at Golden Ring Barrack in Baltimore County.

TFC Toatley's parents resided in the county, and Lieutenant Grissett was assigned to personally escort them to the Washington Hospital Center, in D.C., where he was on life support. TFC Toatley was being kept on artificial support, allowing his family time to be with him before the inevitable. Ray asked that I accompany him as I was familiar with Ed's parents. TFC Toatley's parents were taken by a trooper to the Waterloo Barrack. Ray met me at my home, and I drove us both to the barrack. We chose to take the most direct route to Washington via the Baltimore Washington Parkway, I-295.

As luck would have it, I-295, was undergoing major road construction. Although I was expected to expedite, I had to use caution. I couldn't afford to have an accident, or cause a flat tire. It was difficult to imagine what Mr. and Mrs. Toatley were feeling silently sitting in the backseat, knowing their world had suddenly been shattered.

When we finally arrived at the hospital, it was a madhouse. Ray and I had to push through the throng of law enforcement officers, and others who had come out of respect. We led the Toatleys to the area where Colonel Mitchell was standing by to greet them privately, before accompanying them to say goodbye to their son, and our fallen brother.

Thanks to a cooperative effort by the MSP, FBI, U.S. Marshals and the NYPD, the suspect Kofi Orleans Lindsey was apprehended two weeks later in Brooklyn, New York. Ed was an energetic, hardworking trooper, who loved working undercover. The department posthumously promoted him to corporal. In tribute to his memory, the Coalition of Black Maryland State Troopers, named an award for Ed. The "Corporal Ed Totaley Award," is given to the academy's recruit who best personifies perseverance, in overcoming personal obstacles in order to graduate from the academy. The award has recently been adopted by another concern, and presented on behalf of the "Friends of Corporal Edward Totaley."

Later in July 2001, I was promoted to Captain, and remained as the commander of ISSU. There were four other lieutenants behind me on the list, promoted to captain as well. In confidence, I was told when the assignments for those being promoted to captain was under discussion, my name was being tossed around like a hot potato.

The main person tossing of course was the new FOB chief: Yes, that would be the former major I had when I was the commander at the Rockville Barrack. I thought it was rather funny myself. I couldn't be skipped over, and I was more than happy to remain as commander of ISSU. So in the end, it all worked out for everybody.

During the year, the state experienced a significant public safety concern over the threat of Anthrax laced letters being mailed to different government locations. One particular day, there was a purported threat of a likely Anthrax attack in Baltimore City. The attack was to occur at a specified time. The city police announced they were hosting an emergency conference to develop a strategy in response. Executives representing the surrounding public safety agencies were invited to participate in the conference. Any related emergency in the city, could have similar consequences in the surrounding jurisdictions as well. I received a message to report to the "Third Floor," and meet the FOB chief in the conference room.

When I met with the lieutenant colonel, he informed me of the purported Anthrax threat. He said the MSP would participate with other agencies at Baltimore City Police Headquarters. There the alleged threat would be monitored, while an action plan was developed, and implemented if necessary. The lieutenant colonel said they were originally going to send another captain, but he opted for me. He said he wanted someone who was "level-headed, and used good judgement." When he implied I was "level-headed, and used good judgement," I sarcastically turned around to see if someone else had entered the room.

I thought to myself, "Who is he trying kid?" This was no newly redeveloped evaluation of my abilities on his part. I knew he didn't think much of that other captain, or me. So this was either a case of I was the lesser of two evils, or (and I'm being facetious), I was expendable in the event something bad happened. The lieutenant colonel stated I was to contact him immediately with any information of an actual emergency.

Pardon my cynicism, but borrowing from former NFL head coach, the late Dennis Green's famous quote: "He was who I thought he was." Fortunately, the threat was apparently a hoax, or an attempt to see how the police would respond to the possibility of such a threat.

One of the most intriguing instances of irony I encountered, came when a request was forwarded to me for an audit of the in-car camera program at the JFK Highway Barrack. The in-car camera program began in June 1999. The barrack was the only one in the state with the cameras. The request came personally from the FOB chief. The JFK Highway Barrack commander, was my former lieutenant in CID, who objected to my promotional consideration, while I was assigned to the Waldorf Barrack.

Apparently disturbed over the manner in which the program was being administered, the bureau chief met with me and my assistant commander, Lieutenant Eugene Winters. The meeting took place inside the Administrative Hearing Unit's conference room, in Building "G." I only point out the location of the meeting, because of what transpired next. It reminded me of something straight out of a dramatized, high-level secret meeting, to plot someone's career demise. Lieutenant Winters and I were seated on the side of the table where the hearing officers sat during an administrative hearing.

Several minutes later, the lieutenant colonel entered the room, accompanied by his staff lieutenant. As the lieutenant colonel sat on the opposite side of the table, his lieutenant walked over to a corner of the room, and stood there as if he were a body guard. We glanced over at the lieutenant, as the lieutenant colonel settled in his seat behind the table. Before he began, the lieutenant colonel looked to his right, and then his left, as if to instinctively ensure no one could hear what he was about to say.

Leaning forward slightly, he began explaining how the barrack commander was a "pain in his ass." The lieutenant colonel said he wanted us to conduct an audit of the in-car camera program. He didn't go into any particular details, other than to say there were problems with the program.

So a request that could have been handled over the telephone, required a meeting with a bureau chief, accompanied by his staff lieutenant? What was the big secret? Perhaps the lieutenant colonel was just in the neighborhood, and decided to pop in because he missed my "level-headed" company. I tapped Gene's foot under the table as to say, "Can you believe this guy?" It was pretty apparent the lieutenant colonel wanted ISSU to hand him the barrack commander's scalp on a platter. Correcting the problem was just a bonus.

As I didn't get that dubious F and I material he said he kept on me, apparently the lieutenant colonel didn't get my memo: The one that said we weren't there for his personal attacks upon members of the department, who were no longer in his favor. After assuring the lieutenant colonel we would get started as soon as we could, they left. Gene and I remained in the room, and humorously wondered if he really thought we would be part of his dirty work.

True to his fundamental nature, when you were out of his plans, it was "curtains" for you. I had personally seen what he was capable of stooping to. Perhaps he knew how the lieutenant had earlier tried interfering with my promotional consideration, and thought I'd be willing to take this opportunity to retaliate.

Satirically, I would be refereeing a bout between two of my detractors, who were now duking it out administratively. To ensure he would win, the more powerful opponent secretly plotted a fix behind closed doors. You can't make this stuff up.

After the meeting, I telephoned the lieutenant, and informed him of the requested audit by his bureau chief. I advised him that my staff and I would be coming up there not to lambast anyone, but to help them find and fix the problem; or at least make the necessary recommendations to correct the deficiencies as required.

I also told the lieutenant that when we ended a day's audit, any uncovered issues would be discussed with him, and the program supervisor, so corrective measures could proceed. That way, by the time our report was submitted through the chain of command, their corrective measures would be in place, or at a minimum underway. However, I made it clear we required his full cooperation in order to proceed in their best interest.

The effort between my staff, and the program's supervisor to correct the noted deficiencies, and find the best practices to effectively administer the program, culminated with the audit's success. As usual, our report also acknowledged the positive efforts on the part of the barrack's staff during the audit. This turned out to be quite a learning experience for all, and justified my vision of ISSU's purpose.

Regardless of the outcome, all of this was academic for the lieutenant. Predictably he was relieved of his position as barrack commander, and reassigned to a non-FOB operational position. It appeared the shoe was on the other foot for the lieutenant. He found himself the victim of someone else's distorted sense of self-importance.

Whether the lieutenant deserved it or not, this was a continued pattern for this lieutenant colonel, when it came to the systematic reduction of Black barrack commanders under his command. It wasn't much longer after that before the lieutenant colonel retired. With my handkerchief in hand, waving briskly, I stood on that pier happily bidding him and his rowboat a fond farewell...figuratively speaking that is.

Chapter 54
Snake Oil and State Police Don't Mix

By January 2003, we had a new governor who appointed his own choice for superintendent. In the hands of this wonder drug for the ages, the department experienced its most negative existence I had witnessed during my 35 years. He was a caricature of everything the state police wasn't. A boasting windbag who would find himself in federal prison before it all was said and done. It appeared the new governor was more interested in repaying political favors, than appointing someone of unquestionable integrity.

Talk about being given the key to our town; he and his Axis partners were figuratively given the combination to our safe, and tried taking everything in it… including the safe. There were several examples of their ignominious behavior on display in the days to come. Many of their actions came to my personal attention as the commander of ISSU. So even if the following events seem like fiction, I assure you it isn't bad art imitating life.

Apparently everyone but the politicians knew this sky-rocketing police wunderkind was about to crash and burn. It never fails to end badly when you stop wearing the badge, and the badge starts wearing you. The writing was on the wall in capital letters, and it spelled he was corrupted by power. His followers considered him a big-time celebrity, and anointed him as the "Prince of the City."

Yet still mesmerized by a trumped-up reputation established by riding on the coattail of others (especially the innovated Jack Maple and his CompStat methodology), the governor dumped him on our door stoop, wrapped in all of his soon-to-be federally indicted shame. In my view, in order for him to end up on our shores in the first place, he must have sold our duped, expedient-minded politicians the deed to the Brooklyn Bridge.

Like a modern day version of the "Four Horsemen of the Apocalypse," he and his Axis partners flew in with a strategy to divide and conquer; wrongly assuming they could make us in their image. He started out by filling the heads of many impressionable young troopers with visions of uniform changes, and a vow to turn them into a bunch of hard-charging crime fighters.

Next, he would eventually empower through promotions, certain individuals he could have only known about through their associations with the new governor's election campaign efforts. Although he had the authority to do so, he promoted three lieutenants to the rank of major, skipping over all of the qualified captains but one. Then he promoted a captain to lieutenant colonel, skipping over all of the qualified majors. He obviously wanted willing followers.

Those of us who knew two of the opportunistic egomaniacs he promoted, were not surprised when they inevitably morphed into megalomaniacs. To my knowledge, in the department's history, there was one other politically motivated jump from captain to lieutenant colonel. As it was in this disastrous incarnation, that previous bit of cronyism didn't end well either.

The superintendent's private office has its own bathroom facilities. Everyone else uses the various employee bathrooms. One of his Axis partners ("AP-1") decided he too should have a bathroom installed in his office as well. I'm afraid we had to disappoint him. Private bathrooms weren't provided to Axis flunkies. Although AP-1 thought very highly of himself, he soon learned to share the bathrooms with the rest of us, or walk over to the "Third Floor," and use his boss's toilet.

If that wasn't bad enough, AP-1, who was a civilian appointee, not one with police powers, was seen walking around the compound with an automatic pistol stuffed in the waistband of his pants. When this was brought to my attention, I advised that official to tell the "Third Floor" that AP-1 either put it away, or apply for a handgun permit. If neither met his fancy, I would gladly accommodate his arrest. AP-1 also had to have more than one vehicle assigned to him. He was given a sedan, and an SUV. The SUV had to have more emergency lights installed on it, than three marked patrol vehicles combined. After his indicted boss had to step down in disgrace, AP-1 was allowed to remain on the payroll.

Predictably, one afternoon, AP-1 illegally conducted a traffic stop in Anne Arundel County. Questioning his authority, the female operator contacted the Glen Burnie Barrack, and reported AP-1 to the duty officer, Sergeant Phil Nolan. AP-1 now faced being prosecuted for impersonating a police officer. In order to avoid another politically embarrassing headline, for the governor's sake, the department allowed AP-1 to resign instead of charging him criminally.

Another one of these partners "AP-2," approached one of our civilian officials about the existence of an internal fund for use by the new superintendent. AP-2 was informed the superintendent's position had its own line-item in the budget for his official use only. This was the state police, and we had no secret off-line accounts for extracurricular personal expenditures.

I was summonsed over to AP-2's office one morning after they settled in. AP-2 expressed his dislike of a state policy regarding sick leave. In his opinion, in order for our employees to return to work from sick leave, they should be required to provide written medical verification after three days instead of five, as allowed by the state. AP-2 actually suggested I do something about it. Wondering why he was wasting my time, I had to decline, and inform him we couldn't arbitrarily change Maryland Law under the Department of Budget and Management, just because he didn't personally care for it.

In the aftermath of the indictment of his boss, AP-2 left quietly. I don't ever recall seeing the third partner. The only traces of his existence, were the paid for daily newspapers provided to "Third Floor" executives, that were piled outside his closed office door. Like his boss, he too would be making an appearance in the federal court system, according to news reports. 3

3 The Baltimore Sun 6/22/2004

When a trooper in his capacity as the head of a fraternal organization, publicly expressed himself in opposition to their existence, he was transferred in retaliation as an example of their demand for obedience. Then there was the time I saw a federally funded MSP cadet required to wash the new superintendent's personally owned vehicle on state time. The only reason I didn't report this misuse, was knowing them as I came to, they would have taken it out on that poor cadet. This was just a sample of things to come in our nightmare before Christmas.

This political appointee made it very clear he wasn't generally impressed with state police organizations. He even publicly opined he never thought state police were used properly. That was rather funny coming from someone who had to rely on a political favor to even wear a troopers' uniform. It was too bad the bridge leading back to where he came from, was blown to smithereens by the mayor who sent him packing. We would've gladly sent his traveling elixir show back to all of his adoring fans.

In his own words at his first mega rally in our gymnasium, the new superintendent proclaimed that he wanted cops who were more concerned with arresting bad guys, rather than worrying about where pink and yellow forms went. Patrol troopers aren't generally involved in administrative duties. As it was with most of his contrived drooling efforts to denigrate our culture, that was another wasted bit of helium. Like most would-be dictators, it was apparent he enjoyed the sound of his own voice.

As for his disregard for appropriate administrative requirements, perhaps there was a method to this hailed police-savant's madness. Maybe that's how he was able to convince his former employer, that filing certain pink and yellow forms (especially fiscal ones) wasn't terribly important. Another one of his annoying so-called witticisms, was that some of our units were "boutique" in nature. As he reportedly spent a lot of time in one, it was obvious he knew a thing or two about boutiques.

Instead of substance, we got blustering slogans. One in particular was, "You'd better get on my train, or get run over by it." When he finally decided to meet with the department's commissioned officers in the old academy classroom one afternoon (our new academy was in Sykesville, Carroll County), he paraded the three bureau chiefs in front of the gathered audience. One by one, they each got up, and declared how initially they had doubts about his plans for moving forward; But now they all had their train tickets in hand, and suggested we do the same.

His worthless tenure was no enlightenment-to-greatness tour, I assure you. After all, it was his rear, not ours in the crosshairs of the federal government's sights for allegations of criminal conduct. Up to that point, the only plan I saw, was the one where they were trying to establish their iron fist methods, while figuring out what was available for the taking. As bureau chiefs serve at the pleasure of the sitting superintendent, and can be removed without cause, I guess it was either conform, or in the trunk you went for a one-way ride.

Having convinced some of the rank and file he was a cop's cop, and now with the top three executives having their train tickets stamped, he quickly moved to seat his bought and paid for syco- phants, and assorted opportunists into his inner-circle of power; One based on ruling instead of leading. That display of obedience from the bureau chiefs was designed to show those in the room, who was the boss. Now he could predictably move forward with the plotted purge of two of the bureau chiefs, whose train reservations were be- ing permanently cancelled.

The first lieutenant colonel suddenly to be removed under the "serve at the pleasure of" clause, was told rather than come to Pikesville in the waning days of their time left, to work near home until officially retired. The next lieutenant colonel to go was on sick leave, and received a telephone call from the newly installed suc- ceeding bureau chief. The lieutenant colonel was told to have all per- sonal belongings out of the office sooner than later. The third one (famous for a chameleon-like ability to change political affiliations in the blink of an eye) survived until ready to retire, and move on to another career.

With his "night of the long knives" accomplished, the prince made his way around the state sporting an expensive non-issued double breasted leather coat. A coat paid for at the taxpayers' expense. I be- lieve this was one of the uniform changes he promised to get for the troopers. Of course like any self-respecting prima-donna, he had to have his first. It is currently hanging in a closet at quartermasters, as another shameful reminder of political expediency gone wrong.

Eventually becoming wise to his confidence game, some of his once fascinated audience now with inquiring minds, began asking questions about the rumors of his impending troubles with the feder- al government. Attempting to quell these embarrassing questions, the prince conceitedly quipped: "You can indict a ham sandwich." How prophetic was that now-infamous drivel. No pun intended, but he was right on the "Grey Poupon" with that one.

To really spice up his tough guy routine in front of another audi- ence of troopers, he boasted that you weren't a real cop, until you got your head busted on some street (he named) located in the Bronx, New York. This exemplification of egomania may have titillated some of our newer inexperienced troopers, but in reality, it was nothing more than the boastings of a pompous blowhard to most veteran troopers. That's what can happen when you start believing your own press clippings, and expedient-minded politicians beat a path to your door.

Certain he had found the right people to do his bidding when he wasn't around, our hero left the department's day to day operations in the hands of those who weren't only delusional, but completely voided of common sense. During the first winter days it snowed, the newly promoted FOB bureau chief, actually called around to the barracks demanding to know why the number of issued citations were low. One of the newly promoted majors wanted to take a subordinate's SUV because it was nicer than his. As Lord Acton said, "Power tends to corrupt, and absolute power corrupts absolutely."

Fed up with this buffoonery, on my own time, I wrote and signed an open letter which circulated around the department, denouncing those particular individuals who forgot how to be troopers (if they ever really knew how). Incensed over my comments, one of the subjects who was not spared (my old friend, the "Town Liar" from Glen Burnie), expressed there should be a reprisal for my comments. I sent word that if the truth hurts, then those responsible needed to start acting like state troopers, not storm troopers.

It was getting to the point that all the promises were becoming a fading memory, and the foundations of their little fiefdom began showing signs of wear. There were no boots and breeches, no leather coats, no overhauling of the department in his self-glorified image; just plenty of his putrid lip service. By now, the prince's bare keister began glowing like a hot coal in the dark. Even some of the on-the-fringe upper-echelon followers, began grumbling negatively about this sham of an administration. One afternoon, three majors suddenly found themselves demoted for this sign of defiance. With his minions firmly entrenched, they were prepared to give those of us they didn't tolerate, a "fresh one" across the face if necessary. Not surprisingly, morale became dismal.

One morning, several people passing by the executive building, noticed there was damage to the front of the superintendent's assigned Dodge Durango SUV, parked in his designated space. Subsequently, rumors began spreading that the damage resulted from his operating the vehicle while under the influence. This allegation made its way to Annapolis, and the governor's office. Unbeknownst to me, the governor's legal counsel summonsed the commander of IAU (who was one of my subordinates) to his office in Annapolis.

Lieutenant Eric Danz, was personally assigned to investigate the allegation. Lieutenant Danz was under strict orders not to disclose his involvement, or anything about the investigation with anyone, including his supervisor, until the matter was concluded. Lieutenant Danz's investigation found that the superintendent failed to comply with the department's rules and regulations, pertaining to damaging an agency vehicle. Secondly, he failed to report the damage through the proper channels, pursuant to departmental policy. There was no evidence to support the allegations of DUI.

Subsequently, Lieutenant Danz was called to the "Third Floor," and lambasted by the recently installed FOB bureau chief, for having the audacity to sustain charges against the superintendent. Later that evening, I received a page from Lieutenant Danz, asking me to call him. Jokingly, Eric began the conversation telling me he was in the trunk of the superintendent's vehicle being taken to some unknown location. Speaking seriously afterwards, he told me he had been transferred. Surprised, I asked if he got promoted.

He said, "No."

I said, "I didn't know you wanted a transfer out of IAU."

Lieutenant Danz said he didn't, and told me his transfer came after a meeting with the FOB chief. It was then he told me about the IAU case. Eric said he wanted to tell me, but was prohibited by the legal counsel's directive.

Meeting with Eric the next morning, I learned the entire story. I found it hard to believe that the superintendent's staff of handpicked sworn members, didn't inform him of the department's policies regarding damage to our equipment. It was probably more of the case they tried, and were ignored. In his alternative universe, the rules didn't apply to the prince. That was the final straw for me. I told Eric to leave it with me.

Later that evening, I telephoned the duty officer at executive protection in the governor's mansion. I requested to be connected to the legal counsel's office. The counsel's administrative aide answered my call. After a brief explanation of my reason for calling, she connected me with the counsel. I apologized for what may have seemed unorthodox, but assured him I was justified to do so.

Taking that at face value, he asked how he could help me. I told him I was Lieutenant Danz's immediate supervisor. Getting to the point, I asked if he was satisfied with Lieutenant Danz's investigation. The counsel said he was. I asked him if he could explain why my lieutenant was being transferred. The counsel said he didn't understand. I explained the manner in which we were normally transferred. I told him retaliation was not on the list of accepted practices.

I informed the counsel that the order had to come from the department's executive level. I said whoever was responsible, violated an existing executive order, protecting employees from reprisal in situations like this. The counsel's conversation became guarded after that. He requested I prepare, and submit a report describing the nature of my allegations, and forwarded it to his personal post office box. I told him I already had the report in hand, and would do so immediately the following day.

The next morning, I was watching the news while getting ready for work. The department's PIO was giving an interview to a news concern in front of the executive building. The PIO director stated that in reference to the removal of Lieutenant Danz as commander of IAU, the personnel action was in error, and immediately rescinded.

Later that morning, I telephoned the office of the governor's legal counsel to inform them of what I was sure they already knew. I did however thank them for their attention, even though it was all a big "misunderstanding." It was so comforting to know our friends on the "Third Floor" got the message, that putting our troopers (especially those with integrity) in the trunks of vehicles, was no longer an option.

In April 2004, my ISSU assistant commander, Lieutenant Gene Winters, retired from the department after 33 years of service. I have to absolutely acknowledge him as the one the most important troopers in my career. Although I didn't know him when he came to ISSU, right from the start we got along famously. It was like we had known each other for years. Some of our escapades still make me laugh today.

Gene wasn't all fun and laughter though. When it came to getting the audits done, no one was better. I've made many a friend over the years in the MSP, and he remains as close as any. I was honored that Gene invited me to be with him and his family on December 9, 2019, when the urns of his mother Elsie and his father retired Army

Major Earl Winters, were buried with military honors at Arlington National Cemetery in Virginia. That was really something very special to be a part of.

Chapter 55
Will No One Rid Us of This Contemptible Prince?

In December 2003, United States' Attorney for Maryland, the Honorable Thomas DiBiagio, indicted the governor's chosen one on three criminal charges.4 As usual, I was watching the early local news broadcasts while getting ready for work. There were announcements of the indictments being reported by the news anchors. I went to my office earlier than usual that morning. It was still too early for most of the employees to be there. I wanted to discuss the reports with the PIO Director, Greg Shipley.

When I got to his office, I saw several of the executive staff sitting inside the director's office. They were watching the news telecast reporting on their boss's indictment. One of them was flipping through a copy of the multi-paged bill of indictment. This wasn't a moment to gloat, but now they all seemed less cocky, and somewhat contrite... well at least for them anyway.

After the prince's conviction and eventual release from federal prison, I read an article in a local news publication reporting he was seeking a federal pardon.5 Once again, I had to ask was anyone outraged over his effrontery. Acting as a private citizen, I wrote a letter to the editor expressing my opinions in response to the article. As was his fundamental nature, this reduced to "court jester" of the airways, predictably lashed out at me using his newly acquired public forum.

4 The Baltimore Sun 12/11/2003
5 The Baltimore Examiner 1/23/09

On the morning my editorial appeared in the newspaper, I received four telephone calls from my MSP colleagues. The initial call was from my friend, retired Sergeant Joe Jenkins. Joe asked me if I was listening to that particular broadcast. Of course I had no idea what

Joe was talking about. I was out of the office conducting an internal investigation. Unbeknownst to me, my editorial had been published. Apparently it struck a nerve. I was told the former federal prisoner, was pouting over my opinions, referring to me as "Stewy," during a diatribe-filled monologue on his morning FM radio broadcast.

Our hero insinuated I was motivated to denounce his all-new brand of snake oil in my editorial, because I wasn't promoted while he was with the state police. He obviously mistook me for one of those fascinated opportunist in his legion of goons. It was even more pathetic, when he publicly acknowledged he had no idea what it was I did. All he knew of me, was that I was "Well dressed, and walked around carrying folders." I'm sorry I couldn't repay the compliment, but we knew exactly what he was doing.

After that, I received three more calls: two from retirees, Major Mike Ziegler and Lieutenant Jack Bowman, and the third from Captain Linda Stascavage. It appeared the broadcast, and my letter to the editor, became the talk of the town locally in police circles. Perhaps he should have asked me what it was I did, when it was just the two of us, on the elevator in the executive building one afternoon.

After receiving his standard "How ya doin?" instead of a salute, he stood across from me in the back of the elevator counting the money in his wallet. I couldn't wait for the elevator to reach my floor. I was fearful that one of those bulging buttons on his ridiculously tight "one-too-many-steaks suit," was going to pop off, and cause an injury.

Once their little plot against Lieutenant Danz failed, he found out exactly who I was, and what I did for the department. To quote my guy, Baltimore's own, the late great Charley Eckman: "You can go to sleep on them cherries!" Thanks to Mr. DiBiagio, I got exactly what I wanted for Christmas that year: A forced abdication, and the return of a real superintendent.

As I served under eleven superintendent's, I was no state trooper only apologist when it came to who was appointed as superintendent. However, I most certainly cared about the character of the lead person wearing our uniform, and representing the department I served. The corner office behind the glass door on the "Third Floor," is no place for a medicine show barker. To be fair, his administration was credited with forming a reincarnation of a special unit designed to detect drugs and guns. That unit is no longer in existence. When he was indicted, I read where politicians and some citizens alike came to his defense, touting the reduction of homicides in Baltimore City while he was there. It's too bad he didn't realize that was his job. Thanks to those officers who risked their lives daily to reduce those numbers of homicides, he got paid very well.

After he fired an officer for sleeping on the job, I remember he said the citizens had a right to expect more from their cops. I guess illegally using an off-line police expense account to accommodate his personal habits, is something that citizens really embrace in their cops… especially if you're the celebrated "Commish." Someone forgot to tell him getting your head busted on some street in the Bronx, wasn't the only criteria for being a "real cop." "Real cops" don't have to worry about getting their heads busted in criminal court by the federal government. Oh well, I guess that's show business.

Chapter 56
Now This Is More Like It!

Forced to move on from his compromised public servant, the governor wisely appointed the person he should have all along, retired MSP captain, Thomas E. (Tim) Hutchins. Tim Hutchins is a retired Army veteran who served our country during the Vietnam conflict. He was a command sergeant major in the Maryland Army National Guard (MANG). In 2003, while serving as an elected delegate from Southern Maryland, the governor appointed him as the Secretary of Veteran Affairs in his gubernatorial cabinet.

With the announcement of Colonel Hutchins as the new Secretary of the Department of State Police, our nightmare before Christmas was officially over. Personally speaking, I was elated. Although I didn't know the colonel when he was a captain, I knew of his reputation as a solid leader, and heard stories of his other sound qualities from First Sergeant Derek White. Derek worked under then-Captain Hutchins, as an instructor in the training academy.

The following day, Derek and I saw Colonel Hutchins briskly striding across the headquarters parking lot in our direction. We exchanged salutes, and the first sergeant introduced me. Derek fondly renewed his acquaintance with the colonel. When Colonel Hutchins smiled and said, "Gentlemen we have a lot of work to do," I knew we were in good hands now. Very quickly, I would see the colonel's unquestionable leadership abilities for myself.

Two disgruntled leftovers from the outgoing administration, also found out about Colonel Hutchins' stability in short order. Unhappy they were stripped of their ill-advised promotions, they began a futile attempt to undermine Colonel Hutchins. After their little cartoonish plot blew up in their faces, they used the remaining sediment of a political favor from their pal the governor. For their benefit, the governor whisked them off to another state law enforcement agency where they languished in self-exile, far away from those of us who could gladly do without them.

During the early part of the colonel's tenure, he reinstated the command sergeant major's rank (CSM). His choice came as no surprise, when he announced that First Sergeant White would be his selection. Command Sergeant Major White, would be the first Black member of the department to hold that rank, which was established in 1923. It was later abolished in 1970, before Colonel Hutchins reinstated it. CSM White would be the colonel's eyes and ears, serving as the senior noncommissioned officer for troopers' affairs.

CSM White was the 45th trooper in our history promoted to that esteemed rank. In 2007, the CSM's rank was abolished once more, by the subsequent incoming superintendent. Although the rank had been abolished before he retired, Derek retired with the rank of CSM in 2009. Officially, he is the last CSM in the department's history to date. After his retirement, Derek went on to become a deputy chief with the Amtrak Police Department. He retired from there in 2020.

Colonel Hutchins also appointed retired MSP captain, Jack Howard as his chief of staff. Captain Howard, a former commander of IAU, came by my office to say hello. He mentioned that the colonel wanted to know what I was looking for from his administration. I told Jack he could tell the colonel, all I wanted was to be treated like a contributing member of the department. Jack smiled and said, "Be careful what you wish for captain."

Although the outgoing regime wasn't concerned with the filing of pink and yellow forms, that didn't deter the Office of Legislative Auditors (OLA) from caring about them. On the heels of their departure, the OLA was paying us a visit. The OLA's audit placed emphases on 14 administrative deficiencies that were repeats from the previous three years.

I was toying with the idea of looking for another assignment. When I received an unexpected telephone call from Colonel Hutchins that changed everything. He told me he understood I was looking for a transfer out of ISSU. The colonel said he needed me to do him a favor. "Of course sir," was my immediate response.

Colonel Hutchins told me of the OLA's pending audits. The colonel wanted me to personally work with the auditors, ensuring that these repeat deficiencies were resolved. The colonel then told me to be ready to go with him to Annapolis, as he had been requested to appear before a legislative committee regarding those deficiencies.

That was the first personal call I ever received from a superintendent.

Standing before the gathered committee, Colonel Hutchins began his statement by acknowledging these issues were inherited, but they were his responsibility to resolve. I was seated at the table to the colonel's right. He looked over and pointed to me, telling the committee, "Captain Russell here, will be in charge of seeing these matters are resolved."

Kindly, the colonel went on to tell the committee members I was a "rising star." I responded to his compliment self-deprecatingly, saying that rising stars usually burnout, and come crashing to earth. There was a shared laughter. In response the chairman called me the "SOP-SOB." This was the first time in my career, I ever appeared before any hearing committee in Annapolis. It was clear I had my work cut out for me. Suddenly, Captain Howard's statement had a haunting realization; but I was getting what I asked for.

The first order of business was to familiarize myself with what was deficient in the eyes of the auditors. While I was in ISSU, we never dealt with the auditors. Entities like IT, the Forensic Science Division, Quartermaster's and Finance Division, were areas the unit hadn't inspected. We were primarily working with the barracks as our priority at that time. Those other entities completed the DLI process locally, and forwarded the report to their respective bureau chief's, who then sent the reports to ISSU to be placed in our master files, once they were reviewed for content.

When the OLA auditors initially met with the department, I was not included in their discussions. I contacted the audit supervisor who conducted the meeting. I requested she meet with me, as I would be working closely with their office to resolve these issues. She wasn't pleased at the thought of having to repeat herself. I politely asked her to consider that it wasn't my fault, and I didn't want to go over her head to get cooperation. Grudgingly, she agreed to meet me at Pikesville, and went over each item, including OLA's expectations to resolve them. As I was taking my notes, I could see that rising star crashing in a hurry.

As part of his plan to address the audit's findings, Colonel Hutchins brought in Larry Guderjohn, to strategically oversee coordination of the combined efforts to address the deficiencies. The colonel and Mr. Guderjohn served together in the Maryland Army

National Guard. Mr. Guderjohn, who retired from the guard at the rank of colonel, was also a Baltimore City police officer at one time.

Although I started off working with two different auditors, the OLA subsequently assigned a senior auditor named Jonathan Finglass to take over and complete the audit. With Mr. Guderjohn's whiteboard displaying the 14 deficiencies, and their phases of corrected measures (red, yellow and "Guder-green"), we began our challenging task. Thanks to Mr. Finglass's expertise, and the combined efforts of everyone involved, over the next few weeks (including weekends) we were able to move forward effecting the necessary corrections.

Early on, Mr. Finglass exhibited a high degree of professionalism, and although genuinely congenial, he was still about his business. Make no mistake about it, he stood his ground when it came to the proper means of addressing a deficiency, but he also listened to reason as well. When he felt we were right, he didn't hesitate taking his office to task about any inconsistencies in their own interpretation of a regulation. Johnathan was an example of what I was determined to establish within ISSU.

When we were finally done, many of the issues were corrected, or on the way to being corrected. We owed Jonathan a great deal of thanks. I know everyone has a different personality, and outlook on the way they go about their business, but he should have given a class on how to get the most out of your efforts by acting like a normal human being. I told him to tell his mother she should be very proud of him. That chance encounter led to an acquired friendship between us, and has lasted well after our time in state service.

With the audit behind us, I got another call from Colonel Hutchins, this time thanking me for getting the job done on my end. I told the colonel this was no one-person show. Cooperation from all the involved personnel in the department was crucial and help make it all possible.

Colonel Hutchins told me he had need of a troop commander for the southern troop. The colonel said he wanted someone he could rely on to handle things timely and correctly. He said I was his choice. Humorously, he admitted he wasn't doing me any favors. As that was the area where he lived, people didn't hesitate to call him if they weren't happy about one thing or another, he said. Favor or not, I was getting what I asked for. Mutual respect from the department's leader, and the opportunity to get things done in support of our personnel.

The southern troop consisted of Glen Burnie, Annapolis, Prince Frederick and Leonardtown Barracks, and the recently constructed LaPlata Barrack, that replaced the defunct Waldorf Barrack. The troop also had five of the department's best barrack commanders in Lieutenants Kevin Hickey, Jerry Jones, Homer Rich, Brian Cedar, and Randy Stephens. The troop also had the distinction of having some of the most qualified first sergeants: First Sergeants D.K. Jones, Livingston Banks, Ron Best, Cliff Hughes, and Roland Butler.

The southern troop also had a first time distinction. Four of the troops' five first sergeants were Black. The troop also had a female detective sergeant, Linda Lozier. This was certainly a noteworthy advancement in the department's stride for diversity and inclusion.

When news of my transfer reached the field, I received a call from First Sergeant Livingston Banks, Glen Burnie Barrack. The first sergeant was a very caring, knowledgeable and hard-working administrator. First Sergeant Banks told me of a civilian employee named Kathy Nadwadney, who was suffering from cancer, but still coming to work. However, Ms. Nadwadney required consideration at times when she didn't feel well. The other administrative civilian staff employees were rallying around Ms. Nadwadney, and gladly pitched in when she needed to step away.

There was a concern that I may have an issue with those arrangements as the incoming troop commander. Although First Sergeant Banks knew me, some of Ms. Nadwadney's supporters at the barrack didn't. I asked the first sergeant to immediately put their fears to rest, as I assured him nothing would change. I also asked him for Ms. Nawadney's telephone number, so I could personally call her, and put her mind at ease as well.

I left a message with her male companion as she was at a doctor's appointment. I was touched to receive a heartfelt note of thanks from her afterwards. I would like to think anyone in my position would do the same thing under the circumstances. Sadly, a few months later, Ms. Nawadney would succumb to her illness. At her services, First Sergeant Banks eloquently spoke of Ms. Nawadney's strength in the face of her fate. The manner in which the barrack rallied around Ms.

Nawadey when she needed it most, was not lost on those celebrating her life.

Just before the transfer became effective, I was in Glen Burnie's area on a Saturday, and stopped by the barrack. The duty officer buzzed me in, and welcomed me aboard. I noticed the PCO had on a surgical face mask. As there was always some type of problem in some of the older barracks, I thought that might be the cause of her wearing the mask. After introducing myself, I asked was she feeling all right. PCO Angie Wells, told me she was feeling under the weather. I asked if she needed to go home.

PCO Wells thanked me for my concern, saying she could manage. PCO Wells didn't want to leave the barrack without a PCO, because she was concerned for the safety of her troopers on patrol. It had been six years since I was assigned to a barrack. Although I always had the utmost respect for our civilians, this instance would turn out to be an exceptional moment for me to witness.

I told PCO Wells that I didn't know what the future held, but wherever I was in the department, if I could ever repay her dedication, not to hesitate calling upon me. More so than not, these were the types of civilians we had; unselfish, underpaid, and dedicated to the MSP. It wasn't until a few years later, I found out that PCO Wells had been fighting cancer, and was dealing with her condition at that very moment we met.

On my first day as troop commander, I was en route to the LaPlata Barrack which would be my headquarters. After hearing a radio transmission directing troopers to respond to the scene of a fatal accident, I headed there as well. Upon my arrival, I saw the results of someone else's disregard for safety. A grandmother and her teenaged granddaughter, were killed instantly when an oncoming vehicle crossed into their lane, colliding with them head on. The operator causing the accident was driving on a suspended license. He too was killed.

Colonel Hutchins was in the area, and upon hearing the call he also responded. As required, the Accident Reconstruction Unit responded.

One of the barrack's brand new troopers just out of the academy, and her Field Training Trooper (FTT), were the initial responders. I asked the new trooper if she was ok. The trooper who had prior military experience said she was fine. I told her to take a good look at the aftermath of how one violator can take the life of innocent people, who were simply driving down the road minding their own business. I said if she ever doubted the importance of doing her job well, she should always remember what she saw here today. "We can't stop everything, but never take what we do for granted," I said.

A few weeks later, I was notified that we would be receiving a first sergeant on a temporary bases at the Glen Burnie Barrack, to replace First Sergeant Banks, who was being transferred. First Sergeant Keith Runk, a veteran of the Special Tactical Assault Team Element (STATE), would be replacing the steady First Sergeant Banks. First Sergeant Runk's reputation for leadership proceeded him. Like Livingston, Keith would be a stabilizing force. With his background in tactical elements, I envisioned his experience would be a benefit when it came to addressing officer safety concerns, especially to our newer troopers.

One of our most important traditions occurs when a retired member of the department, sworn or civilian, and in some cases, a family member of an employee passes. In honor of the deceased, the department provides available resources if the family desires to have a uniformed presence at the funeral, or memorial services. As a paramilitary custom, when a retired trooper passes, we perform casket watches as well as provide police escorts to the cemetery for sworn and civilian personnel if desired.

When I was notified that retired First Sergeant Lou Saffran passed, I assigned First Sergeant Runk to liaison with the family. It was always my desire when possible to involve the most junior troopers as pallbearers. It presented a symbolic gesture of the future paying tribute to the past. I felt it was very important to teach our newer troopers the significance of honoring our past, and never forgetting the importance of this tradition.

In the days after, we received many compliments from a number of retirees, who said they felt the old traditions were fading with the newer generation of troopers. One particular public comment came from a retiree who as far as I knew, never had many good things to say about anything. I was told he actually said we made him proud. I was happy to hear that. The last thing I wanted was for the retirees to feel they had been forgotten. Not long after, First Sergeant Runk returned to the Special Operations Division. Keith was promoted to lieutenant before he retired in 2020. Like most troopers, Keith still keeps the MSP near to his heart with no apologizes. He is a dear brother, and a man after my own heart.

We were closing in on another four years, and that meant there was another governor's election looming. One afternoon, I was walking across the parking lot at Pikesville. I was approached by First Sergeant Tom McElroy. The first sergeant was the president of one of MSP's fraternal police organizations. When he suddenly asked me if it was worth it, I had no idea what Tom was referring to. He told me rumor had it, I was one of two names sent to the governor's office by Colonel Hutchins, for promotion to major.

First Sergeant McElroy said it was purported that my name killed the request. Apparently, my confidential telephone call to Annapolis in defense of Lieutenant Danz who was "mistakenly" transferred, had been revealed. I told Tom someone had to stand up to those Gestapo agents. I said, "If you can't stand up for your people when they are right, what do they need you for." I ended the conversation telling Tom if that were true, and that's the kind of governor he was, then perhaps he wouldn't be one much longer. I never inquired about the rumor. If that's what really happened, I'm sure I wasn't the first, nor would I be the last.

In January 2007, a new governor was elected. The governor appointed another former trooper as superintendent. Colonel Terrence B. Sheridan, retired from the MSP in 1995, as a lieutenant colonel. Eventually he became chief of the Baltimore County Police Department serving there for eleven years, before returning to the MSP under the new governor. I continued in my capacity as the southern troop commander, until I got a telephone call in late November from the new FOB Chief, Lieutenant Colonel Matt Lawrence.

As usual, I took my vacation towards the end of the year. Lieutenant Colonel Lawrence telephoned asking if I minded stopping by his office. It was almost history repeating itself. Many years ago, I got a telephone call from his father Captain Will Lawrence when I was assigned to SSD asking me to report to his office.

Captain Lawrence reached me at home while I was on leave. He asked if I was going to be in the area of SSD Headquarters sometime that day. I advised the captain I hadn't planned on it, but I'd be glad to stop by that afternoon. I didn't wait for the afternoon. As soon as I got dressed I headed for the office.

The whole way driving down to SSD, I'm wondering what I did wrong. I told myself the captain didn't sound angry; and he even identified himself as "Will." Perhaps the captain had an important case for me, and didn't want to discuss it over the telephone, I thought.

I was on pins and needles. When I got there the captain apologized for making me come out on my day off, but he had to administer a random urine drug test for me, as my name had come up on the list for testing. Captain Lawrence said he couldn't alert me about the test. He then said I could refuse the test. I told the captain I was so nervous, I could pee in 10 cups. I was just happy nothing was wrong.

When I arrived at his office, I told Lieutenant Colonel Lawrence that story. This time however instead of urinating in a cup, I was told that Colonel Sheridan wanted to make me an acting major. I was speechless. When Colonel Sheridan came into the office, he asked me what I thought. I told Colonel Sheridan I was honored and ready.

The colonel said he wanted to see how I handled the position first, and he would see about making it permanent at the proper time.

Colonel Sheridan then wanted to know what I was doing that coming Friday. Although I would still be on vacation, without hesitation, I responded, "Whatever you want me to do!" My first assignment was to represent him at an upcoming Pennsylvania State Police Academy graduation in Harrisburg. On February 27, 2008, Colonel Sheridan permanently promoted me to major. I would be one of the two assistant bureau chiefs responsible for the barracks.

As region commander for the eastern half of the state, I had thirteen of the 22 barracks. Major Rob Turano had the remaining nine in the western part the state. I have to say that my position was enhanced by the excellent command staff I had assigned to the region. My troop commander on the Eastern Shore, was Captain Marty Koerner. He was the ideal leader, as evidenced by the respect he earned from those he commanded. There wasn't a better troop commander in the department, or a better person to have as a friend.

In the years that followed, many of those I had the pleasure to command, moved on to top positions as bureau chiefs, chiefs in other departments, and some have been elected as county sheriffs. One of my barrack commanders who was later a captain in my troop, Jerry Jones, would become superintendent of the MSP in 2020.

One afternoon, I received a telephone call from Mr. Sam Burgess, the Communications Section's administrative officer. Mr. Burgess asked if I could help a PCO in my region, who was having trouble getting her transfer to his section navigated through the red tape. I was happy to look into the matter as I would for anyone. Accordingly, I saw that the transfer was honored. What made my effort very special, was when I learned the PCO was Ms. Angie Wells: The same PCO who refused to leave her post, despite being more ill than I could have ever imagined at the time. Ms. Wells who had bravely fought a reoccurrence of two types of cancer, would sadly succumb to her illness a few years later. I'm so happy I was able to keep my promise to her.

Effective July 1, 2008, all three of the bureau chiefs were scheduled to officially retire. On June 27, Colonel Sheridan, Majors Bill Pallozzi, Rob Turano and I, attended the retirement luncheon for Lieutenant Colonel Bob McGainey in Harford County. Near the end of the program, the colonel was notified that Prince George's County Police Corporal Richard Findley, had been struck and fatally wounded by a stolen pickup truck.

Colonel Sheridan wanted to return to Pikesville, and reach out to their chief, Melvin High. The colonel requested Bill, Rob and I respond back as well. After contacting Chief High, the colonel advised he was ready to prepare the forthcoming promotion/transfer lists. As this task was usually handled at the bureau chief's level, he designated the three of us to prepare the promotions, and transfers from the standing respective lists.

While we were sitting in the conference room, the colonel asked Major Turano to step out of the room. As Prince George's County was in Rob's region, I just thought he was giving him an update on the matter involving Corporal Findley. When Rob returned he didn't say anything. He just kept his head down, and continued focusing on our task. A few minutes later, the colonel opened the door again, and asked me to come to his office.

A few weeks prior, in anticipation of the announced en-masse retirements of the three bureau chiefs, Colonel Sheridan held interviews in his office with the department's eight majors. All the majors were being considered for the three lieutenant colonel positions.

During my scheduled interview, I jokingly told the colonel he must have thought I had a lot of nerve showing up, especially since he had just promoted me to major only five months before. The colonel said he wanted all the majors to participate in the interview process.

But now, as the colonel began talking about his need to fill the three bureau chief positions, I honestly thought he was giving me the courtesy of telling me I may be considered the next time, which was perfectly understandable. When the colonel told me I was to be his recommendation to the governor for the position as chief of the Homeland Security Investigative Bureau (HSIB) that was the last thing I expected to hear.

I thought my promotion to major was special, but this was truly a great honor. Once more, I was very grateful to Colonel Sheridan. The colonel said he had also selected Bill (who already knew) and Rob as the chiefs of the Support Services Bureau (SSB), and FOB respectively. Now I knew why Rob sat there looking the way he did.

When I returned to the conference room, again joining the other two future lieutenant colonels, we all knew our fortunes had just been changed drastically. There was an ecstatic, but quiet sense of the moment. We tempered our personal joy, in the wake of the tragic death of Corporal Findley. With the superintendent's position being number one, we would be the next three top officials in the department. Based on the seniority of our promotions to major, Bill was number two, I was number three, and Rob was number four. We continued putting the lists together, and presented it to the colonel for his final approval, before it was forwarded to Annapolis.

On June 29, the accused in Corporal Findley's death, Ronnie White, was found dead in his cell at the Prince George's County Detention Center. The medical examiner ruled the cause of death as strangulation. This gave voice to speculation, that White's death may have been perpetrated in retaliation by the police. Chief High contacted Colonel Sheridan, and requested the MSP conduct the investigation into White's death, in order to maintain the propriety of an impartial investigation. The colonel accepted, and my first duty as the acting bureau chief of HSIB, was to meet with Prince George's County police officials. Later that evening, I attend a press conference where it would be officially announced that the MSP would be investigating the case into White's death.

The lead investigator in the case was Sergeant Mike Grant, a second generation trooper. Sergeant Grant's father was the late Major Gus Grant, whose background was also in investigations. The investigation determined that the on-duty correction officer who found White (who had hung himself in his cell), failed to seek medical care for White, or notify his superiors of the emergency. The officer falsified an incident log, and a witness statement, claiming that White's body wasn't initially discovered, until after the inmates' meals were being served by another officer. Sergeant Grant's investigation found no evidence that White's death came at the hands of any county police officials.

On July 1, in front of family and friends, we received our promotions as the new bureau chiefs. For me the best part of this ceremony, was that my mother got to be there and witness it for herself. It brought back memories of the days when I telephoned her only saying I would be away on some case. My mother would always ask why I always had to be the one going on these dangerous assignments. I'd just sigh and say, "It's my job momma."

After we hung up, I knew I must be taking some years off her life with worry. But that day, she got to see the culmination of the things she taught me about responsibility, compassion for others and giving your best. I told her we came a long way from that day in 1974, when I came running home upsetting her nerves over wanting to be a state trooper. My wonderful mother passed this life on June 13, 2012.

As a lieutenant colonel, my experiences both individually and collectively could best be described as it is in the opening paragraph of Charles Dickens' novel, "A Tale of Two Cities": "It was the best of times, it was the worst of times." The worst nightmare for any police agency is reporting that one of your own has died in the line of duty. During my tenure as a bureau chief, we tragically lost four members of the MSP to on-duty deaths.

On September 8, 2008, one of our medic-vac helicopters encountering inclement weather, crash landed in a wooded area in District Heights, Prince George's County. Onboard was the pilot, retired MSP Corporal Stephen Bunker, and flight paramedic TFC Mickey Lippy. Others onboard were Emergency Medical Technician Tonya Mallard, Waldorf Volunteer Fire Department, along with patients Ashley Younger, and Jordan Wells. Of those on-board, only Ms. Wells survived the crash.

On May 21, 2010, TFC Shaft Hunter, Waterloo Barrack, was on night patrol, when he was killed after his patrol vehicle ran into the rear of a tractor-trailer rig, parked on the right shoulder of southbound I-95, in Howard County. I had the honor of escorting the medical examiner's vehicle carrying TFC Hunter's body to their office in downtown Baltimore City. As I observed the autopsy looking down from the above gallery, it was a reminder of just how fragile a life can be. It was my privilege to remain there with TFC Hunter, until a shift of troopers relieved me, and maintained watching over our fallen trooper. The ritual would continue while the family made arrangements for his final mortuary transition.

On June 11, 2010, I received an after midnight call from the headquarters duty officer, informing me that TFC Wesley Brown Forestville Barrack, was murdered while working part-time security at a local restaurant in Prince George's County. After the suspect Cyril Williams was removed for his disruptive conduct, he returned with an accomplice, and fired a handgun at TFC Brown, who was standing outside talking on his cellphone. In the next few days, the Prince George's County Police, the MSP, the Department of Parole and Probation, and several other federal and local allied agencies, exhausted every effort to locate the suspects. Thankfully, those efforts culminated in the arrest of both suspects.

During these most difficult times, we call upon the commanding officers of those who died, to rise above their own grief and emotional burdens, in support of the families and the troopers, whose own senses of reality have hit them square in the face. As a guide, the department's manuals provides us with a practical application when preparing for the ensuing services that honor our fallen heroes. What the manuals can't provide however, is having an innate sense of compassion within you.

I want to acknowledge all of our commanders who have met that challenge in the past. During my time as a bureau chief, Major Andrew McAndrew, Commander of the Aviation Command, Lieutenant Danny Truitt, Commander, Waterloo Barrack, and Lieutenant Crystal Carter, Commander, Forestville Barrack, displayed impeccable leadership, carrying the weight of those tragedies on their shoulders. Whether it was dealing with the circumstances surrounding the cause of death, the aftermath of the emotional impact on the families and our personnel, or ensuring the services were as flawless as possible, they each met the challenge in the highest traditions of the MSP.

Chapter 57
The Maryland Lottery Wasn't the Only Numbers Game
in Town

One of the more necessary evils for me in the coming days occurred once a month. The governor was a proponent of the CompStat process he imported from New York City, when he was the mayor in Baltimore City. At the state level it was referred to as StateStat. I wasn't opposed to the intended accountability factor of the proceedings. What I took exception to, was the unnecessary manner in which the governor's staff went about their business. They unquestionably thought they were very important, and we were there to serve their desires for a second term... even before they completed the first one.

The MSP is the state's repository, and disseminator of information gleaned from public safety reports, involving criminal and accident related data. The data is submitted by the police departments throughout the state. The collected criminal related information is documented by our Central Records Division (CRD), and statistically reported as required, to both state and federal agencies respectively, as part of the FBI's Uniformed Crime Reporting (UCR) program. Regarding traffic safety, CRD and the State Highway Administration (SHA), each maintain a database, derived from the statewide accident data submitted to, and approved by the MSP. This data is then used to initiate important future highway safety programs.

The governor, and some of the same people he brought with him from his previous administration in Baltimore City, oversaw the city's management of these same documents for submission to the MSP. How ironic it is, that this administration received numerous letters from us, notifying them about their failed oversight when it came to the inaccurate or untimely submission of these same forms. Sitting in a different seat, now they demanded perfection from all the contributors across the state. Their convenient lack of memory, was only exceeded by their wealth of hypocrisy. When I would hear them criticizing other jurisdictions, I remember thinking to myself, "Boy, they've got a lot of nerve!"

My first two years dealing with these StateStat staff members, was as chief of the HSIB. One of the main enforcement operations they focused in on was warrants. They felt that emphases should be placed on the apprehension of suspects wanted on outstanding warrants as a measure of reducing crime. This was certainly nothing novel on our part. As mentioned in Chapter 27, the MSP was a member of the warrant task force in Baltimore City.

The governor felt the same type of effort should be implemented in the D.C. Metro area. As required, we explored the opportunity for a consolidation of resources with the U.S. Marshal's Service in Prince George's County. There was a great benefit to working with the marshals' service. The marshals funded the operation, and deputized the other non-federal members of the task force, allowing them to arrest defendants outside of Maryland.

My chief of staff Captain Brian Cedar, conferred with his counterparts in the marshals' service, Matt Burke and his supervisor Rob Fernandez. With the full cooperation of the marshal's service, the Capitol Area Regional Task Force (CARTF) was created. As there were a number unserved violent offender warrants maintained by the county's sheriff's office, they were more than happy to provide CARTF access to those warrants.

Our two supervisors, Detective Sergeants Tom Lubinski (Baltimore), and John Vanhoy (Prince George's), were exceptional troopers, who possessed the leadership skills we trusted to get the job done, without unnecessarily risking officer safety in the process. I was very proud of the performance of both units. Apparently so was the governor.

When he was provided with the statistical data during the early stages of the marshals' task force in Prince George's County, the governor sent an email to Colonel Sheridan stating his profound approval. When the colonel shared a copy of the email with me, I did likewise with the task force. At the next StateStat session, the governor's chief of staff (COS) appeared unimpressed with the effort of our task force.

At the conclusion of my presentation, he wanted to know if that was all of the arrest they made for that period. I advised him that was more than enough in keeping with officer safety. The COS then made the mistake of sarcastically asking me what he was going to tell the governor about my answer. Opening my folder, I took out a copy of the email from the governor, and told the COS, "Why don't you tell him,"… and I began reading the email. Not expecting that response, the COS quickly interrupted me. He obviously didn't want to play that game with me anymore, and moved on to the next bureau chief.

As someone who served warrants, I knew all too well how much more dangerous it had become. Just days before appearing at a later session, an FBI agent was killed attempting to serve a warrant in Pennsylvania. In 2006, I vividly recall responding to the scene where TFC Eric Workman, had been shot while his task force attempted to serve a fugitive warrant in Baltimore County.

TFC Workman was flown by our medic-vac helicopter to the University of Maryland's Shock Trauma Center in Baltimore City. TFC Workman had a bullet lodged just two centimeters from his spine. Thankfully after three months of rehabilitation, Eric was able to return to full duty. So I was in no mood to hear insinuations my troopers could do more, from someone whose job was being a buffoonish numbers pusher in the safety of his office.

During the re-election year, we had to deal with another individual who was the succeeding COS. When they were exploring the possibilities of another stat gathering operation, I advised them we would consider the feasibility later, as it would take time to facilitate the logistics. He remarked, "We can't wait, we have to put points on the board now." I informed him that my troopers' safety was more important than his "points on the board." Arrogantly, he responded that my "rhetoric" was unwelcome.

Evidently, the COS was unaware of the lesson I learned early on playing their little games. If you agreed to comply with their suggestions, there was no going back. On the record, you were held to whatever you previously agreed to carryout. So I wasn't about to commit to anything I felt uncomfortable with, before I considered the operational ramifications. I'll say this for that village idiot of a COS, he didn't mind telling us to our faces what his true regard for us was.

Even in response to their most absurd spit-balled suggestions, when you tried your best to amicably educate them on a subject, they had to have the last word. More times than not, it was a stupid one. It was fortuitous for them to inherit us, not the other way around. Surprisingly, somehow the MSP didn't dissolve into oblivion after they were no longer in office.

Early on in their tenure, one of their chief complaints came because one of the three homicides under our investigation at that time was still open. As any responsible police official will tell you, one is too many. But they had a considerable gall to breath in our faces about that one case. It was no secret how they ran away from the 276 homicide victims in 2006, before heading south to Annapolis; and only as the "lessor of two evils," when it came to gubernatorial candidates I might add.

Condescending as they were, having to deal with them came along with the position I accepted. I didn't want to cause Colonel Sheridan grief, but I had to protect the troopers under my command from these political hacks. After my first two years as the chief of HSIB, the colonel switched bureaus between Lieutenant Colonel Pallozzi and me. Bill was chief of the Support Services Bureau (SSB). Afterwards, Bill and I sat looking at each other. He had never been an investigator, and I hadn't dealt solely with personnel, and other related administrative matters.

Although cause of the switch was never spoken, I knew I was fortunate that Colonel Sheridan only moved me to another bureau. I'm sure I put the colonel in an awkward position with the governor, due to my outspoken challenges to their disregard over officer safety. Especially, when I voiced my exception to having our troopers considered as just the means to their political "points on their board."

With my transfer to SSB, I now had overall command of the support and administrative functions in the department. One of these functions was the Licensing Division. The division's mission could become as political as you could get. I use to say it was the only division where careers were killed in the line of duty.

Guided by state and federal laws, the division conducts investigations concerning the sale, transfer, and registration of firearms and electronic listening devices. The division also regulates security guards, and private detectives and their agencies as well, just to name a few of the division's responsibilities. The division has three sections consisting of Firearm Registration, Handgun Permits, and License Services.

One of the requirements as regulators of the statutes created by the Annapolis lawmakers, was an occasional mandate to appear before committee hearings to justify our positions on the enforcement of the laws they created. One of the more controversial requirements that was a constant source of ire to the public, concerned our policies when citizens applied for a permit to legally carry an approved handgun. By statute, the applicant had to prove they had a "good and substantial reason."

Depending on your circumstances, you could easily feel you met this requirement. However, there are only a few delineated reasons that the department accepts. The legislators left it up to the department to make that determination. So naturally, when applicants who felt they met the criteria were denied, they were unhappy with us. We would then be inundated with calls, and letters from politicians taking umbrage on their constituents' behalf.

The issue as I saw it, was our right honorable friends in Annapolis knew that by leaving it up to the department to determine what qualifies as a "good and substantial reason" (instead of defining the criteria themselves), who the voters would be upset with. Of course when left up to any responsible police department's judgement, they should err on the side of caution and common sense, when deciding what constitutes valid reasons for legally carrying a concealed handgun; especially in this litigious society we live in.

At my first hearing as the new bureau chief, that and the issue of whether Maryland should accept requests to enter into an agreement of reciprocity from surrounding states, was debated. These states sought to make their handgun carry permits legal in Maryland, by accepting ours in a reciprocal agreement pact. One issue for us was that in Maryland, you are prohibited if you have been convicted of a felony. In some states, what we considered a felony, may be considered a lesser offense in those respective states.

Another issue near and dear to the hearts of our politicians, came when unhappy citizens showed up in the gallery, having previously expressed their willingness to move to another state; One with a more citizen-friendly handgun carry permit requirement. The threat of loss tax revenue got their undivided attention very quickly. The hearing would be chaired by a delegate, who I had several unrelated dealings with by telephone and letter. He was a well-known advocate, and self-interpreter of second amendment rights, as they pertained to the "right to keep and bear arms."

When I was told of the hearing, I met with Major Jack Simpson one of my assistant bureau chiefs. Major Simpson had command of the Records Command (Licensing Division, and the Central Records Division). The major selected the division's assistant commander, Lieutenant Jerry Beason, to state our positions, and answer any questions on the department's behalf.

With the delegate sitting at the table to his right, and the unhappy citizens in the audience behind him, Lieutenant Beason skillfully answered all of the questions put before him. But the one exchange that stands out to me even today, was when the delegate displayed a power point slide of an outline of a United States map on the screen. On the map, each state was colorized with one of three colors representing each state's laws regarding the issuance of handgun carry permits.

Some states were "No permits required to carry." Others were "Shall issue a permit to carry," or "May issue a permit to carry." Maryland is a "May issue permit" state. Obviously feeling Maryland should be a "Shall issue state," the delegate confidently asked Lieutenant Beason if he viewed this as a constitutional matter. Calmly, and without the slightest hesitation, Jerry responded by asking the delegate if his question was a rhetorical one.

Jerry continued by saying that if the matter was simply about the constitution, then the country would more than likely consist of the colors representing either "No permits required states" or "Shall issue states." He reminded the delegate we didn't make the laws, we only enforced them. That straight forward response was a classic, and let the air out of the room.

I wanted to stand up and cheer, but decorum prevailed. I just smiled with pride. Even the delegate had to smile awkwardly at Lieutenant Beason's response. The delegate who had just outsmarted himself, knew he had met his match. In a political environment, setting the record straight is not always welcomed by those setting the agenda. But there was no denying it this time. The delegate's attempt to control the narrative was set straight; and Lieutenant Beason saw to it personally.

Jerry would retire as the assistant commander of the Quartermaster's Division. Previously as a first sergeant, he had been the assistant commander at Forestville and Prince Frederick Barracks respectively. As a lieutenant, Jerry was an auditor assigned to the Inspection Support Services Unit, and also commanded the Waterloo Barrack. We have remained friends in our retirement. Once in a while when we hear from each other, we discuss the good old days, and resolve all the current issues facing the world. Just like old times.

Chapter 58
Et Tu… Eh Major Brute?

Just prior to my transfer from HSIB to SSB, I began having inter-personnel discord within my ranks. Simply put, my assistant bureau chief responsible for the criminal functions, felt he should be the bureau chief. As it was my nature to give my staff the autonomy to do their jobs, I treated him no differently. However in the end, that wasn't enough to earn a mutual loyalty between us.

There was an occasion, when I gave the major a directive to carryout. This directive was from Colonel Sheridan. Thinking the major had followed through, I got a rude awakening one afternoon in the colonel's office. Colonel Sheridan had just returned from out of state. Somehow he was made aware of the major's failure to carry out his order, even though I wasn't.

Colonel Sheridan asked me if the major had completed his required task. Having spoken to the major before the colonel's return, the major assured me he had followed through as required. So naturally, I told the colonel "Yes sir." When Colonel Sheridan told me that the major failed to do so, I was speechless. I told Colonel Sheridan that that wasn't possible. I said the major assured me that he had. I asked the colonel to give me the opportunity to follow up with the major, so I could get to the bottom of this.

I telephoned the major, and asked if it were true that he didn't proceed with his assignment as ordered. Although his "I didn't think it was right," attitude only exacerbated my disbelief and anger, I knew this was my responsibility. I could only imagine the ramifications to come. Before deciding what to do about the major's audacity, I had to take that long walk back up the "Green Mile" to Colonel Sheridan's office. I knew the major had a personal dislike for dealing with some of the things we had to do logistically with Baltimore City, but as long as it wasn't an issue over safety, I would tell him it was just another day at the office.

Since I was not always a happy camper when it came to accommodating an occasional harebrained decision from Annapolis, I gave the major the benefit of the doubt. Of course it didn't go well for me with the colonel; but I was determined to bring the major along without relying on drastic measures. Unfortunately, I was mistaken. I decided to have a personal meeting with the major, after a planned staff meeting at HSIB Headquarters.

Innocently enough, my staff meeting with the major, that included my chief of staff Captain Cedar, the major from Drug Enforcement, another captain, and a lieutenant, began amicably. That was until I heard what was on the lieutenant's mind.

The MSP was part of a joint Alcohol Tobacco and Firearms (ATF) operation. She and another lieutenant were overseeing different aspects of our involvement. It was known that both lieutenants took exception to some of the ATF's methods, but those matters had been previously resolved at my level.

The lieutenant started off questioning my lack of support in her favor. I had no idea what she was going on about. No matter how I tried (even backed by Captain Cedar) to convince the lieutenant she was laboring under misinformation, the lieutenant was having none of it. The lieutenant was referring to a prior meeting with ATF agents in Baltimore City. The meeting had been scheduled to discuss two recent operational concerns between their agents, she, and the other lieutenant assigned to the operation.

More so than the other lieutenant, she was the main focus of this meeting in Baltimore. Due to a traffic backup, the lieutenant was detained. After waiting for about 20 minutes, she still hadn't arrived. I knew enough about these issues to address them accordingly, so we began our discussions. I made it clear we supported the lieutenant's stated position. After a brief exchange, both sides agreed any differences were procedural, so there was room for clarifying them, without an unwillingness to continue our involvement in any future joint operations. The agents accepted our position, and everyone was prepared to move on from there without any subsequent acrimony.

As the meeting was winding down, the lieutenant finally arrived, well after the schedule starting time. She wanted to reopen the discussion, but as it was late for everyone, I wasn't going to belabor our defense of the lieutenant after the fact. That had been effectively done on her behalf, and there was no reason to revisit what had been settled. I said as much when she arrived, and told her we would have a discussion subsequently. I accompanied the lieutenant back to her vehicle in the parking garage. While we were walking, I gave her a brief synopsis of what was said, and assured her of my support for her actions.

I told the lieutenant that her concerns were addressed, and the agents understood them. I said despite the blowback, she was right to bring her concerns forward. This was more about their protocol versus ours, I said. Since this was their case, we had to be mindful of that. The lieutenant didn't appear completely satisfied. I had to balance understanding how she felt, versus having the sword of Damocles hovering over my head (in the colonel's office), if I let the lieutenant go off on those agents as she wanted to.

Somewhere between the end of the meeting with ATF, and my visit to HSIB, the lieutenant was led to believe that the agents and I had belittled her before she arrived. The lieutenant was very vehement about her accusations. I immediately knew somehow the major had his dirty hands in this. I was aware the major disagreed with not letting the lieutenant have her say, but that wasn't his call to make.

The major was present during the meeting with the agents, and knew exactly what was said. So there was no mistaking my support on behalf of both of our two lieutenants. The major had to be the person who intentionally misled her. That was the last insubordinate act I planned on tolerating from him, and this time I left no room for doubt in his little calculating mind. For the other two staff members who were unconnected to this ordeal, regrettably they were placed in an uncomfortable situation. I did apologize to them afterwards.

Once that fiasco was over, I headed back to my office. Predictably that heated exchange made its way to the "Third Floor," before I returned to Pikesville. Colonel Sheridan summonsed me to his office. I was sure he had already been given the sordid details (undoubtedly including eyewitness accounts). In a moment of counseling, Colonel Sheridan insisted that I shouldn't have addressed the major that way in front of the other staff members. I told the colonel our meeting didn't start out as a counseling for the major, but in all accounts, things got a little out of hand. Although I accepted the colonel's position, I figured there was more to come.

Instead of charging the major as I should have for his initial infraction, I tried to reason with him. I was fond of using the old wise saying: "No good deed goes unpunished." Despite seeing the major's treachery right in front of me, I elected to appeal to a better nature he obviously didn't possess. That was my mistake, and my punishment to accept.

On the heels of my verbal sparring with our StateStat benefactors, and now this internal strife in my bureau, I wasn't surprised when Colonel Sheridan announced he was switching bureaus between me and Bill Pallozzi. As I said earlier, I knew I was fortunate to maintain my position as a bureau chief. Unfortunately for the lieutenant, after my transfer, she was left unprotected. The major who she trusted more than me, personally saw that his new bureau chief had her reassigned to another bureau soon after.

The major's double-dealing also extended to the other lieutenant involved in the ATF's investigation. When Captain Cedar heard this lieutenant express his displeasure over my lack of support as well, he tried to convince the lieutenant that was not the case. Unfortunately, the lieutenant was also under the spell of the major's lies.

During the course of the ATF's operation, the lieutenant telephoned me late one evening to inform me of a decision he made based on his concern over their operational methods. After hearing his explanation, I agreed under the circumstances, he was right to hesitate committing our resources. I asked if his decision affected the safety of the operation. The lieutenant said it didn't, and he gave the agents the courtesy of explaining his decision before securing from the staging area. I was sure the agents weren't happy, but they were kept informed, and according to the lieutenant, the safety of the operation was not compromised. That was very important.

Aware the lieutenant's decision wasn't going to go away quietly, I telephoned the colonel's chief of staff, retired MSP Lieutenant Colonel Tom Coppinger. I gave him the story as related by the lieutenant, and told Tom I supported the lieutenant's decision. The next call I got was from Colonel Sheridan. To say he was not pleased is an understatement. Evidently, the colonel had been contacted by the ATF's special agent-in-charge, prior to telephoning me.

I couldn't get a word in trying to explain what I knew, before the colonel abruptly hung up on me. I jokingly told people he acted like I stood him up on a date or something. The next day, there was an impromptu meeting held in the conference room. Apparently it was not intended for me to be there. Thanks to some sort of guilty conscience I suppose, the major gave me a heads up.

In attendance at the meeting was Colonel Sheridan, COS Coppinger, the major, the lieutenant, and last but not least, one of Colonel Sheridan's civilian staff members, Kevin Davis. Mr. Davis is a retired Baltimore City police homicide detective. After the prin-ciples had their say and the facts were on the table, it the lieutenant acted in the best interest of the department after all.

Although there was no denying the lieutenant was right, the colonel still didn't seem fully convinced. That was until Kevin gave his blessings, and told Colonel Sheridan he (Kevin) would have done the same thing under the circumstances. Saints be praised! Finally, there was verification, validation, and vindication.

Having taken an earful from Colonel Sheridan for sticking up for him, I didn't understand how the lieutenant came to the conclusion I hung him out to dry. Once again, I knew the major had to be somewhere lurking in the shadows. Sometime later, the lieutenant was promoted to captain, and became the commander of the Licensing Division. It was after that, the new captain admitted to me he underestimated my support for him. He apologized for his lack of trust in me. Like that other lieutenant, he too learned their friend the major was the true Brutus in the room. I must give the major his due: He was an equal opportunity backstabber.

Because of confidentiality, I didn't describe any specific details on the ATF's investigation. I do want to make it clear, this account was no criticism of those agents or the ATF. Any lack of agreement on the part of our personnel was merely a difference of opinion, based on the levels in which both agencies operated. Once there was an open and frank discussion regarding those differences, it was back to business as usual, with no loss of genuine regard between our two agencies, or our personnel.

Chapter 59
Pay No Attention to the Shiny Man Behind the Curtain

After the 2011 governor's election results were in, it became apparent the incumbent governor got his "points on the board," and was re-elected. Later in August, Colonel Sheridan would unexpectedly retire. The colonel and I got by some tight situations, and differences of opinions. I will always appreciate him for giving me the opportunity to perform at the department's second highest level.

The colonel's announced retirement left the big question as to who was going to replace him. There was one name that quickly surfaced. Not too many people had heard the name before, but I had. What I heard about him from trusted sources wasn't at all flattering. I received a voicemail message from this same individual on my cell phone, the Sunday afternoon following Colonel Sheridan's departure. Not surprisingly, his message said he had been appointed superintendent by the governor.

The message went on to say he heard a lot about me, and was looking forward to working with me. Whatever he heard, it would soon become apparent someone forgot to mention my integrity wasn't for sale. I immediately returned his call and we spoke congenially for a few moments. As it has been stated, bureau chiefs serve at the pleasure of the superintendent. So it was nice to hear I wasn't immediately being replaced. I certainly had more than enough time to retire. Even though I was getting close to the mandatory retirement age of 60, I still loved being a trooper. I thought, "Oh well, let's see what we have here." It didn't take long to see this shiny new minted coin from the governor's hip pocket, was the latest master of the "Old Charm City Two Step," to be left on our door stoop. However, unlike his expelled 601 East Fayette Street alumnus, he didn't ascend upon us like the "Four Horsemen of the Apocalypse."

He was more subtle, and said the right things coming into a new situation initially. Attempting to negotiate his way smoothly, he came in the company of two former troopers who retired from the MSP as majors. They were two trusted allies who had worked with him in their post-MSP careers. Although it had been several years since these two majors retired, the new superintendent obviously felt they provided him with an immediate creditability, and the insight to navigate the environment, and our culture.

At the superintendent's first StateStat, the governor decided to stop by. The governor took advantage of his impromptu visit, to express his views on the lack of success by the department, regarding the recruitment of minorities. Although he used the word "minorities," the governor's subsequent comments focused in on "African Americans."

Voicing a most uninformed and irresponsible observation, the governor said our academy system "was not advantageous to African Americans." Was the governor being a champion of the under-represented African Americans of the world? Perhaps in the governor's opinion, Black people were incapable of managing the stringent methods employed to prepare troopers for their duties.

I suppose since the governor was in his domain surrounded by paid loyalist, and other state employees, he was in the habit of saying whatever he felt without fear of contradiction. Still new to the department, the superintendent sat there in vain trying to offer some response. Seated two spaces to the superintendent's right, I raised my hand to attract the superintendent's attention. As recruiting, and the academy were under my command, I wanted to respond.

When you are one of the highest ranking officials in any governmental department, there is an expected sense of decorum you must maintain in the presence of other government officials, especially the governor. I certainly didn't want my indifference towards the governor's stated position, to exceed my wish not to get off on the wrong foot with the new superintendent. However, as the only Black person in the room of about 15 people, I wanted to make my feelings clear to the governor, and set the record straight.

First, in a respectful tone, I factually explained how the governor's assessment was flawed. When he countered by trying to compare our academy system to other police academies, I told him he couldn't reasonably do so. State police have a different mission;

one that requires troopers to train differently, beyond the basic elements of those academies that allow recruits to go home at the end of their day, I said. Additionally, because our recruits come from many areas in and out of the state, it was also unreasonable, to expect us to require some people who may live several hours away, to drive back and forth during training.

Our academy is all about preparing our recruits for their future in the department, I told him. This wasn't about some antiquated tradition intended to keep "Black people" out, I said. I dared tell him that the real issue was the lack of our competitive pay scale when prospective candidates were making career choice decisions. I added that we had sought the opinion of a professional consulting firm who echoed that same sentiment.

The firm concluded they wouldn't recommend the department to its Black clients, primarily based on the pay discrepancy, when compared to the other major police departments in the state. So as far as I was concerned, it boiled down to a financial personal choice, not the governor's perceptions attributed to the restrictive nature of our academy's format.

For good measure, I informed the governor that as someone who went through both styles of academy training, I could assure him the state police knew exactly what they were doing in the field of training. Having concluded my expert position, I now addressed a personal issue. The governor whose mouth opened before his brain kicked in, unintentionally or otherwise, had just insulted Black people in my opinion.

I inferred that he apparently felt Black people were incapable of enduring the same requirements, or hardships as our counterparts from other races. After the red left his face, and returned to its normal hue, he chose not go any further. The governor ended with the last word saying, all he knew was there weren't many "African Americans" in the last academy class. With that being said, he left the room in a bit of a huff.

The MSP, and eight other state-level law enforcement agencies were represented by the State's Law Enforcement Officers Labor Alliance's (SLEOLA) Memorandum of Understanding.6 Matters involving wages, hours, and other related conditions of employment, are negotiated by designated SLEOLA members, for these nine state-level police agencies. Some of Maryland's other major city and county fraternal police employee organizations, helped negotiate contractual conditions with the benefit of "binding arbitration," in their agreements.

Once an arbitration was settled upon between the local government, and the police agency concerning their employees' salary increases, binding arbitration meant the decision was final. There was no binding arbitration agreement between SLEOLA, and the state government. We got what they gave us. Having the ability to negotiate their salary structure in good faith, certainly gave our allied agencies the leg-up in the ability to recruit qualified candidates; minority or otherwise.

When Colonel Sheridan reassigned me as the chief of SSB, I along with the director of human resources, retired MSP Major Don Lewis, ensured our recruiting section took great strides to ramp up our efforts in all available venues, trying to encourage qualified Black candidates to join the department. Through the leadership of First Sergeant Jimmy Russell, our efforts sincerely doubled. But when it came to the bottom line for some, our reputation, traditions and cultures weren't enough in today's economy.

The truth told, other state police departments across the country were also experiencing the same issues when it came to recruiting qualified Black candidates. Despite the challenges, thanks to First Sergeant Russell, and the members of our recruiting section, Sergeant Keith Phillips, TFC Crystal Miller and TFC Travis Nelson, the MSP was recognized for our overall efforts in the difficult market of recruiting minorities. Representatives from other state police departments reached out to us, inquiring about our recruiting methods used to seek qualified minority candidates.

Jimmy is a second generation MSP trooper. His father James and I met during my second year on the job. TFC James Russell sadly passed from a health related condition, while still on the department in 1984. Jimmy proudly chose to follow in his father's footsteps years later. After achieving the rank of lieutenant, Jimmy commanded the North East Barrack in Cecil County. Now a captain, he serves as the commander of our Automotive Safety Enforcement Division. Like so many others I've been privileged to mentor, he continues to personify what it means to be the type of leader who leads from the front: An effective, caring leader, who earns the respect of the people under his command, and the department.

6 SLEOLA MOU

Curiously enough, the governor's public concern about opportunities for "African Americans" in the state police, didn't quite measure up privately, when it came to the selection of troopers for his hand-picked executive protection staff. Out of the 33 total troopers from the ranks of TFC to captain, there were only three Blacks assigned to the section at that time. The only other "African American" on his protective staff, was a retired police officer from Baltimore City, he brought with him, and employed as a civilian.

The origins of the MSP began in 1921. By the time this governor was elected in 2007, and re-elected in 2011, the department was in service for 86 and 90 years respectively. We've never had a superintendent who is Black. In 1957, the department appointed its first Black sworn member, when Milton S. Taylor applied, and was accepted. It was almost 10 years before the department hired another Black applicant. Achieving the ranks of lieutenant and captain, he became the first Black commissioned officer in the MSP, before retiring in 1982. We lost a true paragon of equality, when Captain Taylor unexpectedly passed in 2016.

It was my privilege to speak at his services, thanks to his daughter Ms. Lisette Taylor. Captain Taylor's legacy is an indelible fixture in department's storied history. In his tribute, the department adopted my idea, to honor his legacy. Thanks to the blessings of the superintendent at that time Colonel Bill Pallozzi, and with the guidance of Lieutenant Colonel Dalaine Brady, the "Captain Milton S. Taylor Humanitarian Award" was developed: An award presented to a sworn member of the department, who best personifies the meaning of giving back to enrich the lives of others in their communities. The inaugural award was received by a most deserving recipient from the North East Barrack. TFC Kelly Seafeldt, was recognized for her kindness, and personal generosity to a local family in need of health and residential assistance.

I suppose as the alleged champion of "African Americans," the governor had to soothe his social conscious by denigrating our academy. He didn't stay in the room long enough to say how he planned on having more "African Americans" in executive protection, or a Black as the superintendent; or help us get a more competitive pay scale, under his tender loving care.

Later that afternoon in the "Third Floor's" conference room, the superintendent and I were engaging in conversations about the promotional system as it related to the Blacks on the department. As promotional testing was also within my command structure, I was happy to enlighten him to the facts. He wondered aloud if our testing process gave equal footing when it came to "African Americans."

The superintendent began uttering hyperbole similar to what the governor said at StateStat. I thought to myself, he and the governor obviously have no clue, so where was all of this coming from. Besides, his initials were "MLB not MLK," so I didn't need any insincere history lessons on the plight of Black people from him, or the governor.

I told the superintendent we weren't separated by race here, adding "Brown v. Board of Education" took care of that years ago. Please understand it's not that I objected to having a genuine conversation about the equal treatment of Blacks, but that business from the governor and the superintendent was just a lot of self-serving rubbish.

I politely informed the superintendent that the department provides every trooper with the same study information to help prepare them for the promotional process. The members of the testing unit knew their business, and ensured our system could withstand any challenge regarding its fair application. I told him how the unit also solicited critiques after each testing cycle. When it was viable, they acted upon any suggestions within our fiscal, or practical limitations. I said the unit's commander Captain Ken Hasenei, and his staff, Debra (Madam Director), Cogan, and Catherine (Miss Kitty) Butta, were also available to help, or discuss issues concerning any aspect of the process for anyone requesting help.

This discussion thankfully ended when I directed his attention to the 19 8x10 framed pictures of himself, and past superintendents on the wall to his right. I told him within the last 16 years, we had Black members hold every position in the department except his; and that's been for the last 90 years, I said. In 1995, beginning with the late Lieutenant Colonel Ernest Leatherbury, Sr., and including myself, there were four lieutenant colonels who were Black in the department's history.

After his retirement in 1997, Lieutenant Colonel Leatherbury served as chief of the Princess Anne Police Department, until his untimely death in 2003. He is survived by his son a second generation trooper, Lieutenant Ernest Leatherbury, Jr. Before Ernie Jr. retired, he was commander of the Salisbury Barrack. In 2016, he was appointed as the deputy superintendent of the state's Department of Natural Resources Police, thanks to a recommendation by the current lieutenant governor.

We in the upper command, were waiting to hear what direction the new superintendent had in store for the department. Soon he revealed his manifesto's three main priorities. They included creating a CompStat process within the department, and enrolling us in a system of accreditation. The third, a plan devised to justify recommending we consolidate with the Maryland Department of Transportation Authority Police (MDTAP), was nothing more than a tired old dusted off act of illusion, and deception.

After his departure from the Baltimore City Police Department, the new superintendent was named chief of the MDTAP by this same governor who had just appointed him superintendent. This certainly meant he was intimately involved in failed previous considerations, and desires by the governor to see this proposed consolidation come to fruition. The MDTAP is responsible for providing law enforcement services on MDTA highways and facilities throughout the state, in addition to providing contract services at BWI/Thurgood Marshall Airport, and at the Port of Baltimore.

In the meantime, we had a greater priority of concern. In 2008, a necessary upgrade in the department's ammunition required a change in the sidearm, the state mandated we carry. Those same used, but serviceable handguns were donated to an allied state law enforcement agency: The Maryland Capitol Police Department (MCPD). Subsequently, MCPD exchanged those handguns for a newer model, from a different manufacturer.

Once again, we were required to use the state's same choice of manufacturer to supply our replacement handguns. The manufacturer developed a totally different model, and provided them at no cost as our new sidearm. Unfortunately, these newly developed handguns would later become the source of safety concerns for the department.

By late October 2009, this prototype's lack of durability became evident. In October 2010, after being briefed regarding the reoccurring issues with this model, Colonel Sheridan responsibly directed that a detailed account of all prior, and ongoing issues with this handgun be formally documented. Meanwhile in the field, personnel began voicing frustration over the problems, and the potential risk to their safety using this handgun.

Captain Scott Wayne, Commander of the Inspection and Compliance Division (formally ISSU), was appointed to head this project. Additionally, our Legal Counsel Unit was kept abreast of the results related to the ongoing issues. At some point their opinion was sought regarding any contractual concerns that needed to be considered. In short, they opined there were no legal obligations that prohibited us from discontinuing business with the manufacturer, or keeping the weapon. As usual, the only obstacle proved to be a human one, motivated by political expediency.

Captain Wayne was also a member of the department's Special Tactical Assault Team Element (STATE). Lending his own firearms expertise, Captain Wayne prepared a comprehensive report that covered over a two-year period, documenting all aspects of testing supervised by the Training Division. The report also compiled all of the observed mechanical, and material failures attributed to this model as well. There were several meetings held between me, and the quartermaster's director retired First Sergeant Nate Beam, and our agency armorer, retired Corporal Tim Rosso. Subsequent group meetings also included Captain Wayne, and representatives from the manufacturer.

Working earnestly (try as they may), the manufacturer couldn't overcome our concerns with the model's safety, and lack of reliability. Despite the anticipated political fallout, Colonel Sheridan directed Captain Wayne and me, to meet with the manufacturer's representatives, and politely inform them of our decision to move on from their company, and our continued use of those particular handguns.

In the meantime, a focus group was convened in July 2011. The group consisted of STATE team members, the Firearms Training Unit, the Training Division, Quartermaster Division's Procurement Section, and the department's armorer. The group's purpose was to discuss, and compare several reliable police-tested handguns for consideration, as our replacement sidearm. The group reached a unanimous choice, and reported their findings to Colonel Sheridan.

When Captain Wayne learned that Chief Phil Palmere, MCPD, was able to upgrade from our donated handguns, and outfitted his department with the same new model we were now considering, he reached out to the chief. Next, understanding our general funding budget constraints, Colonel Sheridan directed our chief financial officer (CFO), Mr. John Draa, to provide funding using our forfeited asset sharing program's accumulated funds.

Through this program, property seized by law enforcement, can be forfeited, and processed through a series of civil forfeiture laws. By way of equitable sharing, a percentage of fiscal seizures can be returned, or shared with state and local law enforcement agencies. After determining the cost involved to outfit the entire department with the new handguns, and any ancillary equipment, Mr. Draa provided the necessary funding, which would go on to gain approval by the state's Board of Public Works (BPW).

Everything was moving forward, when Colonel Sheridan unexpectedly retired in August. As the colonel set the acquisition in motion, we were prepared to carry on with the approved purchase, and our plan to implement procedures for a departmental conversion to the new safer sidearm… so we thought.

Early on, I tried to engage the new superintendent about the necessity to move forward with the purchase, which now required his approval. I can only speak of my own interactions with him, but he didn't seem to be quite as concerned as his predecessor was, over our two-year odyssey with that defective handgun. Despite the detailed voluminous volumes of documentation that were available for his attention, the superintendent seemed disturbingly reluctant to get involved. This was a far cry from Colonel Sheridan, who put officer safety above all.

Instead, the superintendent seemed intent on questioning the validity of our information, when confronted with the facts. Strangely enough, the officers at the transportation authority where he just left, were no longer carrying that same model of handgun we were trying to move on from. Thanks to his predecessor Chief Gary McLhinney (who was appointed by the previous governor in 2003), the transportation authority officers were carrying the same sidearm we were trying to acquire. If the superintendent thought I was going to ignore my responsibilities to keep his favor, he was mistaken.

Moving forward with one of his own priorities (the push for consolidation), his two retired majors facilitated focus group sessions, designed for us to determine what were the advantages, and disadvantages of consolidation. One particular morning most of the commissioned officers (captains, majors and lieutenant colonels), were required to meet at the Commercial Vehicle Enforcement Division's (CVED) Headquarters in Linthicum Heights, Anne Arundel County.

Most of the rank and file, were probably vaguely aware that in November 2010, a report to the Maryland General Assembly's Senate Budget and Taxation Committee, and the House Appropriation Committee, was generated to study the feasibility of a consolidation between the MSP, and the Maryland Department of Transportation Authority Police (MDTAP). This study also explored the same feasibility of a consolidation between the MDTAP and the Maryland Department of Transportation (MDOT), and with the Maryland Transit Administration Police Department (MTAP).

The study pointed out, that as the second largest law enforcement agency in the state government (behind the MSP), the MDTAP was the only one to operate off-budget. As the MDTAP was a non-budgeted entity, the General Assembly had little oversight over their jurisdiction, policies and budget. The study which began in September 2010, concluded there were only two advantages, and seven disadvantages regarding any consolidation of the aforementioned entities.

Along with fiscal complications, some noted differences in personnel pension systems and training requirements were recognized as disadvantages, just to name a few.7 The report was prepared with the cooperation of the MSP, represented by Colonel Sheridan, state budget committee members, MDOT's Deputy Secretary, and the chief of the transportation authority police who was now the superintendent. I was not personally aware of the report's findings. I had heard talk of a study regarding consolidation though. I can't say for sure, but I believe not many in the room had an opportunity to review the report's conclusions either.

7 Maryland General Assembly's Senate Budget and Taxation Committee, and the House Appropriation Committee Report, 2010

I can say for sure the superintendent knew about the report's conclusions, because he participated in the study. Regardless, they still proceeded with this pretense telling us we were being given the chance to voice what we thought were the pros and cons. For years, there was always an occasional rumor surfacing about a combining of our resources with MDTAP. As the MSP didn't accept laterals from other police agencies, probably most troopers gave no credence to the rumors.

It was known that some of MDTAP's officers wanted take home cars, and to be considered state police without going through our academy. Speaking for myself, I was against that notion. I also knew many other troopers were against it as well. Call it what you please, that was a fact.

We were divided into groups to discuss our points of views. During the individual group discussions, our responses were written on blank easel chart pads. At the end of the allotted time, the groups regathered to evaluate our documented thoughts on the subject. After the overall review and discussion, the majority saw no benefit to the MSP.

When I asked how we were expected to provide responses to something of this nature on the fly, one of the retired majors announced that it was the superintendent's wish to give us the opportunity to come up with responses. He added that if we couldn't come up with anything ourselves, then the superintendent would gladly provide his own considerations. It was obvious they knew something the rest of us didn't. I suggested they share the "big secret" with the rest of us. Perhaps then we could counter with some informed responses, I said.

I was told that wasn't the purpose of the exercise mandated by the superintendent. Of course at that time, I was unaware of the results of that 2010 General Assembly's report; A report which took a combined high-level government committee to study. One that featured personnel and equipment resource charts, fiscal graphs, and knowledge of any legal ramifications, collected from all of the participating agencies involved.

This contrived think tank, reeked of an all new shell game appearing right before our eyes. It became obvious in short order, that this new version of an "all-knowing wizard," and his two "merry illusionist," were bent on making the department in his image, only stopping occasionally to provide a tiny glimpse behind the curtain. Fortunately, some of us in leadership roles, weren't distracted by shiny objects, or shiny people like this superintendent.

Chapter 60
Aw, C'mon Colonel

Shortly after assuming command of the SSB, I inherited an administrative matter involving the incorrect disposal of antiquated IT equipment. After my review, I prepared a report which included an explanation of how the equipment was mishandled, and a solution designed to prevent any reoccurrence. There was no pilfering involved, just administrative inefficiency. My report was not completed until just after Colonel Sheridan's unexpected retirement. Procedurally, the report would be reviewed by the superintendent for his approval, and forwarded to the Secretary for the Department of General Services' (DGS) office, officially closing the matter.

After my report was submitted to the new superintendent for his attention, one of the retired majors brought it to my office wanting to know why the superintendent had to sign it. Not understanding why a retired MSP major wouldn't know the simple answer to that obvious question, I told him Colonel Sheridan wouldn't want to come back and sign it, so it's up to your boss. I was making a facetious reference to the new superintendent, who liked referring to himself as "Boss."

For example: If you had an issue, he suggested you come to him and say, "Hey boss I need this, or hey boss I'm having an issue meeting your timeline." Since we weren't on a prison chain-gang looking for a bathroom or water break, I chose to reframe, and stuck to the more desirable paramilitary title of "colonel" or "sir."

I said to the retired major, "I inherited the problem from Lieutenant Colonel Pallozzi, and he's not signing it." I told him no one was going to hold this matter against the superintendent just walking in the door. I thought that made sense. That was until the other retired major serving as the chief of staff (COS), paid me a visit with the same question. I was told the superintendent didn't see why he had to sign the report.

I know it had been a few years since those two had been with the department, but this was more about common sense than anything else. Although I had to write the report, the superintendent's signature was required as an acknowledgement of the incident, and corrected measures to be taken, I explained. As the report had to end up with another cabinet secretary at the superintendent's level, that was the procedure, I said.

I even offered to discuss my report with the superintendent, to assure him everything was aboveboard. But the superintendent's issue was having to sign the report, because it didn't happen under his tenure. If there was a practical, or factual issue with the report, I could understand this back and forth drama.

Apparently that wasn't good enough. The superintendent called the state office complex in Baltimore City, and convinced someone at DGS, to allow me to sign the report as his "designated authority." The COS tried to justify the superintendent's reluctance to signing off on the report. No longer caring, I reminded the COS his "boss" didn't have much of a problem signing off on that dubious city retirement pension in 2005, having only 15 years of service.8 With a cheese-eating grin on his face, the COS said, "Aw, c'mon colonel."

Grinning back, I told the COS only people winking and nodding say, "Aw, c'mon," when confronted with facts. Evidently, the new superintendent never heard of the old leadership principle that says: "You can delegate authority, but you cannot delegate responsibility."

8 "Baltimore Police union sues over controversial pension deal" WBAL News 9/17/2007

On the eve of the superintendent's scheduled appearance before the Senate's confirmation hearing committee, I was contacted by retired MSP Captain Tom Williams. Tom was the department's civilian liaison for governmental affairs. He informed me that my presence at the confirmation was required by the governor's office. I jokingly asked if it was because they needed someone to serve the hors d'oeuvres afterwards. Amused by my comment Tom laughingly told me to behave myself. Later that afternoon, I passed the superintendent in the hallway. Anxiously he asked me if I was going to be at the confirmation that evening.

Pretending I didn't know what he was referring to, I asked:

"Be where sir?"

He said, "At the confirmation."

I said, "I didn't know you wanted me there."

The superintendent said, "Yes, I'd really like you to be there."

In jest, I asked if it was because they needed someone to serve the Hors d'oeuvres afterwards. The superintendent just stood there with a blank look on his face a few uneasy seconds. His expression changed when I began laughing, and told him I was just kidding with him. Looking relieved he said, "Oh man you got jokes." He may have thought so.

When I arrived at the hearing room that evening, I noticed the curious selection of myself, Lieutenant Colonel Pallozzi, (who at one time was the commander of executive protection), the COS, and last but not least, Captain Linda Stascavage (a holdover from Colonel Sheridan's executive staff). I say it was curious because two of us were Black, one was a White male, and the other a White female. I thought it was a nice ratio, but certainly not an actual representation of his entire upper-management's makeup.

Just after my arrival, Captain Williams and I met outside the meeting room. Still in a playful mood, I asked him where I could find the white serving jackets. The poor man pleaded with me not to joke around in that setting. I apologized. Ever since then, whenever Tom and I occasionally run in to each other, we still have a good laugh about that exchange.

Finally, the confirmation started. Most of the members on the committee were Black, and from Baltimore City. Glowingly, they extolled their praises upon the superintendent, noting his prior service in Baltimore City. It made me wonder how this former champion of justice in the "city that bleeds," was deemed such a powerful piece of manpower; yet his position there was purportedly in jeopardy. I began thinking how unbelievable these politicians are. These are some of the same people responsible for rubber-stamping the confirmation, of a soon-to-be indicted miscreant, as our former superintendent in 2003.

As no one asked for my opinion, it was on with the show. One particularly unhappy senator from Prince George's County, cast her lone disapproval of his affirmation. In a fit of what turned out to stem from a previous personal agenda against the department, her little tantrum was only a temporary setback. Obviously, none of her senate colleagues cared about her petty personal grievances, and the appointment became official soon after; and so that was that.

One afternoon, our CFO Mr. Draa, stopped by my office asking for my advice on a matter that he was confronted with. Mr. Draa was one of the executive staff members brought in by Colonel Sheridan, upon his return to the MSP as superintendent. I found Mr. Draa, who is a retired Baltimore City Police lieutenant, to be a man of integrity, as one should be in a position of trust.

Early on, it became evident he was a great asset to the department. Through his efforts to provide adequate, but responsible funding for needed resources, Mr. Draa showed how much he really cared about the troopers. It wasn't long before John and I became very good, and trusted friends.

Mr. Draa said he was looking for guidance on a sensitive matter. He told me he was in possession of a Form 17, with a letter attached to it. The Form 17 was slid underneath the door to his office while he was out. The Form 17 which was from the COS, simply directed Mr. Draa to "Take care of this." There was no explanation why, just the directive.

Mr. Draa explained that the attached letter was from an allied police chief, who had recently entered into a contractual agreement with the state through the Board of Public Works (BPW). The chief's department used our federally funded cadets, to pose as under aged buyers of alcoholic beverages from targeted liquor stores in his jurisdiction. This is something that the department accommodated upon request, in our effort to provide assistance to allied agencies.

The requesting agency agreed to reimburse the department, as MSP cadets' hours and salaries are compensated through federally funded highway grants. Based on the content of the letter, it appeared the chief was under the impression he was exempted from honoring payment of the contract. Evidently, somewhere between the chief signing that contract, and the arrival of the new superintendent, the chief was led to believe he was no longer obligated to his contractual agreement with the state.

Undoubtedly surprised by the billing invoice he received, the chief sent the letter to the superintendent asking for the relief he presumably expected. Now it's a well-known fact that the state won't take kindly to nonpayment of financial obligations, especially contractual ones. Although I didn't know the chief personally, I was familiar with him. I told Mr. Draa, who had also been an experienced investigator, this wasn't a hard one to figure out. I told John to give me the documents, and I would take care of it for him.

I placed a telephone call to the chief. When he returned my call, we exchanged pleasantries, and renewed our passing acquaintance. I informed the chief that I was in possession of his letter to the superintendent regarding his outstanding invoice. He went deafly quiet. I continued by asking the chief who told him he was exempted from paying it.

Measuring his words carefully, as I'm sure this was a most uncomfortable conversation, I had to be direct with the chief, to keep the conversation moving. I asked him was it the superintendent. Attempting to put his mind at ease, I explained that my inquiry was just a formality. I added there would be a need for the appropriate documentation placed in his file, in the event of a fiscal accountability audit.

Predictably, the chief uttered the "winking man's" favorite reply: "Aw, c'mon colonel!" I informed the chief that the legislative auditors were on our compound on an unrelated matter, as we spoke. I assured him that as I was once the head auditor for the department, I didn't take fiscal audits lightly. Now sure I knew the answer, again I asked the chief was it the superintendent who told him he was exempted from honoring the invoice. Finally, the chief ineluctably answered yes.

Respecting his position, I assured him that was all I required. If that's what he was told, then all was fine. I thanked him, and ended the call. I later learned from a member of the chief's department, that the chief immediately made inquiries about me through a trusted source. I'm sure what he heard in response, didn't make him feel any better about the situation.

I met with Mr. Draa, and told him what I had suspected was true. I knew from their time in Baltimore City together, the chief was the superintendent's right-hand man back then. Unfortunately for the both of them, that bit of surreptitious business as usual wasn't recognized by BPW; as they both found out.

Trying to take the higher road, I prepared a Form 17 to the COS for the superintendent's attention. I informed him of my knowledge of the situation. I simply recommended that if the superintendent desired to exempt the chief from his remuneration of the invoice, some documentation was needed in the event of an audit. Nothing I wrote had the slightest intimation of any intentional or ill-advised wrongdoing. I was merely protecting the department, and a civilian who was needlessly placed in a precarious situation.

Conversely, I did what the COS should've done. Instead of sneaking the problem under the door, and dumping it on Mr. Draa, he should have informed the superintendent of proper protocol. When my Form 17 was received, the COS lashed out at Mr. Draa, chastising him for not following through as directed. Obvious what the COS really meant, was that Mr. Draa shouldn't have involved me in that backroom under-the-table scheme. When Mr. Draa told me about the COS's reaction, I asked the COS to meet me in the conference room.

With Mr. Draa present, I asked the COS what was wrong with my Form 17. Figuring I upset their little applecart, it came as no surprise when he arrogantly said that my Form 17 was insulting. The COS actually tried defending this matter as merely a desire on the part of the superintendent, to perform an "in-kind act" to an allied agency. I showed him a copy of the contract between the chief and BPW. I told the COS that BPW would deem it a kinder act if the chief paid his bill.

The COS continued to defend the superintendent's gesture. Thinking I was stupid, uninformed or both, he referred to the superintendent and chief, foolishly declaring: "It's not like they know each other or something." Instead of laughing in the face of this prized fool, I enlightened him on the facts of life between the chief, and the superintendent. I wanted to say stop being a yes man, and tell his "boss" that bit of "the rules only apply to everyone else," went out with the Axis partners in 2003. It became obvious the COS's eyes had become glazed over. He was in too deep, so why bother. I looked over at Mr. Draa and said, "I guess this meeting is adjourned sir."

Ironically, when I was a new corporal, the COS (back when he was an ambitious, ladder-climbing detective sergeant) once told me he thought I had the ability to go far in the department. He was surprised however, when I didn't know a particular form by its designated form number, during our conversation. He said policy knowledge was important to my potential growth. I suppose in his current incarnation as a civilian, the shift in his principles were available at the right price.

As the ongoing issues with the handguns became increasingly troublesome, our lack of success to get the proper attention from the superintendent was growing tiresome. Despite earnest on the fly modifications by the manufacturer, episodes of varied malfunctions continued to occur. Always close by the superintendent, was his faithful COS, dutifully wanting to keep his boss cloaked in public plausible deniability about those handgun related issues.

After a letter from the manufacturer was received by the governor dated July 20, 2011, the new superintendent was directed to prepare a response on the governor's behalf. In his response to the manufacturer's representative, the superintendent thanked them for personally meeting with him (superintendent), on August 17, 2011. In his letter, the superintendent acknowledged the status of several required modifications, noting that all but one had been resolved at that time.

Regardless of the superintendent's extended olive branch, we were still experiencing episodes with that weapon's defective nature. On November 18, the superintendent attended a scheduled session intended to test several recently modified handguns. Also in attendance were representatives from the manufacturer. The shooters were all highly trained, and qualified MSP personnel.

Immediately, there were noted issues with the newest modifications. Even the company's representatives had to finagle one of the new parts, in order to have it just barely function properly. There were other noted malfunctions that also occurred during those series of test phases. In his detailed written account about these latest failures, the commander of the Training Division, emphatically stated: "There should be no further effort given in finding solutions to the [myriad of] problems with this weapon." The report's conclusion urged we move on to a safer handgun.

In an email to the superintendent dated February 8, 2012, Mr. Draa informed him that on February 7, members of the STATE team participated in their scheduled night course firearms qualifications. Of the 17 shooters, 15 experienced numerous malfunctions. A total of 87 malfunctions occurred while shooting this course. Once more, Mr. Draa highly recommended that the department move forward to secure a different handgun immediately.

On February 10, the superintendent emailed Mr. Draa requesting he seek guidance from our legal counsel. The superintendent wanted them to provide a legal opinion that had already been given, before his arrival as superintendent. The two main legal concerns had already been addressed. By now, everyone involved but the superintendent, seemed to know where the department stood legally. This was a colossal waste of time. In a documented timeline, Captain Wayne had painstakingly assembled hundreds of documents in great detail, relating to every noted concern.

The information was available when the superintendent first arrived. Instead, he dubiously doubted what he was told. Did he doubt what his own eyes told him at that training session? Certainly he couldn't deny what he witnessed personally. Anyone other than a political appeaser, would have acted in the best interest of safety. As the state's procurement contract with our newly selected manufacturer was due to expire in June 2012, we didn't have the luxury of unnecessarily retracing our steps.

One morning before a scheduled CompStat session, Captain Wayne stopped by my office. He was obviously troubled by a call he just received about another round of malfunctions. I told the captain I too was growing tired of this, and afraid it was just a matter of time before someone might get hurt. I told Captain Wayne I'd take care of it that morning.

CompStat was held in the old academy classroom at Pikesville. The superintendent seemed chipper as he sat next to me, greeting me with, "Hey man how are you doing?" Just before the last barrack commander made his presentation, I leaned over to my right, and asked the superintendent if he had a minute after we finished. As the room cleared, I asked the other two bureau chiefs if they would remain along with Captain Wayne.

By now, the COS couldn't react fast enough to derail this impromptu discussion. I announced to everyone that the captain had been informed of the latest round of serious issues with our handgun, and it was critical that the superintendent hear about them immediately. Captain Wayne had given me a copy of the latest documented issues. I gladly gave the superintendent my copy. He informally perused the document as Captain Wayne described the latest round of noted issues. Judging by the superintendent's body language, he appeared uneasy, as well as unhappy.

After thanking Captain Wayne, the superintendent briskly left. I don't know if he was angry over the manner in which I handled this, or genuinely concerned about the captain's report. At that point, I really didn't care if he didn't appreciate my rouse. The lives of troopers were at stake, and he was going to hear this bad news, not behind closed doors in secrecy, but in front of witnesses.

I'm not suggesting the superintendent had no regard for our safety, but he was the only one in the room who could do something about it. Up to that point, there was no indication he had. Nothing he came with as his agenda, was more important than this. As only the superintendent and his little triumvirate knew what was going on, I'm not exactly sure what transpired afterwards.

Not long after though, the superintendent finally relented, and gave me the authorization to move the proposed acquisition forward. Nevertheless, that bit of capitulation was full of unwarranted micromanaging, and undue anxiety on their part. Simply put, we were going to do it his way from that point on. The first few days were spent working closely with my recently appointed director of the QMD. First Sergeant Nate Beam had retired in his civilian capacity as director, prior to Colonel Sheridan's departure.

With Colonel Sheridan's concurrence, my recommendation to elevate the head of our procurement section was approved. Alice Thompson, became the QMD director. Mrs. Thompson was a recognized expert in her field even before joining the MSP from another state agency. Even so, the superintendent who didn't know the first or last thing about her business, had to try and bend us to his will.

Early one morning, Captain Wayne said he needed my opinion on something. The captain was directed by the superintendent to personally involve himself in the procurement of the new handguns. Noticing the look of concern on my face, Captain Wayne knew I understood his problem. Scott said he tried explaining to the superintendent that he (Scott), had no knowledge about procurement procedures, and how it would also be highly improper for him to involve himself. As commander of the compliance section, and the department's head auditor, it would be a recognized conflict of interest on the captain's part to get involved. However the superintendent insisted.

As a progress meeting was scheduled that afternoon, I told Captain Wayne, I would tactfully attempt to explain to the colonel that at a minimum, he (Scott) was prohibited because he was not trained, or assigned to QMD. The last thing we needed was for some avoidable whim on the superintendent's part, to come back on us in the eleventh hour. During the meeting, no matter how diplomatically I attempted to inform the superintendent of protocol, from his point of view, he wouldn't see it that way.

Becoming more direct, I informed the superintendent that I too was the compliance commander at one time, and Captain Wayne was absolutely correct with his reluctance to follow this request. For some reason, our proper procedures always seemed to frustrate this superintendent. Having to have his way regardless, he said he wanted the captain to be present during any meeting regarding QMD's interaction with the distributor. I tried to calmly explain this wasn't necessary, and it took the captain away from other duties relative to moving forward. Mrs. Thompson and her staff were quite capable of handling their business without Captain Wayne, I insisted.

This exchange unintentionally prompted the superintendent to blurt out how he didn't see any issues with it, as he had already secretly met with the sales representative. I asked the superintendent when did he meet with the sales rep. Realizing it was too late for the superintendent to remove his scuffed up patent leather shoe from his mouth, I asked him when was he going to tell me, or QMD, so we could be on the same page. The superintendent ended the meeting, visibly disturbed that I wasn't under his spell. The last thing we needed was for him being out on his own, doing who knows what, and messing things up with his "Charm City Two Step" interpretation of proper procedure.

In a subsequent progress meeting, the superintendent seemed bothered by the lack of movement since our last meeting. He went as far as challenging the abilities of the staff at QMD. The conference table was a long wooden table. My normal position was at the opposite end, looking directly at the superintendent's designated seated position at the head of the table. Coming to the defense of my staff, I said given the fact they had to keep stopping to answer unnecessary questions from the COS, I thought they had performed especially well.

Visibly disturbed by my defense of QMD's efforts, he sharply asked what did I expect him to say under the circumstances. I looked straight down the table at him. With as much restraint as possible, I told him: "If I were superintendent, I'd be discussing something else ... because those guns would've been in our holsters by now sir." Lieutenant Colonel Pallozzi who was seated to my right along the end of the table, kicked me from under the table and whispered, "Easy Stew."

It wasn't my intent to be insubordinate, but this man was under some delusion that he was an expert on everything. I knew this was a very politically sensitive matter, and probably upset all of his original plans, but this is what he inherited. If he wanted to lead from a safe distance, he should have stayed with the transportation authority police, where they had a safer model for a sidearm.

With the superintendent's benefactor being a lame-duck governor, I'm sure he didn't want to step on any unlikely toes, in hopes of keeping his job prospects alive with a new incoming administration. But I also knew that if the unthinkable happened to one of our troopers, due to any untimely malfunction attributive to one of those troublesome handguns, he'd be the first one sprinting to Annapolis, where he'd wind up hiding under the governor's bed next to the governor.

I had no confidence in his exhibited fundamental nature. Undoubtedly, he would've taken no responsibility, claiming the handguns didn't begin malfunctioning on his watch. If he could avoid signing off on improperly disposed of (antiquated) IT equipment as an innocuous formality, what would happen for something much more serious? I'd seen that movie too many times before, to start trusting someone who was conspicuously dedicated to the preservation of his own posterior.

After the meeting, the COS came to my office, and asked me if I had ever considered changing my position at the table. He said that he thought I should consider another spot, that way there wouldn't be this "manly exchange thing" down the table between me and the superintendent. For once the COS had a spine. He admitted the superintendent was equally responsible for that brief exchange. I told the COS it was the superintendent's prerogative to have the last word on all subjects, but he shouldn't ask questions he didn't want the answer to; especially in front of an audience.

As it was with the governor at StateStat, I answered a fool according to his own folly, as the saying goes. The COS left after that asking me to consider it. I didn't… I had more important things to worry about. Moving closer to our goal, one of the final complications was adhering to the state's Public Safety Code, pursuant to who was legally eligible to purchase our outgoing weapons.

Mrs. Thompson located a local federally licensed firearms manufacturer, who was willing to meet our price, and stipulations about the resale prohibitions. Again, I had the COS hanging over my shoulder, questioning me about the manufacture's ATF certifications. I had to remind him they wouldn't be in business as a federally licensed manufacturer, if they weren't certified by ATF.

Finally, the day came when all the effort culminated in the actual discussion of the purchase, and scheduled delivery. I'm not ashamed to admit this was an emotional moment for me personally. In my travels, troopers were asking me what was going on with the handguns. They were understandably concerned. I promised them reliable people had their backs, and wouldn't stop working to get a safer handgun for them. It was also a relief to see something so important that started in 2010, finally come to fruition. We could now say we kept our promise.

The JFK Highway Barrack was the site of the next scheduled CompStat session. The superintendent came up to me, and privately offered his congratulations for the effort in completing the transaction. I told him the credit went to Mrs. Thompson, her staff, and Mr. Draa. Credit aside, after all we went through, I was just happy it was over.

Prior to the start of the session, I learned that in an attempt to save face with his friend (the chief), the superintendent with hat in hand, had just personally reached out to Mr. Draa, asking if he could help with that unpaid invoice caper. Obviously, when the COS slipped that Form 17 under John's door instead of discussing it with him personally, Mr. Draa was supposed to willingly decipher what "Take care of this" meant. The superintendent and the COS, weren't about to put an explicit ill-advised expectation in writing; so they counted on John's witting cooperation.

As the invoice had to be paid, that could have only meant one thing: They expected Mr. Draa to pay the invoice using MSP funds, instead of insisting that the chief honor his obligations to the state. Imagine having to explain to a state or federal auditor how you perpetrated that bit of fiscal irresponsibility on the basis of favoritism. No wonder the COS tried his best to throw himself on that grenade for his "boss," by insisting this was just some innocuous in-kind act.

Using the handy "serve at the pleasure of" prerogative in his carpetbag of illusions, the superintendent summarily terminated John the following afternoon. In the time honored tradition of "the less who are around to tell what they know... the better," a witness to the deed had to be eliminated.

Obviously this archetype of self-preservation, couldn't have someone of integrity around questioning what any principled person would. Instead, the superintendent brought in a retired sworn member from the MSP to temporarily hold down the CFO's seat, who was just willing enough to be of service until further notice.

On June 1, I received a telephone call from QMD director, Mrs. Thompson. What she was about to tell me was the last thing I wanted to hear. Mrs. Thompson began by saying she was concerned over a telephone call she received from the COS just minutes before. I invited her to tell me about the call, so I could help resolve her concerns.

Mrs. Thompson told me that the COS had just directed her to delay the purchase of the new handguns, with no explanation. I thanked Mrs. Thompson, and told her she did the right thing in calling me. I immediately contacted the other two lieutenant colonels, and asked them to meet me in the conference room. As they were the two enforcement operational bureau chiefs, this latest example of veiled secrecy, affected the majority of their personnel. I wanted them to witness this latest round of games and no fun.

Once we were all seated, I didn't mince words. I asked the COS why did he direct Mrs. Thomson to delay the purchase of the new weapons, without informing me as well. The COS uttered one word "Politics." At that time, there was an ongoing session in Annapolis where our right honorable friends were trying to balance the budget. Whether that was the cause, or just a convenient excuse, I can't say.

Apparently, some genius decided it didn't present a good perception for us to be making an expensive purchase, at a time they couldn't balance the budget. Because of their incompetence, we had to suffer while indirectly, politicians were playing political "Russian Roulette" with our lives. Since this superintendent was more fixated about getting his hands on that untapped revenue over at MDTAP, and starting his own little fiefdom in the process, I guess the politicians thought, "What's a few more weeks since he waited this long."

Pointing to the governor's and lieutenant governor's pictures on the wall, I asked the COS, if a trooper should be hurt because of these defective weapons, which one of those pictures is going to say to that family... "Sorry it was just politics." The COS had become infamous for keeping secrets. When pressed about the truth he wasn't permitted to reveal, the COS's usual reply was, "I'm not going to talk about it."

I reminded him we were in the process of changing weapons almost a year ago, before Colonel Sheridan left. I said, "We had the approval from BPW, and you, and your boss did nothing but get in the way." I suggested he start praying that nothing happen to any of our troopers because of that handgun. I told him the Grand Canyon wouldn't be big enough for them to hide in, if the unthinkable happened: And I meant every word I said.

Although balancing the budget may have been their excuse at that time, what political expedient excuse was there when they walked in the door? Instead of scheming how to hand out free cadets to his friend, or holding forums on consolidation, already knowing the results of the study, the superintendent should have accepted the undeniable facts about our firearms safety concerns, and acted responsibly.

In this superintendent's little utopia, he'd rather do things like host what I referred to as the "Every Other Wednesday Book Club Meetings," in the Forensic Science Division's conference room. There the superintendent's next wave of potential candidates for commissioned officer promotions, had to give book reports on his suggested titles, before an audience of the upper command.

During the first such gathering, he used power point slides illustrating his choice of leadership principles. As he got to the end of his presentation, the last slide was of a flag-draped casket, flanked by two police officers. As the superintendent stood at the podium looking very solemn, simultaneously he had the dimmer switch turned down, slowly darkening the room for effect. Trying to appear somewhat emotional, he asked those of us in the audience to consider if we had honored our commitments, by doing the best we could during our tours of duty. Unfortunately, he was the one glowing in the dark like a hot coal full of hypocrisy.

The last thing we needed, was a phony motivational speaker trying to lecture us on effective leadership. In my opinion, if you are going to talk about leadership, then at least have some first. In my book, effective leadership is about doing more than what's best for your own career. As far as I was concerned, he was unqualified to tell anyone with integrity, how to become an effective leader. As I cared more about my reputation, than being a self-serving abettor, his exhibited brand of so-called leadership, was not for me.

To Colonel Sheridan, and those who from the beginning, worked tirelessly to test, document, and lend their administrative authority, or expertise towards our endeavor to secure a safer sidearm for the department, my compliments go to them all. They deserve a great deal of thanks!

After my retirement, Captain Wayne would deservedly get promoted to major, and command the Special Operations Command. When Scott retired, he went on to become a major with the Special Operations Branch of the Pentagon's Force Protection Agency, located in Virginia. Like so many of the proud troopers I was fortunate to work alongside of and mentor, Scott too remains as one of my dear brothers and friends.

Chapter 61
And Now Presenting the Black Version of "Annapolis' Games with No Fun"

In what appeared to be an attempt to further the discussions on diversity within the MSP, the department received a request to appear before a few committee members of the Black Caucus in Annapolis. They had questions about the number of sworn Black members that were assigned to specialized units, and the number of sworn Black members eligible for promotion to our commissioned officers' ranks. Along with the superintendent, and my trusty sidekick, assistant bureau chief Major Laura Lu Herman, Commander, Personnel Command, we faced questions primarily from the chairman, who was a senator from Prince George's County.

Regarding assignments to specialized units, I explained that you were generally considered to be in a specialized unit if you weren't assigned to a barrack performing patrol or investigative duties. Out of the total population of our 202 Black sworn members, 73 from the ranks of TFC to lieutenant colonel were assigned to specialized units, or 36%. That meant the remaining 129 members, or 64%, were assigned to FOB. The senator still wanted know why the percentage for specialized units was only at 36%.

I told him that field operations had the largest number of all the troopers regardless of the actual numbers, or racial makeup of all our personnel. As the barracks provided patrol coverage, and answered calls for service, they were the priority, I said.

I suggested that the senator consider the following possibility: What if there had been a much higher number of our Black sworn members assigned to specialized units; and during his travels on the interstates to and from Annapolis, he saw little to no Black troopers in uniform, performing road patrol duties. I told the senator he'd have us here explaining why.

Then the senator wanted to start playing mind games. He asked why there were only three Black troopers in executive protection. I said it depended on how many actual transfer request to executive protection from Black members were on file. The senator was told that qualified troopers assigned to executive protection, were handpicked by the governor and his staff, and they got exactly who they wanted. I recommended he pose that question to the governor.

Another committee member, a delegate from Baltimore County, inquired about the number of Black troopers eligible for promotion to the commissioned officers' ranks. Major Herman responded to her question, by explaining that the first commissioned officers' rank began with lieutenant. The rank below that is first or detective sergeant. Of those Blacks who were eligible to test for lieutenant, several chose not to participate for economical, or other reasons, she said.

As a first or detective sergeant, you are still eligible to receive regular overtime as an extension of your shift. At that rank, you may also take advantage of the sanctioned extra duty assignments known as the "Triple A's." Referred to by troopers as the "Triple A's," it stands for the Motor Vehicle Administration (MVA), the National Security Administration (NSA), and the State Highway Administration (SHA).

Once you reach the rank of lieutenant, you are no longer eligible for the department's standard overtime, or for those contractually reimbursable overtime assignments mentioned above. From that point on, as a commissioned officer, you are only compensated for any regular duty extra hours, by compensatory reimbursement time, also known as "comp-time."

Those who don't participate in the promotional process, aren't considered for promotion, Major Herman added. Major Herman warned this predicament would have an overlapping effect on the number of Blacks who were eligible for the next rank of captain as well. Once again, I brought up the uncompetitive salary structures. But as usual, no one on the other side of the table wanted to discuss that.

Speaking of games, the "concerned" senator was a Democratic primary candidate opposing the incumbent U.S. Senator, Ben Cardin for his seat. There was a television news crew to our right, standing near the wall filming our meeting. Once the news crew began packing up to leave, I watched the committee members begin conversing amongst themselves jovially, while Major Herman was still speaking. I must say they had less interest in our answers, after it was apparent the senator got his media coverage at our expense.

Still using the opportunity as a positive attempt to show the department's willingness to accept help in recruiting qualified minorities, I approached the senator afterwards. I heard he was also a pastor with a fairly large congregation in Prince George's County. I gave him several of my business cards. I asked the senator to provide my cards to anyone in his network who may be interested in becoming a trooper, and have them contact me. Major Herman offered her cards as well.

Not surprisingly, neither one of us received a call from anyone recommended by the senator, or the delegate prior to my retirement. Unfortunately for the senator, the percentages of his political ambitions didn't fare as well as our percentages. The senator garnered just 15.7% of the votes, to Senator Cardin's 74.2%.9 Like the reporter said: Once they stopped filming this little so-called fact finding hearing: "That's wrap!"

9 United States Senate Election in Maryland 2012

Chapter 62
To Quote Lieutenant Stacy…

On July 23, 2012, I was scheduled to join speakers from the Prince George's County government, who were giving opening remarks at the National Association of Black Narcotics Agents (NABNA) 35th Annual National Training Conference, held at the National Harbor. I was given this honor by the NABNA, thanks to a recommendation from MSP Corporal Jocqua Shropshire.

Later that afternoon when I returned to Pikesville, I was sitting in my office when HRD Director Donny Lewis, stopped by. I invited Donny to have a seat on the settee in front of my desk. He had a preoccupied look on his face, which wasn't unusual, having to deal with this administration.

I was about to have him tell me what was on his mind, when the superintendent hurried in. He sat next to Donny, and awkwardly began telling me that as he was approaching his first year in office, he now wanted to go in another direction personnel-wise.

Continuing his insincere (break it to me gently) attempt at courtesy, the superintendent said although I did nothing wrong, I would be returned to the captain's rank, thus ending my tenure as a lieutenant colonel. He ended by telling me Mr. Lewis would provide me with my personnel options. With that said, he got up, and abruptly left. As he was leaving, I told him thank you. Of course he didn't respond.

Although sudden, it came as no surprise. Someone of his ilk couldn't afford to have someone like me around with their eyes open. After all, he had just done the same to the former CFO John Draa. If he expected complicity simply because he was in charge, then he did what was best for his sense of privilege. Trying to make it so your former assistant didn't have to honor a state contract was one thing; But as far as I was concerned, disregarding information important to the safety of the troopers under your command, was totally unacceptable.

That left me and Donny, to get past that difficult moment. I got up and sat next to him. I could see the sincere look of regret on his face. The director and I had been friends for a long time, going back to the days when we were shift partners at Westminster Barrack in the early 1980s. I told him not to be sad, we had seen this before. Joking figuratively, I said I read the fine print on the proverbial contract when I accepted the position from Colonel Sheridan. I knew the position was not mine for life.

I told Donny that I had four good years as a bureau chief, and got somethings done to help people. However, I did tell Donny he could tell the superintendent that I wasn't going back to captain. Presumably, I figured the superintendent hoped I wouldn't accept such a demotion, opting to retire instead. At my pleasure, I decided I should retire at my former rank of lieutenant colonel. There was a precedence to do so. Since he evidently wanted me out so badly, that was my price. Donny and I shook hands, and I thanked him for his obvious concern for my feelings.

Minutes later, I found out that I wasn't the only casualty of this house-cleaning purge. When Lieutenant Colonel Pete Landon suddenly appeared at my door wondering aloud what the heck just happened to him, I saw I had unexpected company. Only Lieutenant Colonel Pallozzi would be spared. Bill would go on to become the next superintendent in 2015, replacing the "Boss" under the newly elected governor.

After the superintendent left my office, he walked over to the old academy classroom, where he presided over an impromptu promotional ceremony. My friend Rob Turano would be my successor. Giving credit where it's due; the "Boss" was slick enough to recognize as there were only three bureau chiefs; if he demoted the only Black; he'd better do the same with a White one; to keep the appearance this wasn't personal. Unfortunately, Pete was nominated, and got caught in my backdraft.

It was obvious this was all preconceived. A few days earlier, we had to attend a mandatory seminar about accreditation at the Anne Arundel Community College campus in Glen Burnie. The COS could be seen huddling with the majors who replaced us. In order to say he replaced a Black with a Black, they created an unnecessary fourth bureau, and appointed that major as the bureau chief. That major would become the fifth Black member in our history appointed to lieutenant colonel. The superintendent could now proclaim he and the governor contributed to equal treatment of "African American's" in the state police. After Bill became superintendent, the department eventually returned to its normal compliment of just three bureau chiefs.

I was touched by the kind telephone phone calls, emails and personal contacts I received from sworn and civilian alike, after word got out that I had been replaced. Of course there is always one heckler in the audience, and mine was retired Captain Tommy McCord. Tommy was now a civilian prosecutor in the Office of Administrative Hearings. When I stopped by his office, Tommy asked the "Siri" device on his cell phone should I have been demoted? I had to laugh as the device flickered, but didn't bother to answer the question.

In another bit of humor, I found an 8x10 picture of me and the new superintendent taken at a function in happier days. The superintendent had his arm around me in the picture. On the picture I inscribed the warning "Rob don't let this happen to you!" I gave it to him as a going away present, when I congratulated him on his new position.

As it was customary for retirees, a METERS message announcing my retirement was sent to all MSP installations around the state. For me, it was a reminder how quickly your career can come to an end, even when you've accepted it. I had the distinction of being the last member of my academy class to retire. My message listed my official retirement date as September 1, 2012.

On my very last day, I was removing the remainder of my things from the office. The COS, who was on leave the day I was relieved of my position, came by my office to check in. He asked if I was ok. I told him the same thing I told Director Lewis: Exempted ranks aren't yours for life.

Ever the superintendent's bagman, the COS had the effrontery to ask me what I thought about the superintendent coming to my retirement party, and present me with my retirement credentials. In one last act of civility, rather than tell him what I really thought, I told the COS no thanks. I had a real superintendent (Colonel Hutchins) attending who would do me the honor, I said. No poor excuse for a superintendent, was going to appear before my family and guest, trying to redeem himself at my expense.

That afternoon when I returned my issued equipment to QMD, a number of the staff members were also very kind in their expressions of regret, over my retirement. By this time, the ordered delay to purchase, and deliver the new weapons had been conveniently rescinded. Before I left the counter, our chief armorer Sergeant Charlie Hahn, in a very kind act, extended me the tribute of being issued one of the new weapons on an MSP Requisition Form 111.

The one he chose had the lowest serial number, which meant it was the first one stamped in the lot. He assured me the troopers knew I had their backs, and I was most respected, and appreciated for it. Of course I had to give it right back, but it was a moment I will absolutely never forget.

It made me recalled my brief conversation with First Sergeant McElroy at Pikesville earlier in 2004, when he asked me if it was worth not being promoted to major, because I dared stand up for a subordinate. That moment at QMD was a reminder of how important making a difference the right way can be. This was no sacrifice on my part; I was doing what I got paid to do. I wasn't there to be a politician; I was a police executive, whose top priority was to take care of our sworn and civilian men and women, who were protecting our citizens.

Sadly, it seemed the department needed to be protected from some of the politicians, and the ambitious appointees in their pockets. I have been asked if I was bitter at the department for how my career ended. I learned a long time ago, not to hold acts by individuals perpetrated against me as the department's fault.

I had just finished waxing my assigned vehicle Car 3, when Major Herman was dropped off at my resident to pick it up. She wanted it to be reassigned to her. This signaled the official end of my 35 years. As we hugged, she said she'd see me at my retirement party. Laura Lu thanked me again for our friendship, and said she appreciated all I did for her during her career.

One's career as a state trooper doesn't end any better than that. As she drove off saluting me, I knew I was saluting a future lieutenant colonel. Gladly I was right. She was promoted under Bill Pallozzi's administration when he became superintendent. Lieutenant Colonel Herman was the second woman to hold that rank in our history.

It was finally over. There were no regrets, and nothing left on the table. The MSP had help define me, as I helped define it. I made a great many friends for life: And I was blessed to survive my years of service. I truly lived my dream.

I remember when I had to appear at traffic court in BelAir, Harford County one afternoon in 2002. I saw my first barrack commander, retired Lieutenant Elwood E. Stacy standing in the lobby. The lieutenant was the head court bailiff at the district court at that time. I walked over, and reintroduced myself. I think he remotely remembered me. The lieutenant noticed the railroad tracks (captain bars) on my collar.

Genuinely smiling he patted my shoulder and said, "You made the right choice didn't you?" Lieutenant Stacy then said something very inspiring. Referring to himself, he said: "I was born to be a trooper… I just wasn't old enough at the time." No one could have said it better. Lieutenant Stacy passed in 2020, but his sentiment lives on for many of us who felt the same way he did.

In the MSP we have a saying that goes: "Once a trooper, always a trooper." So for all of those who have any questions about my feelings towards the Maryland State Police, I'll just quote Lieutenant Stacy: "I was born to be a trooper…I just wasn't old enough at the time," unquote.

As I've said throughout, our civilians are the best anywhere. I had three of them as part of my immediate bureau staff. They are Jackie (Go Ravens) Jackson, Frances (Miss Fran) Campbell, and Margaret (The Ring Leader) Ringley. I had the privilege of their counsel, skillset, friendship and loyalty throughout my career, especially in my last four years on the "Third Floor." I owe them a great deal of thanks and respect. I really couldn't have done it without them.

Chapter 63
"Where Are My Troopers?"
A Tribute To Mrs. Shirley Howard

When one of our civilian employees my dear friend Bonnie (FW) Beisser approached me about helping out with the Children's Cancer Foundation (CCF), that was one of the best things that ever happened to me. The CCF based in Owings Mills, Baltimore County, started in 1983, when Shirley Howard found out that Johns Hopkins Hospital in Baltimore City, was short on funding to keep its children's cancer unit open. Working with her late husband Bill, and several others, they got together to form the foundation. From that point on, the CCF became her passion.

Under Shirley's leadership, Bill and other parents awarded funding to a variety of facilities throughout Maryland and Washington, D.C. for the past 30 years. Institutions like Johns Hopkins Hospital, the University of Maryland's Medical Center, Sinai Hospital, the Children's National Medical Center, and the Georgetown Lombardi Comprehensive Cancer Center, benefited from the CCF's benevolence. A number of doctors, including renowned pediatric neurosurgeon Dr. Ben Carson, began their careers with grants from the foundation.

Jeffrey Toretsky, a professor in oncology and pediatrics at Georgetown University's Lombardi Comprehensive Cancer Center, received a grant from the foundation, allowing him two additional years of laboratory training as a pediatric oncology fellow at the National Cancer Institute when funding was tight.10 Joseph Wiley, chief of pediatric hematology and oncology, and chairman of the pediatrics department at the children's hospital, said Shirley poured her heart and soul into the foundation and was always willing to help others over her own interests. His first research grant came from the foundation. "Shirley demonstrated for me just how much one person with enough desire and commitment can make a difference," he said.

Although Shirley passed in August 2012, she will not soon be forgotten. The CCF is credited with helping children's cancer treatment make major strides forward in her lifetime. Shirley who was 88 at the time of her death, almost single handedly raised more than $30 million for treatment and research as the executive director of the CCF for 30 years. 11

Close to the hearts of many troopers was a young man named Robbie Robertson, the son of retired First Sergeant Darrell Robertson. Much like a trooper, Robbie was bravely fighting his battle with leukemia. Several troopers rallied to help sponsor the CCF's activities, and events in support of Robbie.

Although Robbie would sadly lose his fight in 1988, many of us in his memory, continued to support the CCF at their annual events in the following years to come. As many of the troopers began to retire, that left Bonnie, me, and a few newly added troopers and volunteers, mainly Joy Squires, her husband Chip, my immediate family, and my in-laws to carry on the tradition at the events.

While our volunteers paired with CCF workers, the troopers and I provided security measures, especially for the performing celebrities. Shirley was always energetic, and sometimes anxious because she wanted everything just right at these events for her "kids." Although she was small in stature, Shirley had a heart as big as the galaxy. When she needed the presence of a trooper, or didn't see you, we would hear her loudly call out "Where are my troopers?"

Thank you Shirley. You were there when children with cancer needed someone the most. Like many of us who were honored to do our humble best to help you, your "wonderful kids" and their families will never forget you.

Acknowledgements
The MSP's 76th Graduating Class, 1977

Phillip Andrews, George Barney, Jr., Denise Bays, Garrett Berge,
Paul Bomgardner, William Brooks, III
Gary Chatfield, Carlton Cobb, Filmore Corbin, Jr., Ronnie Creel, Dennis
Deal, Dennis Delp, Norman Eklund, John Ell,
Jeanmarie Fasone, Paul Feryus, Charles Finney, Jr., Martin Flowers,
Vaughn Foreman,
John Gainey, Reginald Gilliam, Leonard Glenn, Jr., Theodore Gray,
James Harmon, Constance Harris, George Harrison, Jerome Jankowiak,
Joann Jerome, Brian Jones, Robert Kerr, George Lewis, Jr., Alan
Michael, Matthew Miller, Maynard Miller, Kevin Mooring,
Douglas Morgan
David Nickens, Darrell Niner, Richard Norman,
Nicholas Plazio, William Presgraves,
David Reier, Stewart Russell,
Jerry Scarborough, Robert Sharp, Jr., James Standifer, William Starvis,
Joseph Ungvarsky, Herbert Uzzelle,
Willem Van der Heyden, Burton Ward, Mark Ward, Vonzell Ward,
David Weisman, Hilliard Williams, Stanley Wilson

In Memoriam:
Charles Brown,Sr., Ricky Dell, Larry Karnes, Greg May, Robert
Milbourne, Eric Monk, Richard Nock, Charles B. Smith, William
Updegraff, Jr., Heber Watts, Jr.

"They Do so Much More"
Troopers I Worked with During My Career Not Mentioned:

Gary Aschenbach, Rich Arnold, Tim Aronhalt, Jeff Alexander, Anita Allen, Toya Adams, Mike Allred, Otis Ashton, Tim Adams, Charlie Alvera, Karen Alt, Gerald Ables, Mike Alt
Dave Briscoe, John Banzhoff, Joe Branhan, John Branham, Randy Bounds, George Beisser, Winfield Baker, Dante Briley, Tom Bailey, Laura Beck, Barbara Barnes, Willie Benton, Mike Boyd, Rick Barilone, Kathleen Barilone, Holly Barret, George Brantley, Marc Black, Doug Baralo, John Burton, Arthur Betts, Dwayne Boardman, Shane Bolger, Rodney Byrd, Rusty Biddle, Henry Burns, Gary Bachtell, Ricard Bachtell, Don Beads, Earl Beville, John Beville, Harvey Brent, Brian Bonnell, Elizabeth Beck, Bill Bernard, Walter Barnes, Sha Brown, Herman Bethel, John Bollinger, John Boyd, Ed Buell, Bill Barron, Richard Bruns, Gary Bromwell, Ray Bond, Ron Beavans, Edward and Joyce Bilbrough, Robert Bambary, Clarence Bell, Paul Benson, Gary Berkrbile, John Blades, Jr., Shannon Bohrer, William Bokel, Bob Bosley, Bill Bonarski, Kim Bowman, Leroy Barton, George S. Butler, Lawrence Brown, Billy Byrd, Morris Brown, Mike Brady, Patrick Brady
Rudy Chapman, Eric Corbin, Mike College, Ray Clasing, Greg Crosland Gary Carpenter, Greg Cullison, John G. Cook, Eric Claxton, Donny Cupe, Roland Cothorne, Chris Corea, George Colbert, Mike Cartner, Jeff Claycomb, Roger Cassell, Joe Consoli, Ira Click, Wayne Cusimano, Mike Cusimano, Mark Cummings, Darryl Clark, John Casey, Mark Carter, Sam Cottman, Linda Conner, John Carhart, Sonya Clark, Mike Cain, Gary Cofflin, Ben Cohey, Chuck Cave, Sam Capecci, Gordon Cottman, George Cunningham, Scott Collier, Doug Cawman, Norm Cochran, Chuck Creswell, Brian Curley, Vernon Conaway, Joe Collins, John Collins, Laura Childress, Brandon Cuomo, Blake Cuomo, Calvin Cullison, Rannie Conner,
Ray Cotton, James Culp, Henry Cumberland, David Czorapinski, Lee Caple

Doug Dodds, Mark Donisi, Jay (GRC) Diggs, Norman (Clint) Dofflemyer, Christina Darienzo, Michael Dornberger,
Marvin Dorsey, Billy Dunston, Gary Davis, Mike Dawson,
Miguel Dennis, Earl Dennis, Tom Dentry, Joe Davis, Jim Dewees, Chuck Demby, Bruce Dana, Mike Davey, John Dunn, Bob Devers, Tom Dupczak, Ron Diggs, Ron Dixon, Doug Doak, Ray Domico, George Douglass
Jeff Eyler, Harry Edwards, Daniel Everett, Edward Eicher, Andrew Eways, Mike Evans
Bob Finn, Frank Fornoff, Wes Forchion, Ernie Ford, Mike Fluharty, Larry Faries, Gary Foster, Doug Forrester, Mike Fischer, Karen Fourtune, Chris Finn, Neil Franklin, Mitch Frye, Steve Foster, Dave Frazier, Francis Friedel, Jr., Bobby Friend, Larry Fulton,
Leon Foremen
Dr. Delaphine Green, Julie Guyer, John Greene, George Green,
Larry Grasso, Jesse Graybill, Predi Garcia, Jeremiah Gussoni, Wellington (Sgt. Rutlidge) Gray, Mike Gordy, Bill Gordy, Tony Gaines, Jeff Gahler, Thomas Gardner, Paul Gerstner, Bob Gunter, Mervin Gooch, Jerry Gooding, Mary Griffies, Al Goode, Jeff Green, Cameron Gibson, Steve Geppi, John Glorioso,
Tracy Hart, Vicky Harrison, George Hall, Phil Hinkle, Mike Harrington, Janet Harrison, Charles Horner, Pat Guidash, Dave Hopp, Jessie Haas, Diane Hanson, Rudy Hanson, Mike Hawkins, Charles Hinnant, James Hockett, Scott Hinkley, Ken Harry, Tom Hejl, Don Harrison, Erwin House, Chad Hymel, Carlos Hall, Raymond Hale, Hayes, Wendell Highsmith, Emerson Hoopes, James Harris,
Ed Humphries, Harold Harbold, James Harvey, Vernon Herron
Robert Iman, Craig Ingram, Joe Ireton
Cynthia James, Mike Jones, Bill Johnson, Bobby Jones, Sean Jackson, Dean Jones, Jim Joyce, Charlie Jones, Bill Jacobs,
Ray Johnson,
Walter Johnson, Mujaihid Jones, Mark Judge, Wesley Jefferson, Dwight Johnson, Steve Jessee, J.J. Johnson, Greg Johnston, Suzanne Jordan, Steve Johnson, Vones Jamison
Rick Klebon, Marty Knight, Jerry Kriener, Ralph Kabernagel, Sandy Kestner, Gerald Kreiner, Marta Koock, Scott Keyser, Fran Konzel, Bob Kirk, Gary Kulik, Donny Knott, Walter Kerr,
James Krionderis, Paul Kelley, James Kerns, Mike King,

Richard Jackson

Frank Lioi, Graham Lang, Ernst Lassard, Ron Lewis, Duane Lee, Eddie Luers, Mike Lewis, James Laisure, Wesley Lutz,

Virginia Lewis, Dwayne Ligghtsey, Robert Lemerise, Bob Lukiewski, Linda Lozier, Jason Leichtman, Padraic Lacy, Bill LeFevre, Bob Lipsky,

Bobby Lankford, Anthony London, Jimmy Lee, Kevin Lambert, Al Liebno, Joe Little, Tommy Long, Vernon Love, Douglas Lowery, Chuck Lukoski, Cindy Lewis

Mike Mattingly, Howdy Martin, Brett Moore, Danny McLain, Rodney Morris, Chuck Moore, Darryl Morgan, Buddy Mowbray, Sarah Mastronardi, Mark Mowbray, Mike Mann, Charles Mackey, Carl Miller, Robert Mondor, Bonnie Morris, Don McCord, Charlie Mays, Jimmy Mayo, Sean Morris, Kevin Moriarty, Gary Manos, Suzanne Mazan, Bruce MacLean, Bob McQueeny, Phil Metz, Jimmy Mitchell, Steve Moyer, Tony (Hootie) McClendon, Timothy McDonald, Danny Mabry, Scott Mergenthaler, Gar Menefee, Mike Myers, Joe McCrea, Alan McLeod, Teresa Marion, Dan McCarthy, Vernon Murray, Gary Mounts, Antonio Malaspina, John Maiello, Ray Milburn, Jack McCauley, Mark McGuire, Chuck Martin, John Mooney, Betty Mooney, Robert Myers, Bill Miller, James Martyn, Joe Masci, Andy Mays, Greg Mazzella, Aaron Michael, Merrill Messick, Frank Moran, Doug Morris, Tom Murrill, Mike Mullin, Jim Matteo, Bob McAfee

Russ Newell, Phillip Nickerson, Brian Newcomer, Gerald Newman, Mickey Norman, Rick Nash, Dan Nelson, Khris Nelson,

Kevin Opher, Steve Outten, Nicholas J. Over, John O'Neill

Kenny Pollack, Danny Poist, Art Porter, Tony Parker, Dave Perry, DaVaughn Parker, Al Payton, Maureen Patterson, Dallas Pope, Bob Parrott, Earl Phillips, Mike Powell, James Pyle, Krah Plunkert, Ronnie Presnell, Earl Page, Dale Petty, Fred Phelps, John Psota John Pietanza, Ron Prematta, Joe Pruitt, Dan Peters, James Pilchard, Mitch Parke, Norman Pepersack, Gene Paluzzi, Vicky Patton, Mike Panos, Gary Prochaska

Paul Quill, Francisco Quisay. Dewayne Queen

Thornie Rouse, Dave Reichenbaugh, William Reaves, Brian Reider, Dave Ruel, Ian Rola, Angie Rutledge, Dean (Go That Way) Richardson, Scott Rice, Steve Reynolds, Tony Romaro, Joe Ryan,

Jay Robinson, Scott Robinson, Mark Roadheaver, Anthony Rounds,
Warren (Rinky) Rineker, Ron Riggin, Phylis Roberts,
Dewight Rolley, John Reburn, James Rinehart, Sciana Roach,
Frank Rose
Dana Smoot, Harold (Rick) Sullivan, Dave Sexton, Chris Sexton,
Todd Sexton, Brian Smith, Pete Spaulding, Ron Small, Joe Saboury,
Bob Smalok, Charles Stevenson, Jeff Stevenson, Nayim, Sadik,
Jeffery Stevens, Tony Smith, Margo Shank, Scott Saunders,
Chris Sasse, Bob Smith, Mark Sroka, Aaron Stein, Brandon Stein,
Vinson Smith, Dwight (EE Jr.) Styles, Max Schulte, Walter Smith,
John Sawa, Kim Smith, Earl Starner, Larry Schuyler,
Richard Sullivan, Robert Simpson, Bernie Spangler, Rick
Sczerbicki,
Byron Scott, Frank Smith, Adam Stachurski, Walt Schulz,
Francis Shanks, Bruce Smith, Marty Smith, Danny Shell,
Harry Smith, Randy Smith, Cynthia Smith, Lake Scott, Morris
Shank, Vickie Szimanski, Yolanda Stockton, Warner Sumpter,
Morgan Storey, Bill Szimanski, Vernon Serro, Dennis Seymour,
Wayne Scriber
Wayne (The Big Ragu) Totaro, Craig Talbot, Bob Thomas, Mike D.
Thomas, Mike W. Thomas, Mike Thompson, Gary Tracy,
Dion Talley, Craig Tyer, Craig Thompson, Charles Travers,
Stephen Tom, Norma Trass, Bruce Tanner, J.D Thomas,
Jeffrey Thomas, Mike Tagliaferri, James Tucker, Bruce Tucker,
Terri Taylor, Mike Torbert, Mickey Tarr, George Taylor, Larry
Titus, Chuck Troutman,
Jarris Taylor
Ken Thrasher, Ken Tregoning, Gail Treglia, Susan Topper,
Elmer Tippett, Roger Thibaudeau, Larry Tolliver
Damon (Mt. Airy Mauler) Vinson, Rick (New York) Vercera,
Julio Valcarcel, Tim Vitito
Pete Williams, Mark Williams, Gerry Winner, Andy Winner,
Kenny Ward, Ray Wojcik, Don Welker, Scott Wilson, Craig
Williams, Brian Whitehead, Lenny Watts, Mike Wann, Devita
Washington, Frazier West, Phylis Wert, Sylvia Wright, Dave (Big
Boy) Washington, John Wilhelm, Tanya Wingfield, Tom Wardrope,
Steve Wilson, Lloyd White, George Ward, Ernie Wilkinson,
George Webster, Leslie Williams, Brian Wiley, Dave Waltemyer,
Sam Washington, Doug Wehland, Steve Wright, John Wooters,

Tom Woodard, Scott Wilson, Irv Washington, Lloyd White, Jr.
Darron Whitehead, Fabian White, Scott Whitney, Jeff Wobbleton,
Jim Wobbleton, Julian Wooden, George Webster, April Wilson,
Richard Waters, Frank Webber, Charles Wernz, John Wisniewski
Dave Yohman, Beth Youngren, Scott Yinger, Charlene Yinger,
Adrian Yancy

In Memoriam:
Tony (Hawk) Bell, Doug Buckalew, Tom Bosley, Eldon Budnick,
William Brooks, Gary Betzing, Mel Coleman, Jimmy Daucher,
Bob Dandridge, Pat Drum, Kirk Daugherty, Bobby Ellis, Ted Evans,
Jim Galyon, Gary Girton,Mike Gavel, Bob Guary, William Gerwig,
James Gulley, Don Hoffman, Elmoses Harvey, Mike Haas, Steve
Hassett, Phil Henry, Carl Harbaugh, Bernard Haywood, Chris
Hohenstein, Dave Horan, Hoyt Jones, Meredith Jones,
Fred Kirckhoff, David Keller, Charles Kirkpatrick, Al Knott,
Ray Leonard, Charlie Lester, Dave Michael, Ralph Morgan,
Charlie Masimore, Chester Miller, Avon Mack, Ronnie Mosco,
Dante Nettles, Joe Over, Jimmy Ostovitch, Tony Pokorny,Ron Petty,
Bob Pepersack, Warren Pitt, Vanessa Pinder, Pride Rivers,
Mike Ridgell, Robby Robinson, Bobby Scruggs, Steve Sugg,
Jadie Sinclair, Melanie Shockley, Charley Skuhr, Ed Schulz,
Tom Smith, Barry Smith, Yoandry Singh, Juri Tammary,
George E. Taylor, Danny Thomas, Bob White, Carol, Warner,
Tracy Wiser, Wilbert Travers, Robert Tunney, Lloyd White, Sr.,
Robert Weisenmiller, Michael Washington

Maryland State Fire Marshal's Office:
Bill Barnard, Joseph Flanagan, Alan Gosnell

In Memoriam:
Joe Zurolo

Attorney General's Legal Counsel:
Mark Bowen, Sharon Benzil, Nichole Gatewood, Ron Levitan,
Betty Stemley, Jamie McGuirk Cooney, Kim Rice, Sheri Smith

In Memoriam:
Brenda Jackson

They're Always There When We Need Them

This is a special thank you and acknowledgement to Mr. Howard Gersh who came in as the department's prosecutor with Colonel Sheridan's new administration. Mr. Gersh made an immediate impact on creating a professional addition to the department, and became my trusted ally and good friend. Before coming to the MSP, Mr. Gersh served as the department prosecutor for the Baltimore County Police. Prior to that, he was at one time the chief prosecuting attorney in the homicide unit with the Baltimore City State's Attorney's Office, and also served as a federal prosecutor. Howard was also a professor of law for over 40 years at the University of Maryland's School of Law. My brother, and dear friend PCO Jeff Bridges, has been a lifeline on the radio to hundreds of troopers for 55 years. Jeff has been a night patrol staple, and always a welcome voice over the air. Like all of our PCOs and other support employees, he represents what is best about the MSP. We are all the better for our dedicated civilians. They're always there when we need them.

Maryland State Police Civilians Who I Worked with in My Career Not Mentioned:

Clare Alford, Dr. Donald Alves, Tonya Austin, Matt Abbott.
Gayle Bennett, Jim Bise, Melody Brooks, Dorthy Bennett, Kesha Brooks, Pam Bowles, Mary Bear, Carol (FHA) Billian,
Pat Buckland, Wayne Broseker, Johanna Broussard, Linda Byers, Mary Bruns, Howard Blake Dwight Bowers, Diane Bell
Donna (MPF) Cobb, Frances Carey, Deborah Cooper, Dave Cantrell, Mark Cook, Missy Cobb, Ron Calebaugh, Pam Clark, Edwyn Corley
Dalene Drum, Verna Davidson, Gary Davis
Bill Ebare, Teresa Eitel, Carroll Evans
Leslie Fortson, Wayne Frisby, Rene Frazier, Charlene Foster, Patrick Franz
Patty (Old Bud) Garrish, Janet (Miss Vine) Galyon, Mike Gartside, Marty Gordan, Mark Gangi, Dirk Griffin
Amy Hager, Cee Cee (Put that stick down) Holland, Deborah (TOPF) Horton, Carol (# 24) Herron, Diane Hill, Luvenia Heflin, John Hahn
Florence (Toots) Johnson, Deborah Jeffries, Nancy (Hon) Jones, Rita Jones, Bill Jones, Marlene Jenkins
Chu Kim, Dan Katz, Sharon Kreitzer, Salisha Khan, Jenne Klein
Terry Long, Henry Lindsey, Tom Lawson, Frank and Don Leister, Patrick Linnehan, Rachal Leon, Cathy Lopresti, Marcie Lieberman, Anna Lieberman, Brenda Lyons
Denise (B) Masimore, Troy (Fur Coat) Maker, Dave Manning, Diana McIntyre, Terry Martindale, Linda Metzler, Mark McKenzie, Peggy Mekins, Michelle Miller, Tracie Moultrie, Carol Moore, Margaret Michel, Kathleen Miralles, James Mable, Olga Maddox
Bill Nugent
Linda Oller
Gregg Presbury Jr., Terry Poole, Gene Phipps, Carla Proudfoot, Frances Peterson
Carrie Robinson, Walter Reich, Gene Ridgell, Mike Roosa,

Elena Russo
Karen Siegman, Sherri Smith, Torin Suber, Kim Scarlett,
Karen Schneider, Denise Scherer, Dora Smith, William Simpson,
Michele Singhas, Tony Stevens, Ann Sanders
Marie (Next Window Please) Taylor, Jay Tobin, Lana Turner
Tom Vondersmith, John Vespa
Ida (Madam Director) Williams, Darrell Waller, Joe Webster,
James Webster, Diane Webster, Ken Webster, Tom Willis,
Karen Waters, Larry Worden, Jill Watts, Rosalind Williams,
Vickey Wells, Betty White.
Emma Young, Richard Yienger
Sharon Zacks

In Memoriam:
Ellen Davis, Janice Horner, Dr. Philip Phillips, Tom (Consiglieri)
Przybyla, Sara Plovsky, Gloria Webster, Andy Jackson, Billy Moses,
Donald Bailey, Mary Lou Griffiths, Bernie Wise,
Betty (Don't call us) Johnson, Bob Meekins, Jay Teipe,
Jerry Alderman, Robert Nilles, Liz Crawmer, Joe Kopera,
Richard Bruckman, Marionette Shorter, Betty Nelson, Gus Wetzel

Volunteers In Police Services (VIPS):
Iris (Mrs. I) Katz, Paul Browning, Norman Greenberg, George
Hartig
Jim Betts

In Memoriam:
Jay Bonder, Marvin and Mary Ellen Martindale, Russell Sears
Beno Robinson

Chaplains:
Father Karl (Elvis has left the building) Chimiak,
Reverend Mike Adams

Acknowledgment to Our
Valued Allied Partners and Departments Not Mentioned:

Annapolis City Police:
Zora Lykken, Frank Palumbo

Baltimore City Police:
Wayne Jones, Mike Smith, Kirk Fleet, Derek Day, Mack Smith
Donald Worden, Jay Landsman, Rick James, John Gavrilis,
Floyd McCargo, Keith Matthews, Bobby Potts, Dwight Randall, Floyd
Jones III, Henry Martin, Jessie Oden, Melvin Russell, Vernon Holley,
Gomez Greene, Fred Bealefeld, Dean Palmere, James Shields,
Sheppard Schwartz, Jeff Rosen, Arthur Cook, John Gavrilis, Gregory
Eads, Mike Dunn, Barbara Hunter, Helen Butler, Sharon Marr,
Bernard Ralph, Cliff Macer, Kevin Brown

In Memoriam:
Lt. Darrell Duggins (my neighbor), Raymond Shipley (my early mentor
when I was a cadet), Joe Shaw, Odis Sistrunk, Edward Dix, Timmy
McShane.

Baltimore County Police:
Rick (Dr. J) Flieshman, Gerald Brooks, Larry Stallings, Mike McCleese,
Brian Matthews, Sara Ward, Charles Fleet, Rodney Speights, H.F.
Greenlow, Robert Derbyshire, J. Douglas Dunlap, Stanley Harmon,
Gary Settle, Mike Crabbs, M.B. Koffenberger, Michelle Pomfret,
Donald Lee,

Chaplain:
Rabbi Norman Lohenthal

In Memoriam:
Gwen Parrish, Karen Shelton

Baltimore City Sheriff's Office:

Keyota Washington
In Memoriam:
Luther (Sonny) Smith

Bel Air Police:
Wallace Harward, Joe Swam

Charles Hickey School:
Stephanie Conyers

Hampstead Police:
Ken Russell

In Memoriam:
Durwood Sites

Howard County Police:
Herman Charity, Bobby Jones, Mark Paterni, Paul Rappaport

In Memoriam:
Bobby Jones, Paul Rappaport

Prince George's County Police:
Mike Blow, Mark Magaw, Kevin Davis

Maryland Transportation Authority Police:
John Foster, Glend Maguire, Ronce Alford, Eric Garrison, Joseph Scott,
Greg Prioleau. Steven Benner, Errol Etting

In Memoriam:
Marshall Carroll

Maryland Natural Resources Police:
Alphonso Hawkins, Wayne Jones, Mance McCall

Maryland Transit Administration Police:
Earlene Ward, John Robert Stanley

Maryland Army National Guard:

John Casey

Maryland Department of Military:
Pere Jarboe

Maryland Department of Public Safety Corrections:
Lamont Edwards, Janet Willis, Jessie Ballard, Doug Cloman, Allison Gilford, Phylis Merriweather, Jodie Stouffer

Maryland National Capital Police:
J.M. Johnson

Maryland Treasury Department:
Dave Parris, Theodore Vaughn

Maryland Emergency Management Agency:
Teresa Chapman

Maryland Department of Labor and Licensing Police:
William McMillian, Larry Summerville

National Security Administration:
Mike Talbert

C&P Telephone Security:
Paul Brashears

Delaware State Police:
Matt Engler, Charles Rynkowski

Florida Department of Law Enforcement:
Al Dana

New Jersey State Police:
Bob Cuomo, Ron Kirby, Dwight Payne

New York State Police:
Michael Prunty

New York City Police:
Stanley Schiffman, John Tierney

Pennsylvania State Police:
Thomas Lyon

In Memoriam:
Ron Sharpe

Exeter Pennsylvania Township Police:
Clarence Swoyer

Metro Dade Florida Police:
Paul Kuiper

Palos Heights, Illinois Police:
Charles Hankus

Metropolitan D.C. Police:
Ralph Ennis, Kenneth Kendall

U.S. Attorney Maryland District:
Harvey Eisenberg

Federal Bureau of Investigations:
Louis Borges

U.S. Drug Enforcement Administration:
William Athas

U.S. Department of Defense National Security Agency:
Jim Heathcote

U.S. Customs Service:
Earl Cottman

U.S. General Services Administration:

Manley Stampler

U.S. Postal Inspection Services:
Melvin Carter, Gregory Campbell, Burt Foster, Elmer Mooring

U.S. Attorney Delaware District:
Edmond Falgowski

U.S. Office of Foreign Missions:
D. Clay Hays, Stephen Mitchell

U.S. Marshals Service:
David Thomas

U.S. Secret Service:
Carl Pearsall, Todd Kreisher, Ryan Myett, Dennis Martin

U.S. Department of Transportation:
Taft Kelly

Social Security Administration Inspector General:
Gary Williams

Government of the Virgin Islands Department of Law:
Thomas Fick

John Jay College, New York:
Eli Silverman, Ph.D

To My Loving Friends

I also want to mention those who became my family as they adopted me and I'll be forever grateful for my time with them. One of my earlier junior high school friends was Barry Morgan. Very soon I met his mother Miss Margie Morgan Parker who became like a Godmother to me. She is a wonderful person and I think it was me who adopted her rather than the other way around.

At City College High School I met Ralph Vines. Ralph and I have been like loving brothers since 1971, and remain so today. We have experienced a lot together over the years, and if I can count on anyone it is Ralph.

While working part time at Sears, I met Mrs. Elizabeth Castle a phone operator. Soon after I was introduced to her husband Mr. John when came to pick her up after work. They had a large family of children and made me a part of it. Mrs. Castle was a Baltimore City School crossing guard during the day. They too were extra special and kind people. Unfortunately I lost touch with them. I later learned that Mr. Castle passed in 2016. Mr. and Mrs. Castle exemplified true value of family, and they shared their values of love with me.

In 1975, when I was a cadet in Baltimore City, I met Carolyn Green later to become Carolyn Thomas. Carolyn was a fingerprint technician there. Later she would join Maryland's Public Safety and Correctional Services performing the same functions at MSP headquarters in Pikesville. While attending the academy in 1977, we would meet again. Carolyn was like a "slightly older" sister. If I got on her nerves she'd say, "Don't make me smack you!"

After Carolyn married a future trooper named Mike D. Thomas they had a daughter and son that I became Godfather to. My dear friend and big sister passed in 2019. Coincidentally, I also have another set of Godchildren from another trooper named Mike W. Thomas and his late wife Sybil. They both worked at the Westminster Barrack. How's that for irony?

In 1975, I also met Cassandra Parrish, Patricia Scott and Azeri Perry at Baltimore City Police Headquarters. They all worked for the central dispatch in communications. The four of us would become great friends. Eventually I lost contact with Pat and Azeri but Casey and I would maintain our relationship for 43 years. She was wonderful, and very important to me, as was her brother Keith and her daughters Andrea, and Kelly, and her mother the late Miss Lois Patterson. "Bunny" as her family lovingly called her, left us untimely in 2018. What she meant to me personally is beyond words, and I love and miss her dearly.

Carroll (JP) Phillips was a WWII Marine veteran and a United States' Secret Service Agent (Truman through Nixon). JP was an MSP Volunteer in Police Services (VIPS) when we met. JP and his wife Betty became my dear friends very soon after. I had the honor of becoming their power of attorney in 2010, until Betty and JP passed in 2012 and 2015 respectively. I recall the early days when I stop by to visit them. They could often be found sitting in matching recliners in their den. JP would get up and offer me his recliner. Their standard poodle Bianca would have none of it at first, but she got use to me very soon.

Dr. Cyril Byron was a retired WWII Army Air Corps veteran and a member of the famed Tuskegee Airmen. Dr. Byron resided in my neighborhood. After I had the honor of meeting him, "Doc" invited me to go with him to various Tuskegee Airmen events. I had the time of my life meeting these paragons of our history. I will never forget those privileged moments. Doc adopted me too, and with his two sons Cyril Jr. and Jeffery we became a foursome. Sadly "Doc" passed in 2015. Like all of those we've lost, their memories will live on in my heart.

Through my association with Children's Cancer Foundation, I had the privilege to meet Dr. Ben and Candy Carson and their sons BJ, Murray and Rhoeyce. Throughout the years I worked with the Carson's Scholarship Fund providing security at their events. Dr. Carson's contributions as a world renowned pediatric neurosurgeon are well documented. Since 1994, through the family's Scholarship programs, they have promoted academic excellence in many deserving young men and women, ensuring a brighter future for the world in which they will live.

Other Life Long Friends:
Mr. Melvin Carter, Mr. James Davis, Mr. Lawrence Melo,
Mr. George Colbert, Deborah Dorsey, Mike Stevenson, Terry Hunt,
Brian Shea, Mrs. Saundra King, Cyndi Grove, Mrs. Odella Oliver,
Mr. And Mrs. Joseph Dyson, Pastor Stephen Thomas Jr. Rev.
Dr. Laura Lee Morgan, Keith Henry, Art Jackson, Mike Johnson,
Freda Jones, My Zion Baptist Church of Christ Family,
Turners Station, Cherry Hill and Govans Community Friends, My
City, College, High School Friends, and Josh Smith.

In Memoriam:
Doris Rich, Mr. And Mrs. Harold Calhoun, Pastor Stephen Thomas
Sr., Mr. James Oliver Sr. and his son Jay Oliver, Mr. and Mrs.
William Huggins, Mr. Ernest Bannon, Sterling Smith

My Doctors:
Dr. Thomas Lynch, Dr. Jonathan Schreiber, Dr. Stanley Silber,
Dr. Robert Zawodny

The Cover Artwork

Besides including the state flag and a likeness of my retirement badge, I wanted to include a Rudis sword. Mainly because I received one from members of our Special Tactical Assault Team Element. (STATE: the name of our elite SWAT team). Presenting a Rudis to retiring STATE members is standard within their ranks. It was my great privilege to be presented one upon my retirement. That was a great honor, because I've been the only non-STATE member to ever receive one. So I wanted very much to thank them again and make it a part of my cover artwork. Turning to my cousin Kenny Russell (kennethrusselldesigns.com) who is a professional graphic artist, I sent him the most elementary example of my lack of drawing skills. Employing his artistry, he brought my concept to life in a way that surpassed my expectations. Thank you Kenny!

About the Rudis

In ancient Rome when gladiators honorably achieved their freedom from slavery or retirement from the games, they were presented with a wooden sword called a Rudis. The Rudis represented the gladiator's honor and strength. I want to thank the Purple Heart Armoury who crafted the Rudis I received, for allowing me to use the likeness of their product on the cover.

Thanks to My Fellow Authors

James Cabezas, "Eyes Of Justice"

John Poliks, "Charm Bracelets, Snapshot of A Law Enforcement Life"

Ted Jones, "Protect and Serve, Reflections of a Maryland State Trooper"

David Reichenbaugh, "In Pursuit, The Hunt For The Beltway Snipers"

Michael Brown, MD, "The Medical Insurance Virus - The Healthcare Problem in America and the Solution"

Sylvester E. Jones, Sr. "Hunting Criminals to Hiding Them" My Journey to and With the U.S. Marshals Service

Maryland State Police Fallen Heroes

Selfless Service Was More Than a
Slogan… Their Service Will Never Be
Forgotten

Officer John W. Jeffrey - 9/01/1921,
Officer William C. Lochner - 04/20/1923
Officer Raymond P. Eichotlz - 05/21/1923
Officer Hugh K. Painter - 03/30/1924
Officer Albert E. Cramblitt - 10/01/1925
Officer James Noon - 12/25/1927
Officer Clinton R. Rhodes - 01/28/1931
Officer Theodore A. Moore - 09/25/1932
Officer First Class Imla D. Hubbard - 03/04/1933
Officer Joseph E. Kuhn - 04/08/34
Officer First Class Carroll C. Creeger - 12/23/1934
Quartermaster Sergeant Wilbert V. Hunter - 02/07/1936
Officer J.F. Leo Shaab - 07/22/1937
Quartermaster Sergeant Ellsworth D. Dryden - 10/07/1938
Trooper First Class Lauren M. Ridge - 07/14/1950
Lieutenant Leonard N. Brown - 07/07/1958
Trooper First Class Arthur W. Plummer, Jr. - 04/09/61
Trooper First Class Phillip L. Russ - 10/28/1972
Trooper First Class Thomas A. Noyle - 10/28/1972
Trooper First Class Donald E. Parkerson, Jr. - 09/18/1973
Trooper Charles S. Rathell - 09/18/1973
Trooper Milton V. Purnell, Jr. - 05/29/1975
Trooper Mart Hudson, Jr. - 06/16/1975
Sergeant Wallace J. Mowbray - 08/10/1975
Trooper Gregg Presbury, Sr. - 12/17/1977
Trooper First Class William P. Mills, Jr. - 06/08/1979
Trooper Gary L. Wade - 01/30/1982
Corporal Gregory A. May - 01/19/1986
Trooper First Class Carey S. Poetzman - 01/19/1986

Trooper First Class John E. Sawa - 03/10/1987
Trooper Larry E. Small - 03/10/1987
Trooper First Class Eric D. Monk - 04/09/1988
Corporal Theodore D. Wolf, Sr. - 03/29/90
Trooper First Class Mark P. Groner - 10/01/1992
Trooper First Class Edward A. Plank, Jr. - 10/17/1995
Trooper First Class Joseph T. Lanzi - 10/28/1995
Trooper Raymond G. Armstead, Jr. - 03/25/1998
Trooper First Class Edward M. Toatley - 10/30/2000
Trooper First Class Anthony Jones - 10/09/2004
Trooper First Class Mikey C. Lippy - 09/28/2008
Corporal (Retired) Stephen H. Bunker - 09/28/2008
Trooper First Class Wesley Brown - 06/10/2010
Trooper First Class Shaft S. Hunter - 05/21/2011

Stewart Russell grew up in Baltimore Maryland. Influenced early on by the virtues portrayed in the 1950s and 1960s law and order programs, he had a great desire to seek a career in law enforcement. Thanks to a recruiting poster of a Maryland trooper, he set his sights on joining the proud traditions and culture of the Maryland State Police. He joined them in 1977, and loved wearing the uniform of a state trooper. During his first year, he saw the suspected murderer of a trooper, in the custody of a special unit of covert investigators. The sight of those elite troopers motivated his interest in that field of investigation. Six years later he became a covert investigator. Those three years would become some of the most memorable of his career. During those and subsequent years, he would meet and work with some of the best and most dedicated men and woman in public safety. Stewart would go on to work in nineteen different assignments, supervising or commanding ten of them. He held positions in all three of the department's bureaus, while serving under eleven different superintendents. He was the last active member of his academy class to retire. Stewart always felt the MSP was not just a job but a way of life. He retired at the rank of lieutenant colonel in 2012, proudly ending a 35 year way of life, as one of Maryland's finest.

Lieutenant Namon N. Brown (Ret.)
"The Legend"

The famous MSP recruitment poster featuring TFC Brown: The poster I saw riding the bus that help inspire my choice to become a state trooper.

Milton S. Taylor: The first Black recruit in the Maryland State Police - 1957.

Milton Taylor retired in 1982 at the rank of Captain. In 2015 we had a surprise dinner in his honor.
Front row from left to right: Rodney Morris (First Sergeant Ret.), Captain Taylor, Derek White (Sergeant Major Ret.).
Back row: Rudy Chapman (Sergeant Ret.), Namon Brown (Lieutenant Ret.), and Heber Watts (Captain Ret.).

My first assignment: John F. Kennedy Highway Barrack "M" 1977

My mentor, a great investigator, and dear friend: Detective Sgt. (Ret.) Walt Wassmer and his wife Jane

My friend for life: Sergeant (Ret.) Bill Burke. I was honored to present Bill with his MSP vehicle registration plate at his retirement party. Bill was my adult in the room.

The two outstanding men who epitomized leadership, and had such an impact on me at Westminster Barrack, and throughout my career. From left to right: Lieutenant (Ret.) Robert McAfee and Lieutenant (Ret.) Neil Bechtol.

"Ohh No!"
The prankster: Sergeant (Ret.) George A. Butler

The one and only himself:
First Sgt. (Ret.) Peter F. Edge as a new trooper

Pete officiating at our Fallen Heroes Ceremonies 2012, after his retirement.

Criminal Enforcement Section- 1984
I owe them all so very much.

NTF Hagerstown
They were as professional as they come.

Major and Director of our Media Communication Section, my good friend
Greg Shipley. If anyone has made a difference, it's Greg.

"Mac," Detective Sergeant (Ret.) Joe McLeary. They didn't come any better!

Sergeant Bob Sharp (on the phone) and Detective Kenny Dyson, Baltimore City Police
Escape and Apprehension Unit. The best in the business!

Detective Dave Hoffmaster, Alexandria Virginia Police (Ret.). Working good cases and making friends for life go hand in hand in our business!

Valley Barrack Investigation Section: TFCs Efrain Rosario and Doug Zeller, AKA "Whitey and Larry." Crazy and good all in one!

Waldorf CID: Back row TFC Rob Mignogna, Sgt. Willem Van der Heyden. Front: TFC Chip Ewing, me, and TFC Ted Jones. They absolutely got the job done!

My academy classmate, and my assistant commander at the AG's Office and Rockville Barrack,
Captain (Ret.) Rick Norman, at an MSP reunion.

My buddy Lt. Gene Winters, after he announced his retirement.
With Gene, we got the job done and it hardly seemed like work!

The Superintendent
Colonel (Ret.) Thomas E. (Tim) Hutchins: The absolute personifica-
tion of leadership

The Chief Federal Prosecutor for the District of Maryland The Honorable Thomas M. DiBiagio. It was a great honor to meet and shake his hand.

My promotion to Major in 2007, with my troop and barrack commanders. From left to right: Lt. Jerry Jones (currently the superintendent of the MSP), Lt. Homer Rich, Prince Frederick Barrack, Capt. Mike Spaulding, Southern Troop Commander, Lt. Kevin Hickey, Glen Burnie Barrack, Lt. Randy (GD) Stephens, LaPlata Barrack, and Lt. Brian Cedar, Leonardtown Barrack. They set the standards for all others to follow!

The great Annapolis orator: Lieutenant Jerry Beason. He must have learned something from me when I trained him that one late shift at the Westminster Barrack.

Major Laura Lu Herman: One of my three assistant Bureau Chiefs. She would become a Lt. Colonel after my retirement. My trusted sidekick!

Shirley Howard, President of the Children's Cancer Foundation in Baltimore, and MSP civilian employee Bonnie (FW) Beisser. Mrs. Howard recognized the MSP for our continued effort in support of the CCF. Mrs. Howard touched the lives of many children with cancer in her lifetime.

My retirement party 2012: Captain Scott Wayne and Lieutenant Keith Runk of the our Special Tactical Assault Team Element (STATE) honoring me with the presentation a Rudis.

My parents Hazel and Vernon Russell

My beloved momma, Miss Hazel

Oh yea…I was destined to wear the big hat!

Maryland State Police Forever!

In tribute to our Baltimore City High School Classmate, Baltimore City Police Cadet and homicide detective, and our lifelong friend Tyrone Francis. Left to right: Tyrone, Ralph Vines, yours truly, and Warren Cooper: "The Four Musketeers" 2017

In tribute to my best friend Cassandra "Bunny" Parrish 1946-2018. "What I owe you is beyond evaluation."